2005 SUP]

HART AND WECHSLER'S

THE FEDERAL COURTS

AND

THE FEDERAL SYSTEM

FIFTH EDITION

by

RICHARD H. FALLON, JR.
Ralph S. Tyler, Jr. Professor of Constitutional Law
Harvard Law School

DANIEL J. MELTZER
Story Professor of Law
Harvard Law School

DAVID L. SHAPIRO
William Nelson Cromwell Professor of Law
Harvard Law School

FOUNDATION PRESS
NEW YORK, NEW YORK
2005

© 2003, 2004 FOUNDATION PRESS
© 2005 By FOUNDATION PRESS
       395 Hudson Street
       New York, NY 10014
       Phone Toll Free 1–877–888–1330
       Fax (212) 367–6799
       fdpress.com
Printed in the United States of America

ISBN 1–58778–844–6

TEXT IS PRINTED ON 10% POST CONSUMER RECYCLED PAPER

PREFACE

This supplement includes discussion of important decisional law, legislation, and secondary literature that postdate publication of the Fifth Edition in 2003. Significant developments in the past year that are discussed in this supplement include:

- Grable & Sons Metal Products, Inc. v. Darue Engineering & Manufacturing, the Supreme Court's latest word on the scope of federal question jurisdiction under 28 U.S.C. § 1331 as applied to state law claims that incorporate an issue of federal law. Grable replaces Merrell Dow Pharmaceuticals Inc. v. Thompson as a principal case, and a newly revised Note following Grable discusses Merrell Dow and its relationship to the Grable decision.

- Exxon Mobil Corp. v. Allapattah Services, Inc., in which the Court, resolving a conflict among the courts of appeals, interpreted the supplemental jurisdiction statute (28 U.S.C. § 1367) to overrule several Supreme Court decisions by permitting the exercise of diversity jurisdiction in certain cases in which not all plaintiffs (or not all class members in a plaintiff class action) had claims that would in themselves satisfy the amount-in-controversy requirement of 28 U.S.C. § 1332.

- A large number of lower court decisions, rendered in the aftermath of the Supreme Court's 2004 trilogy on military detention, which address many of the questions left open by the Court concerning the use of habeas corpus to test the lawfulness of executive detention of citizens and aliens designated by the executive as enemy combatants and detained either in the United States or at the U.S. Naval Base in Guantanamo Bay, Cuba.

- Exxon Mobil Corp. v. Saudi Basic Industries Corp., in which the Court sought to clarify and restrict the reach of the Rooker-Feldman doctrine—a doctrine that has for some time generated uncertainty and disagreement in the lower federal courts.

- Enactment of The Class Action Fairness Act of 2005, which, among other things, significantly expanded the original and removal jurisdiction of the federal courts in diversity class actions and certain related actions.

- The Supreme Court's latest decisions on the scope of prisoners' postconviction collateral attacks, including Dodd v. United States, Mayle v. Felix, and Pace v. DiGuglielmo (all discussing questions relating to the limitations period), Rompilla v. Beard and Miller-El v. Dretke (both discussing the application of 28 U.S.C. § 2254(d)); Medellín v. Dretke (addressing a recurring question of how habeas courts should deal with claims by convicted prisoners that the state failed to comply with provisions of the Geneva Convention, which requires that aliens who are detained shall be promptly informed of their rights under the Convention); and Rhines v. Weber (giving qualified approval to the "stay-and-abeyance procedure," which permits prisoners with "mixed" petitions to stay exhausted claims while pursuing exhaustion in state court of other claims).

We remind readers that in this supplement, we have followed the same "user-friendly" convention that we inaugurated in the Fifth Edition with respect to our editorial Notes: material in footnotes is intended primarily for scholars and researchers, and our expectation (which we announce to our classes) is that students need not read the footnotes in the editorial Notes unless we specifically indicate otherwise. (We do caution students that they are expected to read the footnotes included in principal cases.)

We are grateful to Elissa Hart, Matt Jones, Stephen Shackelford, and Sharmila Sohoni for able research assistance.

R.H.F
D.J.M.
D.L.S.

July 2005

TABLE OF CONTENTS

*

TABLE OF CASES

Principal cases are in bold type. Non-principal cases
are in roman type. References are to Pages.

*

2 0 0 5 S U P P L E M E N T

THE FEDERAL COURTS
AND
THE FEDERAL SYSTEM

*

CHAPTER I

THE DEVELOPMENT AND STRUCTURE OF THE FEDERAL JUDICIAL SYSTEM

Page 45. Add to footnote 121:

The Court held in Nguyen v. United States, 539 U.S. 69 (2003), that judges of the non-Article III district courts are ineligible to sit on federal courts of appeals under 28 U.S.C. § 292(a), which provides that "[t]he chief judge of a circuit may designate and assign one or more district judges within the circuit to sit upon the court of appeals * * * whenever the business of that court so requires".

Page 52. Add to footnote 166:

But see Barnett, *No-Citation Rules Under Siege: A Battlefield Report and Analysis*, 5 J.App.Prac. & Process 473, 474 (2003)(reporting that following recent changes of policy, "nine of the thirteen circuits now allow citation of their unpublished opinions"). In a further indication of the recent counter-trend, the Advisory Committee on Appellate Rules of the Judicial Conference of the United States voted in April 2004 (by 6–1) to recommend that the Supreme Court adopt a new Federal Rule of Appellate Procedure 32.1 that would bar any court of appeals from specially restricting the citation of opinions that have been designated "not for publication" or "the like". See *Judicial Conference Backs Proposal to Ease Restrictions on Citing Unpublished Opinions*, 72 U.S.L.W. 2626, 2626 (April 20, 2004). But the Conference's Standing Committee on Rules of Practice and Procedure postponed action on the proposed amendment and returned the matter to the Advisory Committee for further study. Among the Standing Committee's evident concerns was whether circuits in which all opinions are available for citation might take longer to dispose of cases than do circuits that bar citation of "unpublished" opinions. See *Judicial Conference Rules Committee Agrees to Propose New E–Discovery Rules*, 72 U.S.L.W. 2766, 2777 (June 22, 2004). Following further study and review, the Advisory Committee approved the proposed rule change on June 15, 2005. See *Key Judicial Panel Approves Rule Change Allowing Citation of Unpublished Opinions*, 73 U.S.L.W. 2761 (June 21, 2005). As this Supplement went to press, the proposal was scheduled for action by the full Judicial Conference at its September meeting, after which, if approved, it would go to the Supreme Court for possible adoption.

Page 52. Add to footnote 167:

See also Pether, *Inequitable Injunctions: The Scandal of Private Judging in the U.S. Courts*, 56 Stan.L.Rev. 1435 (2004) (vehemently attacking the use of unpublished opinions as tending to arbitrariness and inequity).

CHAPTER II

THE NATURE OF THE FEDERAL JUDICIAL FUNCTION: CASES AND CONTROVERSIES

SECTION 1. GENERAL CONSIDERATIONS

Page 64. Add a footnote 3a at the end of the first paragraph of Paragraph (2):

For a detailed critical review of Marshall's opinion, culminating in the conclusion that "[j]ust about everything in Marbury is wrong", see Paulsen, *Marbury's Wrongness*, 20 Const.Comm. 343, 343 (2003).

Page 65. Add to footnote 4:

See also Eisgruber, *Marbury, Marshall, and the Politics of Constitutional Judgment*, 89 Va.L.Rev. 1203, 1205, 1234 (2003) (arguing that Marbury exhibited "great statesmanship" and was "one piece of a more general campaign by Chief Justice John Marshall to define and legitimate a distinctly judicial form of politics" requiring "controversial judgments about publicly contested questions of justice and the common good").

Page 65. Add a new footnote 5a at the end of Paragraph (3):

5a. With the Supreme Court lacking jurisdiction in Marbury v. Madison, would any other court have had jurisdiction to entertain Marbury's claim? A state court could not have issued mandamus relief against a federal official, see McClung v. Silliman, 19 U.S. (6 Wheat.) 598 (1821), Fifth Edition p. 440, and the 1789 Judiciary Act failed to vest the lower federal courts with mandamus jurisdiction, see McIntire v. Wood, 11 U.S. (7 Cranch) 504 (1813). In Kendall v. United States, 37 U.S. (12 Pet.) 524 (1838), the Supreme Court held that the Circuit Court for the District of Columbia, which had been established by a special act, was uniquely authorized to issue writs of mandamus in original actions against federal officials. Based on Kendall, Bloch, *The Marbury Mystery: Why Did William Marbury Sue in the Supreme Court?*, 18 Const.Comment. 607 (2002), concludes unequivocally that the Circuit Court would have had jurisdiction had Marbury chosen to file there. Professor Bloch further speculates that Marbury may have deliberately bypassed the Circuit Court in order to permit John Marshall to issue the precise rulings about Supreme Court jurisdiction and judicial review for which Marbury v. Madison is famous (pp. 625–27). Compare Fallon, *Marbury and the Constitutional Mind: A Bicentennial Essay on the Wages of Doctrinal Tension*, 91 Cal.L.Rev. 1, 52 n.271 (2003) (noting the 35–year gap between Marbury and Kendall and terming it "highly doubtful that the [Supreme] Court, in the politically charged atmosphere of 1803, would have upheld the authority of the D.C. courts to order mandamus relief for William Marbury against James Madison").

Page 66. Add to Paragraph (5) at the end of the first full paragraph:

See also Prakash & Yoo, *The Origins of Judicial Review*, 70 U.Chi.L.Rev. 887 (2003) (arguing that the Constitution's text, structure, and history all support the practice of judicial review).

Page 66. Add at the end of the first paragraph of Paragraph (5):

According to Kramer, *Marbury and the Retreat from Judicial Supremacy,* 20 Const. Comm. 205 (2003), Marshall's opinion in Marbury did not contemplate that judicial interpretations would prevail over those of other branches in all cases, but instead embraced a "departmental approach" (p. 213), under which each branch would decide for itself what the Constitution means: The Supreme Court was thus entitled to decide that the Constitution forbade it to exercise jurisdiction, but the President would have been able to decide for himself whether a court ruling directed to him was constitutionally valid. Kramer cites both Thomas Jefferson and James Madison as among those who subscribed to this view and quotes Madison as follows (p. 212): "The constitution * * * specifies certain great powers as absolutely granted, and marks out the departments to exercise them. If the constitutional boundary of either be brought into question, I do not see that any one of these independent departments has more right than another to declare their sentiments on that point." Kramer concludes that "[t]he current Supreme Court could hardly be more wrong when it cites Marbury" as establishing that its decisions categorically bind other branches (p. 229).

Douglas, *The Rhetorical Uses of Marbury v. Madison: The Emergence of a "Great Case,"* 38 Wake Forest L.Rev. 375 (2003), maintains that the Supreme Court never cited Marbury for the principle of judicial review, for which it is now famous, between 1803 and 1887. Douglas writes: "Marbury's significance today cannot be attributed to the pathbreaking character of the decision. Rather, Marbury became great because proponents of an expansive doctrine of judicial review have needed it to assume greatness." See also White, *The Constitutional Journey of Marbury v. Madison,* 89 Va.L.Rev. 1463 (2003) (tracing historically evolving interpretations of Marbury).[a]

Page 70. Add to footnote 5:

Sabel & Simon, *Destabilization Rights: How Public Law Litigation Succeeds,* 117 Harv. L.Rev. 1015, 1019 (2004), argues that in recent decades the characteristic remedies in institutional reform cases have evolved "from command-and-control injunctive regulation toward experimentalist intervention" combining "more flexible and provisional norms with procedures for ongoing stakeholder participation and measured accountability". According to the authors, experimentalist remedies "create[] opportunities for collaborative learning and democratic accountability" (p. 1101) and thereby avoid many of the problems of judicial competence that critics have thought endemic to institutional reform litigation.

a. Marbury's bicentennial in 2003 occasioned an outpouring of reflections on the decision and its significance. *See, e.g.,* Symposium, *Marbury and Its Legacy: A Symposium to Mark the 200th Anniversary of Marbury v. Madison,* 72 Geo.Wash.L.Rev. 1 (2003); Symposium, *Judicial Review: Blessing or Curse? Or Both? A Symposium in Commemoration of the Bicentennial of Marbury v. Madison,* 38 Wake Forest L.Rev. 313 (2003); Symposium, *Marbury v. Madison: A Bicentennial Symposium,* 89 Va.L.Rev. 1105 (2003); Symposium, *Marbury v. Madison and Judicial Review: Legitimacy, Tyranny and Democracy,* 37 John Marshall L.Rev. 317 (2004); Symposium, *Judging Judicial Review: Marbury in the Modern Era,* 101 Mich.L.Rev. 2557 (2003); Symposium, *Marbury at 200: A Bicentennial Celebration of Marbury v. Madison,* 20 Const. Comm. 205 (2003); Symposium, *Marbury v. Madison: 200 Years of Judicial Review in America,* 71 Tenn.L.Rev. 217 (2004).

For a brief but useful discussion of the diverse practices of judicial review in European nations and a comparison with the American model, see Ferejohn & Pasquino, *Constitutional Adjudication: Lessons from Europe,* 82 Tex.L.Rev. 1671 (2004).

Page 71. Add a new footnote 4a at the end of Paragraph (4).

4a. *But cf.* Driesen, *Standing for Nothing: The Paradox of Demanding Concrete Context for Formalist Adjudication*, 89 Cornell L.Rev. 808 (2004), arguing that much public law litigation involves facial challenges to statutes and other disputes in which individual injury has little relevance to the merits. The author concludes that courts cannot rely on justiciability doctrines to promote wise and limited adjudication, but should instead pursue such "active virtues" as "seek[ing] narrow grounds for decision, confin[ing] themselves as much as possible to briefed issues and rationales, and seek[ing] information needed to understand the broad institutional consequences of many public law decisions" (p. 890).

Page 77. Add to footnote 5:

See also Shannon, *The Retrospective and Prospective Application of Judicial Decisions*, 26 Harv.J.L. & Pub.Pol'y 811 (2003) (advancing policy arguments supporting a firm rule of retroactivity).

Page 80. Add to footnote 2:

See also Casto, *The Early Supreme Court Justices' Most Significant Opinion*, 29 Ohio Northern U.L.Rev. 173, 201 (2002) (arguing that "the early Justices clearly believed that they had a discretionary power" to furnish advisory opinions for the executive branch and that "[t]he only absolute rule that can be teased out of their 1793 letter to President Washington, is that the President is not empowered to require the federal judiciary to provide an advisory opinion").

Page 88. Add to footnote 3:

Healy, *The Rise of Unnecessary Constitutional Rulings*, 83 N.C.L.Rev. 847 (2005), charts an increase in unnecessary constitutional rulings and depicts the pattern as "part of [a] larger trend in which the Court has asserted supremacy over the other branches of government and has come to see its primary role as the declaration of constitutional norms rather than the resolution of ordinary disputes" (935). According to Healy, some unnecessary rulings violate the Article III ban on advisory opinions. He maintains, for example, that for courts in qualified immunity cases to ask first whether the plaintiff has a right, and only later whether the right was clearly established, produces advisory opinions because the decision whether a right actually exists will never determine the outcome and the parties therefore "lack adequate incentive to argue the issue vigorously" (p. 921). How plausible do you find this claim about incentives?

SECTION 2.   ISSUES OF PARTIES, THE REQUIREMENT OF FINALITY, AND THE PROHIBITION AGAINST FEIGNED AND COLLUSIVE SUITS

Page 98. Add to footnote 3:

See generally Parry, *The Lost History of International Extradition Litigation*, 43 Va.J.Int'l L. 93 (2002) (attacking the purported historical foundations for the view that the judicial role in extradition proceedings falls outside Article III and asserting the need for unspecified doctrinal revisions free of "historical baggage").

Page 101. Add a Subparagraph (1)(d).

(d) After Florida courts ordered the withdrawal of a feeding tube sustaining the life of Theresa Marie Schiavo, who had been in a persistent vegetative state for more than ten years (based on a determination, in a proceeding initiated by Schiavo's husband, that Theresa Schiavo would have wanted nutrition and hydration to be withdrawn under the circumstances), Congress adopted an Act vesting a federal district court with jurisdiction to adjudicate any claim by or on behalf of Mrs. Schiavo, but not any other person in comparable circumstances, "under the Constitution or laws of the United States relating to the withholding or withdrawing of food, fluids, or medical treatment necessary to sustain her life." The statute authorized Mrs. Schiavo's parents to sue on her behalf and provided that the district court shall determine all claims de novo "notwithstanding any prior state court determination." It said expressly that "[n]othing in this Act shall be construed to create substantive rights not otherwise secured by the Constitution and laws of the United States or of the several states." In the volley of requests for temporary restraining orders or other emergency relief that followed, both the district court and the Eleventh Circuit–in two rounds of hasty litigation—denied relief on the ground that the plaintiffs had failed to make the requisite showing that they were likely to prevail on the merits, and the Supreme Court twice denied stays. Schiavo ex rel. Schindler v. Schiavo, 125 S.Ct. 1692 (2005); Schiavo ex rel. Schindler v. Schiavo, 125 S.Ct. 1722 (2005).

By directing the federal courts to decide the Schiavo case de novo, did the Act violate a prohibition, traceable to United States v. Klein, against statutes that tell a court how to decide a case or to ignore otherwise relevant issues? By denying res judicata effect to a state court judgment, did the Act run afoul of Plaut v. Spendthrift Farm, Inc., Fifth Ed. P. 100–or did it follow the precedent established by federal habeas corpus statutes that also effectively deny res judicata effect to state court judgments? Compare the opinion of Judge Birch, specially concurring in an order by the Eleventh Circuit denying a petition for rehearing en banc in the second round of litigation, 404 F.3d 1270, 1271–76 (2005), with the dissenting opinion of Judge Tjoflat, joined by Judge Wilson, *id.* at 1279–82.

Page 103. Add to footnote 10:

A recent addition to the literature on the history of the Court of Federal Claims is Resnik, *Of Courts, Agencies, and the Court of Federal Claims: Fortunately Outliving One's Anomalous Character*, 71 Geo.Wash.L.Rev. 798 (2003), which argues that although the non-Article III court of claims was anomalous at the time of its creation, it has ceased to be so as a result of the increasing assignment of adjudicative functions to administrative agencies and to bankruptcy judges and magistrate judges who lack Article III status.

For discussion of a variety of issues involving the Court of Federal Claims and its history, see Symposium, *Proceedings of the 15th Judicial Conference Celebrating the 20th Anniversary of the United States Court of Federal Claims*, 71 Geo.Wash.L.Rev. 529 (2003) (including articles by both judges and scholars).

SECTION 3. SOME PROBLEMS OF STANDING TO SUE

SUBSECTION A: PLAINTIFFS' STANDING

Page 126. Add to footnote 1:

Woolhandler & Nelson, *Does History Defeat the Standing Doctrine?*, 102 Mich.L.Rev. 689, 691 (2004), argue that although "early American courts did not use the term 'standing' much, and modern research tools might therefore convince one that the concept did not exist", early decisions regularly insisted on "proper parties" and "designated some areas of litigation" as being necessarily subject to public rather than private control. The authors thus see the foundations of standing doctrine in a historical distinction between "public" and "private" rights. Although they "do not claim that history *compels* acceptance of the modern Supreme Court's vision of standing", they "argue that history does not *defeat* standing doctrine". *Id.*

Page 136. Add a Paragraph 3(h):

In McConnell v. Federal Election Commission, 540 U.S. 93, 225 (2003), the Court emphasized that the injury necessary for standing must be not only concrete, but also " 'actual or imminent' " (quoting Whitmore v. Arkansas, 495 U.S. 149, 155 (1990)). On this ground it denied standing to a United States Senator seeking to challenge a provision of the Bipartisan Campaign Reform Act that he alleged would hamper his ability to purchase airtime for advertising attacking his opponent, as he contended that he planned to do in future campaigns. Because it would be nearly five years before Senator McConnell came up for re-election, the Court concluded that the "alleged injury in fact is too remote temporally to satisfy Article III standing" (p. 226). Justice Stevens, joined by Justices Ginsburg and Breyer, dissented on this issue. "That the injury is distant in time does not make it illusory," he wrote (p. 363).

Page 138. Add to footnote 21:

Cf. Staudt, *Modeling Standing*, 79 N.Y.U.L.Rev. 612 (2004) (concluding on the basis of a survey of decisions dealing with taxpayer standing that when the applicable doctrine is clear and effective judicial oversight exists, federal district courts render law-abiding and predictable decisions, but that Supreme Court decisions, which are subject to few institutional constraints, tend to reflect strategic considerations).

Page 140. Add to Paragraph (5):

Concurring and dissenting opinions sparred about the reach of ASARCO in Nike, Inc. v. Kasky, 539 U.S. 654 (2003), a case in which the Court (*per curiam* and without opinion) dismissed the writ of certiorari as improvidently granted. Kasky, a "private attorney general" who would have lacked standing under federal law, sued Nike in a California state court under California statutes prohibiting deceptive trade practices and false advertising. The trial court sustained a demurrer based on a First Amendment defense, but the California Supreme Court found that relevant statements by Nike constituted "commercial speech" and thus could furnish grounds for liability insofar as they were false or misleading. Concurring in the dismissal of the writ of certiorari, Justice Stevens, joined by Justice Ginsburg, argued that neither party had standing: Kasky's complaint had alleged no personal injury in fact, and "[u]nlike ASARCO, in which the state court proceedings ended in a declaratory judgment invalidating a state law, no 'final judgment altering tangible legal rights' has been entered" (p. 662 (quoting ASARCO, 490 U.S. at 619)). Dissenting from the dismissal of the writ, Justice Breyer, joined by Justice O'Connor, argued that Nike had suffered an injury "consist[ing] of the threat, arising out of the state court's determination, that [its] speech on public matters might be 'chilled' immediately and legally restrained in the future" (p. 669). (Justice Kennedy also dissented, and thus presumably also thought that Nike had standing, but did so without opinion.) Once it is recognized that a state court defendant may have standing to invoke Supreme Court review even when the state court plaintiff lacks Article III standing, what harms resulting from a state court proceeding, other than the entry of an order against the defendant (as in ASARCO), ought to confer standing on the defendant to seek Supreme Court review? See also the discussion of the Nike case at p. 35, *infra*.

Page 140. Add a Paragraph (5)(a).

The Court cited a desire not to interfere with family relations structured by state law as its grounds for denying "prudential" standing in Elk Grove Unified School Dist. v. Newdow, 124 S.Ct. 2301, an action challenging the School District's policy of commencing each school day with a recitation of the Pledge of Allegiance including the words "under God". Newdow, the father of a girl in the school system, sued to enjoin the practice, which he claimed interfered with his right to communicate his atheistic beliefs to his daughter. But the girl's mother opposed the action, and as a matter of California law Newdow could therefore not bring his action as his daughter's next friend, but only on his own behalf. In an opinion joined by four other Justices, Justice Stevens found that Newdow lacked prudential standing. Without denying that Newdow suffered injury in fact (apparently on the basis that Newdow alleged), the Court emphasized that the outer reaches of Newdow's rights and interests as a parent were governed by uncertain state law and that his interests were potentially adverse to those of his daughter. In finding that federal adjudication would be imprudent, Justice Stevens drew an analogy to the so-called "domestic relations exception" to federal diversity jurisdiction, under which federal courts generally lack jurisdiction to issue divorce, alimony, or child custody decrees even within cases otherwise subject to federal jurisdiction. See Fifth Edition pp. 1271–83. But the Court rested its judgment on standing rather than abstention doctrine: "[I]t is improper for the federal courts to entertain a claim by a plaintiff whose standing to sue is founded on family law rights that are in dispute when prosecution of the lawsuit may have an adverse effect on the person who is the source of the plaintiff's claimed standing" (p. 2312).

Chief Justice Rehnquist, whose opinion on this issue was joined by Justices O'Connor and Thomas, would have upheld standing based on injury to Newdow's right to expose his daughter to his religious views. He thought the abstention doctrine for domestic relations cases flatly inapplicable: "This case does not involve diversity jurisdiction, and it does not ask this Court to issue a divorce, alimony, or child custody decree" (p. 2314). On the merits, all three dissenting Justices would have upheld the School District's recitation policy. (Justice Scalia did not participate.)

Is Newdow an example of purposive use of standing doctrine to avoid a constitutional question on the merits? A defensible or desirable one? See generally Fifth Edition pp. 86–87.

Page 141. Add to footnote 24:

According to Mullenix, *Standing and Other Dispositive Motions After Amchem and Ortiz: The Problems of "Logically Antecedent" Inquiries*, 2004 Mich.St.L.Rev. 703, lower courts are divided about whether the Amchem–Ortiz language categorically bars courts from considering pre-certification motions that might otherwise have led to dismissal for want of jurisdiction. Professor Mullenix argues that a bar to pre-certification motions in all cases would be "perverse," that Amchem–Ortiz did no more than clarify an exception to the obligation to determine standing at the outset, and that "courts should continue to review standing and other jurisdictional challenges at the same time and in the same fashion as those courts did prior to Amchem and Ortiz" (p. 710).

Page 142. Add to footnote 26:

For a useful survey and discussion of issues involving standing to appeal, see Steinman, *Shining a Light in a Dim Corner: Standing to Appeal and the Right to Defend a Judgment in the Federal Courts*, 38 Ga.L.Rev. 813 (2004).

Page 160. Add at the beginning of footnote 8:

Siegel, *Zone of Interests*, 92 Geo.L.J. 317, 368 (2004), traces the cases applying the zone-of-interests test and maintains that it "will continue to [present a frustrating puzzle] as long as the Supreme Court fails to resolve * * * the relationship between the zone of interests requirement and congressional intent". The author argues that the test should be viewed as statutorily mandated by the APA, rather than as a judicially imposed prudential requirement, and that it should be construed to "grant[] standing to all parties injured by agency action unless Congress states otherwise" because this "understanding would best implement Congress' desire to have its laws enforced." *Id.* Do you agree that congressional intent should control? That Congress would ordinarily wish to extend standing to all injured parties?

SUBSECTION B: STANDING TO ASSERT THE RIGHTS OF OTHERS AND RELATED ISSUES INVOLVING "FACIAL CHALLENGES" TO STATUTES

Page 177. Add to Paragraph (4):

The Court, by a vote of 6–3, again rejected a claim of third-party standing in Kowalski v. Tesmer, 125 S.Ct. 564 (2004). The plaintiffs were lawyers challenging provisions of Michigan law that made the appointment of appellate counsel discretionary, rather than a matter of right (as before), for indigent state defendants who pleaded guilty or nolo contendere. In an opinion by Chief Justice Rehnquist, the Court assumed that the plaintiffs had Article III standing, based on the likelihood of lost revenues, but refused to accord them third-party standing to assert the rights of indigent defendants. "The attorneys before us do not have a 'close relationship' with their alleged clients; indeed, they have no relationship at all" (p. 568), the Chief Justice wrote. Nor had the attorneys "demonstrated that there is a 'hindrance' to the indigents' advancing their own constitutional rights" (*id.*). That "hypothesis" was disproved, the Court said, by the success of pro se defendants in asserting their rights in Michigan's appellate courts: "While we agree that an attorney would be valuable to a criminal defendant challenging the constitutionality of the scheme, we do not think that the lack of an attorney here is the type of hindrance necessary to allow another to assert the indigent defendants' rights" (p. 569). An "additional reason to deny the attorneys third-party standing" arose from the *Younger* abstention doctrine, see Fifth Edition, Chap. X, Sec. 2C, which generally prevents "a state criminal defendant from asserting ancillary challenges to ongoing state criminal proceedings in federal court" (*id.*). Because state court criminal defendants could not have brought their own suits in federal court challenging state policies involving the appointment of appellate counsel, to allow those defendants' rights to be asserted on a third-party basis would have allowed Younger principles to be "circumvented" (*id.*).

Justice Ginsburg, joined by Justices Stevens and Souter, dissented. Justice Ginsburg noted that "the Court has found an adequate 'relation' between litigants alleging third-party standing and those whose rights they seek to assert when nothing nothing more than a buyer-seller connection was at stake" (p. 573), and she emphasized the difficulties confronting "indigent and poorly educated defendants" attempting to present constitutional claims in a pro se appeal (p. 574). Justice Ginsburg brushed aside concerns based on the Younger doctrine by noting that the federal plaintiffs had filed their suit before the challenged Michigan statute took effect and thus before the commencement of any state criminal proceeding with which the federal action could interfere.

In light of earlier cases authorizing third-party standing, and the absence of a pending state proceeding that would bring Younger into play when the federal action was brought, is the result in Kowalski explicable on any principled ground?

Page 189. Add a new footnote 3a at the end of the third paragraph:

3a. See also Chen, *Statutory Speech Bubbles, First Amendment Overbreadth, and Improper Legislative Purpose*, 38 Harv. C.R.-C.L.L.Rev. 31 (2003) (arguing that overbreadth doctrine should be deployed to invalidate statutes that are adopted for illicit, viewpoint-based purposes but are written more broadly to appear content-neutral).

Page 190. Add to Paragraph (4):

In a unanimous decision in Virginia v. Hicks, 539 U.S. 113 (2003), the Supreme Court, citing the requirement of "substantial" overbreadth, reversed a decision by the Virginia Supreme Court that had invalidated a state trespass conviction. To deal with rampant crime and drug dealing, the Richmond City Council deeded the streets within a low-income housing development called Whitcomb Court to a public agency, the Richmond Redevelopment and Housing Authority (RRHA), which thereafter posted "no trespassing" signs identifying the property as "private". The RRHA also authorized the Richmond police "to serve notice" on non-resident visitors who could not "demonstrate a legitimate business or social purpose for being on the premises" that they must exit and not return (p. 116). After being given a written notice of exclusion, Hicks came back to Whitcomb Court and was arrested and convicted under a Virginia anti-trespassing statute. On appeal of his conviction, Hicks argued, *inter alia*, that the RRHA's exclusion policy was unconstitutionally overbroad in violation of the First Amendment, apparently because it barred access for leafletting and other forms of protected expression. The Virginia Supreme Court accepted the overbreadth argument. Although it found that the RRHA policy included an "unwritten" exception permitting access for at least some persons wishing to engage in forms of expressive activity beyond the limits of the written policy, it also found that the unwritten exception gave the manager of Whitcomb Court "unfettered discretion", permitting her to "prohibit speech that she finds personally distasteful or offensive" (p. 121) (internal quotations omitted).

In an opinion by Justice Scalia, the Supreme Court reversed. The Court began by construing the Virginia Supreme Court opinion as having held as a matter of state law that the RRHA trespass policy included separate written and unwritten provisions and that these were not severable. Then, focusing on the exclusion policy as a whole, the Court held that it was not substantially overbroad, because most denials of access under the policy would not involve constitutionally protected speech: "both the notice-barment rule and the 'legitimate business or social purpose' rule apply to *all* persons who enter the streets of Whitcomb Court, not just to those who seek to engage in expression. * * * Rarely, if ever, will an overbreadth challenge succeed against a law or regulation that is not specifically addressed to speech or to conduct necessarily associated with speech (such as picketing or demonstrating)" (p. 123–24).

At an early point in its opinion, the Court noted that Hicks had challenged only the RRHA exclusion policy, not the trespass statute under which he was ultimately convicted. Suppose, however, that Hicks had been convicted under a local ordinance that *both* excluded non-residents from Whitcomb Court in terms identical to those of the RRHA policy in Hicks *and* imposed criminal trespass penalties for violation of that policy. If the Virginia Supreme Court held that this hypothetical statute included invalid applications, and that it was not severable (as it held in Hicks), could Hicks's conviction have been allowed to stand, even if the statute was not "substantially overbroad"? Under the "severability" analysis suggested in the Fifth Edition, pp. 181–82, if invalid applications of a state statute are not severable from valid applications, then there is no constitutionally valid rule of law under which a legal penalty for violation of the statute could be imposed, even as to unprotected conduct. If that analysis is correct, how different is the situation in Hicks, in which the applicability of the Virginia anti-trespass statute to persons on the streets of Whitcomb Court depends on a non-severable RRHA policy (governing rights of access) that may have some unconstitutional applications, even if it is not "substantially overbroad"? Can Virginia v. Hicks be reconciled with the Fifth Edition's analysis of severability issues? As a formal matter, Hicks was of course convicted under a state trespass statute, not the RRHA policy that he claimed to be overbroad, but should this make any difference?

The Court reviewed another an opinion of the Virginia Supreme Court in Virginia v. Black, 538 U.S. 343 (2003). In Black, the plurality opinion, without reference to the requirement of "substantial" overbreadth, held that a Virginia statute banning cross-burning with the intent to intimidate was facially invalid. Although the Court invalidated the Virginia statute, a majority agreed that Virginia could ban cross-burnings done with intent to intimidate. According to Justice O'Connor's plurality opinion, the constitutional defect of the challenged statute lay in its provision that any burning of a cross "shall be prima facie evidence of an intent to intimidate" (p. 363). The plurality reasoned that this provision made juries too likely to convict in cases not involving an actual intent to intimidate and, as a result, created an unacceptable risk that political speech would be chilled (pp. 363–67). In a partial dissent, Justice Scalia (joined in relevant part by Justice Thomas) argued that the statute was not facially invalid because not substantially overbroad. In his view, the evidentiary presumption with respect to intent was likely to lead to few constitutionally impermissible convictions, and convictions that rested solely on that presumption would be properly subject to as-applied challenges.

In a footnote, Justice Scalia suggested that a challenge to the processes of proof in a criminal case raises "concerns [that] sound in due process, not First Amendment overbreadth" (p. 374 n.3). Would it have promoted doctrinal clarity for the plurality in Virginia v. Black to have rested its holding on due process rather than First Amendment grounds? Admittedly, the line between the two will not always be sharp. See generally Monaghan, *First Amendment*

"Due Process", 83 Harv.L.Rev. 518 (1970). But does the plurality's failure even to discuss the substantial overbreadth requirement signal its apprehension that this was not a typical First Amendment overbreadth case?[a]

Note that the statute challenged in Virginia v. Black would have made conduct that is affirmatively protected by the First Amendment—such as burning a cross as a form of political speech without intent to intimidate—a basis for inferring that a defendant had committed a constitutionally unprotected criminal act. Apart from the technicalities of the overbreadth doctrine, should the First Amendment bar a state from making expression that may be constitutionally protected the trigger for a presumption that a defendant has committed a crime?

Page 196. Add new Sub–Paragraphs (10)(d)–(f):

(d) The Court revisited the question whether legislation enacted under Section 5 of the Fourteenth Amendment should be subject to facial challenge in Tennessee v. Lane, 541 U.S. 509 (2004) (also discussed at p. 74, *infra*). The case arose when plaintiffs complained that Tennessee and a number of its counties had denied them physical access to state courts in violation of Title II of the Americans With Disabilities Act, which bars governments from discriminating on the basis of disability in providing access to their "services, programs or activities" and purports to abrogate the sovereign immunity of offending states. For legislation to be valid under § 5, the Court has held that it must exhibit " 'a congruence and proportionality between the [constitutional] injury to be prevented or remedied and the means adopted to that end.' " *Id.* at 520 (quoting City of Boerne v. Flores, 521 U.S. 507, 520 (1997)). Under this test, the defendants argued that Title II swept far too broadly by requiring governments to accommodate those with handicaps in contexts in which failure to do so would not violate the Constitution and that it was therefore unconstitutional on its face. In an opinion by Justice Stevens, the Court (by 5–4) rebuffed the defendants' contention that the congruence and proportionality test necessarily authorized a facial challenge: "[T]he question presented in this case is not whether Congress can validly subject the States to private suits for money damages for failing to provide reasonable access to hockey rinks, or even to voting booths, but whether Congress had the power under § 5 to enforce the constitutional right of access to courts" (p. 530–31). According to Justice Stevens, the purpose of the congruence and proportionality test is to ensure that legislation enacted under § 5 does not substantively redefine the constitutional guarantees that it purports to enforce. Prior cases under § 5, including Florida Prepaid Postsecondary Education Expense Board v. College Savings Bank, Fifth Edition p. 196, had involved legislation crafted to enforce a single constitutional right, and a judicial finding that the legislation failed the congruence and proportionality test therefore marked it as invalid in all its applications. See p. 530 & n.18. By contrast, Justice Stevens reasoned, Title II was designed to protect due process rights of access to courts as well as equal protection rights to freedom from irrational discrimination, and the question

---

a. Notably, the plurality left open the possibility that the Virginia Supreme Court, on remand, might offer an interpretation of the evidentiary provision that would "avoid the constitutional objections" and, having done so, might permit the retrial of two of the three respondents in the case (p. 367). If broadly applied, a rule permitting state supreme courts to cure statutory overbreadth by offering saving constructions on remand from the Supreme Court would substantially weaken the overbreadth doctrine. See Fifth Edition p. 189.

whether it validly enforced constitutional rights without redefining them must be determined on a right-by-right basis: "Because we find that Title II unquestionably is valid § 5 legislation as it applies to the class of cases implicating the accessibility of judicial services, we need go no further" (p. 531).

In a dissenting opinion joined by Justices Kennedy and Thomas, Chief Justice Rehnquist argued that Title II exhibited "massive overbreadth" in its extension of rights of access to the disabled in all governmental services and programs, and he would have declared it facially invalid on that basis: "In conducting its as-applied analysis, * * * the majority posits a hypothetical statute, never enacted by Congress, that applies only to courthouses. * * * Our § 5 precedents do not support this as-applied approach. In each case, we measured the full breadth of the statute or relevant provision that Congress enacted against the scope of the constitutional right it purported to enforce" (p. 551). Justice Scalia dissented separately.

Is the Chief Justice correct that the majority's approach "posits a hypothetical statute, never enacted by Congress"? If so, is the situation any different in cases involving § 5 of the Fourteenth Amendment than in other cases in which the Court resolves constitutional challenges to statutes on an as-applied basis? Or is the Court's approach in Tennessee v. Lane peculiar because it asks not whether a statute is valid as applied to particular facts, but whether it is valid insofar as it attempts to enforce one "constitutional guarantee" (such as the right of access to courts) rather than another (such as the right to be free from irrational discrimination)? Under this approach, won't outcomes often depend on how the pertinent "constitutional guarantees" are described? In Florida Prepaid, for example, why wasn't the challenged legislation constitutionally permissible insofar as it enforced the constitutional guarantee against intentional deprivations of property by state officials without due process of law? Note that Justice Stevens had dissented in Florida Prepaid partly on this basis. Is it possible that only Justice O'Connor—whose vote was crucial to the 5–4 majority upholding a facial challenge in Florida Prepaid and to the 5–4 majority rejecting one in Tennessee v. Lane—actually believes that the two cases are distinguishable in their treatment of facial challenges to statutes enacted under § 5?

For approving commentary on *Tennessee v. Lane*, maintaining that no justification exists for abandoning the "ordinary" presumption of statutory severability in Section 5 cases, see Metzger, *Facial Challenges and Federalism*, 105 Colum.L.Rev. 873 (2005).

(e) In a case decided the same day as Tennessee v. Lane, the Court unanimously upheld the constitutionality of a federal statute, enacted pursuant to the Spending and Necessary and Proper Clauses, that criminalizes the bribery of officials of state and local governmental entities that receive at least $10,000 per year in federal funds. Sabri v. United States, 541 U.S. 600 (2004). Sabri, who had been convicted under the statute, argued that it was facially invalid because it failed to require proof of any connection between particular bribes and the squandering of federal money. The Court, in an opinion by Justice Souter, rebuffed this argument on the merits. Even absent a squandering of identifiable federal funds, the federal government retained an "interest" in stopping corruption by the officials of federal grantees: "Money is fungible, bribed officials are untrustworthy stewards of federal funds, and corrupt contractors do not deliver dollar-for-dollar value" (p. 606).

Having resolved the case on this basis, Justice Souter offered "an afterword on Sabri's technique for challenging his indictment by facial attack on the underlying statute" (p. 608–09): Sabri was in essence making an "overbreadth challenge * * * that the statute could not be enforced against him, because it could not be enforced against someone else whose behavior would be outside the scope of Congress's Article I authority to legislate.

"Facial challenges of this sort are especially to be discouraged. Not only do they invite judgments on fact-poor records, but they entail a further departure from the norms of adjudication in federal courts: overbreadth challenges call for relaxing familiar requirements of standing, to allow a determination that the law would be unconstitutionally applied to different parties and different circumstances from those at hand. Accordingly, we have recognized the validity of facial attacks alleging overbreadth (though not necessarily using that term) in relatively few settings, and, generally, on the strength of specific reasons weighty enough to overcome our well-founded reticence. See, e.g., Broadrick v. Oklahoma, [Fifth Edition p. 190] (free speech); Aptheker v. Secretary of State, [Fifth Edition p. 195] (right to travel); Stenberg v. Carhart, 530 U.S. 914 (2000) (abortion); City of Boerne v. Flores, [*supra*] (legislation under § 5 of the Fourteenth Amendment). See generally Fallon, *As-Applied and Facial Challenges and Third–Party Standing*, 113 Harv.L.Rev. 1321, 1351 (2000) (emphasizing role of various doctrinal tests in determining viability of facial attack); Monaghan, *Overbreadth*, 1981 S.Ct.Rev. 1, 24 (observing that overbreadth is a function of substantive First Amendment law). Outside these limited settings, and absent a good reason, we do not extend an invitation to bring overbreadth claims."

Justice Kennedy (joined by Justice Scalia), who joined all of the Court's opinion except the section comprising its "afterword", offered a "comment with reference to it" (p. 610): "The Court * * * does not specifically question the practice [of invalidating statutes on their faces that] we have followed in cases such as United States v. Lopez, 514 U.S. 549 (1995), and United States v. Morrison, 529 U.S. 598 (2000). In those instances the Court did resolve the basic question whether Congress, in enacting the statutes challenged there, had exceeded its legislative power under the Constitution." Justice Thomas concurred in the judgment.

Is there any principled explanation of when the Court will entertain overbreadth challenges and when it will not?

(f) The Supreme Court divided sharply over tangled questions involving facial challenges and the separability of a federal statute in United States v. Booker, 125 S.Ct. 738 (2005). In the "merits" part of Booker, the Court held in an opinion by Justice Stevens (by 5–4) that statutorily mandated impositions of enhanced sentences under the federal Sentencing Guidelines, based on the sentencing judge's determination of a fact not found by the jury, violate the Sixth Amendment. In a separate (5–4) opinion addressing the appropriate remedy, with only Justice Ginsburg joining both majorities, Justice Breyer held invalid the statutory provision that specifically made the Sentencing Guidelines mandatory and determined that this provision should be "severed", with the result that the guidelines became "effectively advisory". *Id.* at 757. (All agreed that, in the light of history, the Sixth Amendment did not bar the exercise of sentencing discretion by judges.) Dissenting from the remedial holding, Justice Stevens (joined by Justice Souter and in pertinent parts by Justice Scalia) protested that the statutory provision making the guidelines mandatory was not facially unconstitutional; although it was invalid as applied to cases in which judges based *enhanced* sentences on facts not found by the jury, it was not invalid as applied to other cases. According to Justice Stevens, the appropriate remedy was therefore to invalidate only those sentence enhancements forbidden by the Constitution and, thus, effectively to force the government to prove to a jury all facts on which it wished to rely at the sentencing stage. (Justice Thomas also dissented from the Court's severability analysis.)

In rejecting the dissenters' approach, the majority appealed to congressional intent: "In our view, it is more consistent with Congress' likely intent in enacting the Sentencing Reform Act (1) to preserve important elements of that system while severing and excising [the provision making the guidelines mandatory] * * * than (2) to maintain all provisions of the Act and engraft today's constitutional requirement [that juries must find all facts pertinent to sentence enhancement] onto that statutory scheme" (p. 768). How persuasive is the argument that a Congress that imposed mandatory sentencing guidelines would have preferred judicial discretion in sentencing to a requirement that juries find all pertinent facts? Even if the Court is right about Congress' "likely intent", what is the source of judicial authority to invalidate and sever a statutory provision that is not facially unconstitutional?

Page 199. Add a new Paragraph (13):

(13) Facial Challenges to State Statutes in Federal Court. Suppose that a plaintiff sues in federal court seeking a declaration that a state statute is facially invalid due to overbreadth or vagueness. Suppose further that the federal court determines a holding of facial invalidity to be unwarranted based on the availability of one or more narrowing constructions that would eliminate the alleged constitutional defect. If the federal court were to furnish a narrowing construction of its own, its ruling would not normally bind a state court in a subsequent action to enforce the statute—even in cases lying outside the federal court's narrowing construction—and thus would afford no protection to the federal plaintiff. In cases of this kind, Buck & Rienzi, *Federal Courts, Overbreadth, and Vagueness: Guiding Principles for Constitutional Challenges to Uninterpreted State Statutes*, 2002 Utah L.Rev. 381, 456–59, argue that federal courts should not merely provide narrowing constructions, but should also rule expressly that the challenged statute would be unconstitutional unless limited to approved applications. According to them, this approach would effectively and appropriately convert a facial challenge to an "as-applied" one. *Cf.* Brockett v. Spokane Arcades, Inc., Fifth Edition p. 190. But in what sense does a court make an "as-applied" ruling when it holds that all applications of a statute beyond its own interpretation would violate the Constitution?

In Hope Clinic v. Ryan, 195 F.3d 857, 869 (7th Cir.1999) (*en banc*), Judge Easterbrook's majority opinion rejected facial attacks on two statutes barring partial birth abortions by noting several possible narrowing constructions, at least one of which the court thought a state court would adopt. Although the court did not specifically adopt any one of those constructions, it directed the district court to issue "precautionary injunctions" against enforcement of the statutes in a contested range of cases. Judge Posner dissented, arguing that the precautionary injunctions were a "novel form of relief" that "violate[d] Article III" by barring the enforcement of a statute that the court had not held unconstitutional. *Id.* at 876–77. Do you agree?[a]

a. The Supreme Court vacated and remanded Hope Clinic for reconsideration in light of an intervening Court ruling on the constitutionality of partial-birth abortion

For discussion of other approaches available to a federal court confronted with a facial challenge to a state statute, see generally Fifth Edition Chapter 10 (discussing abstention doctrines).

Page 208. Add at the end of Paragraph (5):

In Tory v. Cochran, 125 S.Ct. 2108 (2005), the Court ruled that the death of the plaintiff Johnny Cochran did not moot the defendants' challenge to a state court injunction barring the defendants from making derisive statements about Cochran or his law firm in any public forum since the injunction remained in effect despite Cochran's death. (On the merits, the Court then ruled only that the state court's injunction "now amounts to an overly broad prior restraint" (p. 2111) and remanded the case to the state court for further proceedings not inconsistent with its opinion.) Dissenting, Justice Thomas, joined by Justice Scalia, would have dismissed the writ as improvidently granted without reaching the mootness issue, which he described (without further explanation) as "a complicated problem in its own right" (p. 2112).

Page 216. Add to footnote 5:

See also Hay & Rosenberg, *"Sweetheart" and "Blackmail" Settlements in Class Actions: Reality and Remedy*, 75 Notre Dame L.Rev. 1377 (2000) (arguing that the risks of sweetheart and blackmail settlements have been overstated by class action critics and proposing several safeguards to minimize abuses).

Section 5. Ripeness

———

Page 226. Add to Paragraph (2)(c):

In National Park Hospitality Ass'n v. Department of Interior, 538 U.S. 803 (2003), the Court held unripe a suit by an association of concessioners challenging a National Park Service (NPS) rule that deems the federal Contract Disputes Act (CDA) inapplicable to concession contracts. Writing for the majority, Justice Thomas held first (under the two-part Abbott Labs test) that the challenged NPS rule imposed no substantial hardship on the plaintiffs. The Court appeared to acknowledge that various CDA rights and remedies would be valuable to the concessioners if, as they contended and the challenged rule denied, the Act applied to their contracts with the NPS. But Justice Thomas emphasized that because the NPS does not administer the CDA, the challenged rule was not "a legislative regulation with the force of law" (p. 808); that it did not affect "primary conduct" but rather left "a concessioner free to conduct its business as it sees fit" (p. 810); and that even if the NPS rule bound the NPS contracting officer to whom contract disputes would initially be presented, it did not bind either the Interior Department's Board of Contract Appeals or the courts before which the concessioners might assert rights or seek remedies under the CDA (pp. 809–12). With respect to the second prong of the Abbott

statutes. See 530 U.S. 1271 (2000). On remand, the defendant states conceded that their statutes were unconstitutional under the Court's decision, and the Seventh Circuit issued a *per curiam* opinion enjoining all enforcement. See 249 F.3d 603 (7th Cir.2001).

Labs test, Justice Thomas concluded that further factual development would advance the Court's ability to deal with the issue presented, since the CDA might apply to some but not all types of concession contracts (p. 812).

Concurring in the judgment, Justice Stevens would have dismissed the action due to the absence of any allegations of injury sufficient to support standing. Justice Breyer, joined by Justice O'Connor, dissented from the holding of unripeness. According to Justice Breyer, the challengers suffered injury adequate for standing and hardship sufficient to support ripeness, both arising from their need to "plan now for higher contract implementation costs" (p. 818) if they could not realize the benefits available to contracting parties under the CDA; Justice Breyer thought that similar injury and hardship resulted insofar as bidders on future contracts were "forced to pay more" than the contracts would be worth if the CDA did not apply (*id.*). Under the two-part Abbott Labs test, Justice Breyer also maintained that the purely legal nature of the question presented militated in favor of a finding of ripeness (p. 819–20).

If the challenged NPS rule does not bind agency review boards or command deference from the courts, and if the prospect of its application by an NPS contracting officer does not constitute a significant hardship, are there any circumstances under which a challenge to the rule would become ripe?

Page 229. Add at the end of the first paragraph of Subparagraph (3)(b):

The bite of Williamson's determination that a Just Compensation claim is not ripe until a claimant has sought "compensation through the procedures the State has provided for doing so", 473 U.S. at 194, was felt in San Remo Hotel, L.P. v. City and County of San Francisco, 125 S. Ct. 2491 (2005). In an opinion by Justice Stevens, the Court held that after a state court had ruled on an as-applied takings claim, its decision was entitled to preclusive effect in federal court. Noting other contexts in which a plaintiff who would have preferred to proceed in federal court may be required to litigate in state court instead, the Court termed it "hardly a radical notion to recognize that, as a practical matter, a significant number of plaintiffs will necessarily litigate their federal takings claims in state courts" (p. ___). Concurring in the judgment, Chief Justice Rehnquist, joined by Justices O'Connor, Kennedy, and Thomas, opined that the Court, in an appropriate case, "should reconsider whether plaintiffs asserting a Fifth Amendment takings claim based on the final decision of a state or local government entity must first seek compensation in state courts" (p. ___).

Page 241. Add to the penultimate paragraph of Paragraph (3):

The Court cited Lyons as authority for denying standing in McConnell v. Federal Election Commission, 540 U.S. 93 (2003), in which it held that a Senator could not challenge a statutory provision that would allegedly impede his re-election effort in a campaign nearly five years off. In finding that standing required an injury that was not temporally "remote" (p. 226), Chief Justice Rehnquist's opinion for the Court made no reference to ripeness. Neither did Justice Stevens, joined by Justices Ginsburg and Breyer, who dissented on the standing question.

Page 243. Add to Paragraph (5):

In Gratz v. Bollinger, 539 U.S. 244 (2003), the Court upheld the justiciability of a class action challenging the affirmative action policies of the University of Michigan with respect to freshman admissions, even though the class representative claimed continuing harm only from the school's policy concerning transfer admissions. After having been turned down for admission as a freshman, the petitioner Hamacher filed suit challenging the University's undergraduate affirmative action policies. Although he matriculated at another institution, he represented that he would apply to transfer to the University of Michigan if it ceased to consider race as a factor in admissions. The district court certified Hamacher as the representative of a class consisting of all non-beneficiaries of the University's undergraduate affirmative action policies, including both freshman and transfer admissions, who had either been rejected in the past or intended to apply in the future. (A separate challenge to the University of Michigan Law School's admissions policy was rejected by the Supreme Court on the merits in the companion case of Grutter v. Bollinger, 539 U.S. 306 (2003).) Thereafter, the Gratz litigation centered almost exclusively on the freshman admission policy, which included the assignment of 20 points on a 150–point scale on the basis of race.

In the Supreme Court, Justices Stevens and Souter maintained that Hamacher suffered no imminent threat of future injury from the freshman admissions policy and therefore lacked standing to seek an injunction against it. The majority disagreed in an opinion by Chief Justice Rehnquist, who emphasized that Hamacher contested the constitutionality of any reliance on race as a component of undergraduate admissions decisions and that reliance on race was a common element of the freshman and transfer admissions policies. Only the freshman admissions policy used a point system under which all underrepresented minority applicants received 20 points, but "[w]hile this difference might be relevant to a narrow tailoring analysis, it clearly has no effect on petitioners' standing to challenge the University's use of race in undergraduate admissions and its assertion that diversity is a compelling state interest that justifies its consideration of the race of its undergraduate applications" (p. 266).

Following this ruling with respect to standing, the Court held, by 6–3, that the freshman admissions policy was unconstitutional only because it was not "narrowly tailored" to the University's compelling interest in promoting diversity. The Court did not address the constitutionality of the transfer admissions policy.

In his dissenting opinion, Justice Stevens, joined by Justice Souter, cited the Lyons case, Fifth Edition p. 239, in arguing that although Hamacher would have standing to seek damages resulting from his denial of admission as a freshman, he lacked standing to seek an injunction against the freshman admissions policy, because he would never again file an application under it. As the majority noted, however, an obvious difference between the cases is that Gratz was certified as a class action, whereas Lyons was not. Is the real issue whether Hamacher was appropriately certified to represent a class consisting of challengers to *both* the freshman admissions and the transfer admissions policies? The Gratz majority appeared to acknowledge this question, but gave no clear answer, pronouncing it unnecessary to resolve whether Hamacher's entitlement to challenge the freshman admissions policy should be treated as "a matter of Article III standing" or as an issue involving "the propriety of class certification pursuant to Federal Rule of Civil Procedure 23(a)" (p. 263).[a]

a. The Court observed in a footnote that "[a]lthough we do not resolve here whether such an inquiry in this case is appropriately addressed under the rubric of stand-

In a footnote in his dissenting opinion (p. 287 n.6), Justice Stevens posed a hypothetical case in which Hamacher sought to challenge not only the University of Michigan's undergraduate admissions policies (governing both freshman and transfer admissions), but also the Law School's admissions policy. On what grounds, if any, should he have been barred from doing so? *Cf.* General Tel. Co. v. Falcon, 5th Ed. p. 216.

SECTION 6.   POLITICAL QUESTIONS

Page 256. Add to Paragraph (3):

In Vieth v. Jubelirer, 541 U.S. 267 (2004), Justice Scalia's plurality opinion cited an absence of judicially manageable standards as its ground for holding that a challenge to the political gerrymander of Pennsylvania voting districts presented a nonjusticiable political question. Writing for himself, Chief Justice Rehnquist, and Justices O'Connor and Thomas, Justice Scalia did not dispute that "severe partisan gerrymanders violate the Constitution" (p. 292), but he concluded that there were no constitutionally appropriate and judicially manageable standards for determining when state legislatures, which are entitled to give some weight to partisan considerations in designing voting districts, have gone "too far" (pp. 291, 293, 296). The plurality opinion examined a number of possible tests—including those articulated in the plurality and concurring opinions in Davis v. Bandemer, 478 U.S. 109 (1986), a formula proposed by the challengers in Vieth, and those offered in three separate dissenting opinions—and found each of them wanting.

Justice Kennedy concurred in the judgment ordering dismissal of the plaintiffs' challenge. He agreed with the plurality that no constitutionally adequate and judicially manageable standard for identifying forbidden partisan gerrymanders "has emerged in this case" (p. 311) and therefore supported dismissal. Unlike the plurality, however, he declined to pronounce partisan gerrymandering claims categorically non-justiciable (pp. 309–11): "[There] are * * * weighty arguments for holding cases like these to be nonjusticiable; and those arguments may prevail in the long run. In my view, however, the arguments are not so compelling that they require us now to bar all future claims of injury from a partisan gerrymander. * * * That no [adequate] standard has emerged in this case should not be taken to prove that none will emerge in the future."

Writing in dissent, Justice Stevens maintained that partisan gerrymanders should be scrutinized under the same test used to determine the constitutionality of so-called majority-minority voting districts—a test that the Court obviously regards as judicially manageable. Justices Souter (joined by Justice Ginsburg) and Breyer also disagreed with the plurality about the absence of judicially manageable standards and indeed identified the (different) standards that they would apply.

ing or adequacy, we note that there is tension in our prior cases in this regard. See, *e.g.*, Burns, *Standing and Mootness in Class Ac-* *tions: A Search for Consistency*, 22 U.C.D.L.Rev. 1239 1240–41 (1989) * * * " (p. 263 n.15).

As Justice Scalia's plurality opinion acknowledged in response to Justice Stevens' suggestion that political gerrymanders should be analyzed in the same way as race-based gerrymanders, it will seldom if ever be the case that a court could not devise judicially manageable standards if that were the only relevant concern. In the eyes of the plurality, the difficulty with Justice Stevens' proposed standard was not that it was judicially unmanageable, but that it was not "discernible in the Constitution" (p. 295). How helpful is this formulation? Are familiar judicial standards such as strict scrutiny and rational basis review, and the multi-part tests used to apply various constitutional provisions, "discernible in the Constitution", or are they better viewed as formulas devised by courts to implement the Constitution? When the Court cites an absence of judicially manageable standards, is it making a claim about the Constitution or entering a confession about its own inability to craft standards that it regards as both sound and judicially manageable? Justice Kennedy's concurring opinion in Vieth appeared to assume the latter and, for that reason, declined to characterize political gerrymandering cases as presenting political questions, even though he agreed with the plurality that no judicially manageable standard "has emerged" to date. His effort to find a middle ground with respect to justiciability drew a sharp retort from Justice Scalia (p. 301): "The first thing to be said about Justice Kennedy's disposition is that it is not legally available. The District Court in this case considered the plaintiffs' claims *justiciable* but dismissed them because the standard for unconstitutionality had not been met. It is logically impossible to affirm that dismissal without either (1) finding that the unconstitutional-districting standard applied by the District Court, or some other standard that it *should* have applied, has not been met, or (2) finding (as we have) that the claim is nonjusticiable. Justice Kennedy seeks to affirm '[b]ecause, in the case before us, we have no standard.' But it is *our* job, not the plaintiffs', to explicate the standard that makes the facts alleged by the plaintiffs adequate or inadequate to state a claim" (alteration in original). Accordingly, Justice Scalia continued, the lower courts should treat Justice Kennedy's "pronouncement" as if it were "a reluctant fifth vote against justiciability * * * that may change in some future case but that holds, for the time being, that this matter is nonjusticiable" (p. 305). Do you agree?

CHAPTER III

THE ORIGINAL JURISDICTION OF THE SUPREME COURT

SECTION 1. CASES IN WHICH A STATE IS A PARTY

Page 281. Add to Paragraph (2)(a):

For criticism of state immunity from suit by foreign nations, and an argument that the Supreme Court has original and exclusive jurisdiction over suits by foreign nations alleging that states have violated treaties, see Lee, *The Supreme Court of the United States as Quasi–International Tribunal: Reclaiming the Court's Original and Exclusive Jurisdiction over Treaty–Based Suits by Foreign States against States*, 104 Colum.L.Rev. 1765 (2004). The Founders, Lee suggests, addressed the problem of state non-compliance with treaty commitments by empowering the Supreme Court to serve as a "quasi-international tribunal" (p. 1845). The Court would be sufficiently dignified and neutral to serve that role, and adjudication would be preferable to the alternatives of direct diplomacy (which would often require the United States to sacrifice the interests of a majority of states because of the recalcitrance of a few), pressure on states by the federal government (which would be difficult given the strength of ante-bellum states), or war (which the young republic was ill-equipped to fight). Lee suggests that just as the states agreed to submit to suit by sister states to ensure domestic peace, they agreed to submit to suit by foreign nations to ensure international peace. (He acknowledges that the latter consent is not reciprocal, as under international law states would likely have been unable to enforce judgments against foreign nations.) And he argues that such a jurisdiction would not disrespect a state's sovereign dignity, as the opposing party is also a sovereign whose decision to sue requires the exercise of political responsibility.

Lee argues that such jurisdiction was conferred in Section 13 of the Judiciary Act of 1789, a conferral that suggests that Article III extends to such disputes. He also contends that section 13, and possibly Article III itself, mandate exclusive Supreme Court jurisdiction in such cases. For much of the nation's history, he argues, the jurisdiction was broadly recognized (in dicta), but by the time of the Monaco decision in 1934, America's great power status obscured the original reasons for the jurisdiction. He suspects that Monaco was wrongly decided on its facts, but as it involved only a claim to recover on a bond and fell within federal court jurisdiction only because of party-based "diversity", he would read it narrowly as not precluding claims against unconsenting states for violations of treaty obligations.

———

SECTION 3.   EXTRAORDINARY WRITS AND THE ORIGINAL JURISDICTION

———

Page 312. Add to Paragraph (1):

In *Not the King's Bench*, 20 Const.Comm. 283 (2003), Professor Hartnett expressed disagreement with the statement in the Fifth Edition that when issuance of an extraordinary writ is a proper exercise of the Supreme Court's original jurisdiction, no statutory authorization is necessary. Hartnett reads Marbury as indicating "that whether the Supreme Court is empowered to issue a particular prerogative writ depends, in the first instance, on whether Congress authorized it to do so" (p. 293). He then highlights holdings that, absent congressional authorization, prerogative writs may not be issued either (a) by the inferior federal courts or (b) by the Supreme Court, when acting within its appellate jurisdiction. From these and other decisions, he adduces the principle that the Supreme Court did not inherit the power of the King's Bench in England to issue prerogative writs absent legislative authorization.

Does Marbury, in which Marshall thought that Congress had clearly granted the Court authority to issue mandamus, in fact imply that if such authorization had been absent, the Supreme Court would have lacked jurisdiction? And is such an implication supported by the other decisions that Hartnett mentions? Recall that Article III provides that absent congressional authorization, the lower federal courts have no jurisdiction (indeed, that they don't even exist); thus, the need in that setting for congressional authorization to issue prerogative writs is hardly surprising. And while Article III does directly confer appellate jurisdiction on the Supreme Court, it does so subject to "such Exceptions * * * as Congress shall make"; and the Court has long held that an affirmative congressional grant of appellate jurisdiction constitutes "a negation of the exercise of such appellate power as is not comprehended within it." See Durousseau v. United States, 10 U.S. (6 Cranch) 307, 312 (1810). Thus, in the end Congress has an important role in shaping the scope of the Supreme Court's appellate jurisdiction as well. Do the examples on which Hartnett relies establish the need for congressional authorization with regard to the Supreme Court's original jurisdiction, which is not only given directly by the Constitution but also may not be extended or restricted by Congress?

CHAPTER IV

CONGRESSIONAL CONTROL OF THE DISTRIBUTION OF JUDICIAL POWER AMONG FEDERAL AND STATE COURTS

SECTION 1. CONGRESSIONAL REGULATION OF FEDERAL JURISDICTION

Page 340. Add to Paragraph (3):

If Klein's language concerning the impermissibility of jurisdiction-stripping legislation enacted as a means to an unconstitutional end were taken literally, could the result in McCardle be justified? For a discussion of McCardle's political context and a suggestion (though not a conclusion) that surrounding political currents may have influenced the Court's decision, see Friedman, *The History of the Countermajoritarian Difficulty, Part II: Reconstruction's Political Court*, 91 Georgetown L.J. 1, 25–38 (2002). If "the odor of politics" hung about the Court's decision, should it be viewed as "somewhat surprising that the Court's dismissal of McCardle frequently has been invoked as support for the proposition that Congress has broad power to remove cases from the jurisdiction of the Supreme Court"? *Id.* at 36.

Page 347. Add to Paragraph (2)(a):

See also Demore v. Kim, 538 U.S. 510 (2003) (holding that a statutory provision providing that "no court may set aside any action or decision" by the Attorney General and that the Attorney General's decision "shall not be subject to review" did not preclude a habeas corpus challenge to the statutory framework under which the Attorney General acted).

Page 355. Add to footnote 39:

In Demore v. Kim, 538 U.S. 510 (2003), Justice Scalia's protest in St. Cyr that the Court had demanded a "superclear statement, 'magic words' "indication of congressional intent to preclude habeas corpus review was quoted in *support* of the proposition that "where a provision precluding review is claimed to bar habeas review, the Court has required a particularly clear statement that such is Congress' intent" (p. 517). By 6–3, the Demore Court concluded that statutory language barring judicial review of "any action or decision by the Attorney General under this section regarding the detention * * * of any alien" did not preclude a habeas action challenging a provision that mandated detention pending removal proceedings for all aliens convicted of specified crimes. Justice O'Connor, joined by Justices Scalia and Thomas, dissented on the jurisdictional issue.

Page 357. Add a new Paragraph (4) at the end of Subpart D:

(4) Executive Detentions of Enemy Combatants. Apart from any deliberate congressional attempt to preclude jurisdiction, the Executive Branch has contended that the President possesses authority under the commander-in-chief power to order the indefinite detention of "enemy combatants", including American citizens believed to be connected with international terrorist networks, and that presidential orders directing such detentions are either not reviewable by any court or reviewable at most for formal regularity. See pp. 25, 90–114, *infra.*

SECTION 2. CONGRESSIONAL AUTHORITY TO ALLOCATE JUDICIAL POWER TO NON-ARTICLE III FEDERAL TRIBUNALS

Page 378. Add to footnote 1:

Nguyen v. United States, 539 U.S. 69 (2003), held as a matter of statutory construction that judges of the non-Article III district courts for Guam and the Northern Mariana Islands, are ineligible to sit on federal courts of appeals under 28 U.S.C. § 292(a), which provides that "[t]he chief judge of a circuit may designate and assign one or more district judges within the circuit to sit upon the court of appeals * * * whenever the business of that court so requires". If the statute were revised to permit non-Article III judges to sit on panels of the federal courts of appeals, would their participation violate Article III in cases (such as Nguyen) on appeal from non-Article III courts sitting in federal territories? (The Court specifically declined to reach this or any other constitutional question. See p. 76 n.9.)

Page 387. Add a new Subparagraph (8)(f):

(f) "Inferior Tribunals" Account. Pfander, *Article I Tribunals, Article III Courts, and the Judicial Power of the United States,* 118 Harv.L.Rev. 643 (2004), attempts to develop a foundation for non-Article III tribunals in the constitutional text by distinguishing between the language of Article I, which empowers Congress "[t]o constitute *Tribunals* inferior to the Supreme Court", and of Article III, which says that the judicial power of the United States "shall be vested in one supreme Court, and in such inferior *Courts* as the Congress may from time to time ordain and establish". According to Pfander, the "Tribunals" contemplated by Article I are non-Article III tribunals, to be contrasted with the inferior "Courts" authorized by Article III. Although he hedges slightly on the point, Pfander appears to believe that most if not all of the non-Article III federal tribunals with long historical pedigrees have had as their subject matter disputes that either (1) lay wholly outside of Article III (*e.g.,* because the contemplated judgments lacked finality, as was once the case in suits against the United States) or (2) were structured by Congress to lie outside Article III (a condition apparently defined in partly circular fashion by reference to their assignment to non-Article III tribunals, as with cases arising under the Constitution or laws of the United States but assigned by Congress to territorial courts). Pfander approves adjudication by administrative agencies on the separate theory that they are "adjuncts" to Article III courts.

According to Pfander, the constitutionally specified "inferior" status of non-Article III tribunals requires oversight by the Article III judiciary, but the oversight can be exercised in some cases by writs such as habeas corpus or mandamus and need not always take the form of formal "appellate review" or its equivalent. The "inferior tribunals" theory is thus less demanding than appellate review theory in some respects, but it is also more demanding in others. For example, it would not allow the assignment to non-Article III tribunals of any disputes the adjudication of which would have lain "at the traditional core of the judicial power of the United States" (p. 747), even if appellate review were provided.

Pfander's theory appears original in emphasizing the linguistic difference between Articles I and III, and it provides a fair and searching critique of appellate review theory, which cannot explain important elements of current law. But how much analytic bite does the "inferior tribunals" theory possess? As noted, its account of the kinds of cases permissibly assigned to non-Article III tribunals seems at last partly circular. And if administrative adjudication can be justified by the plain fiction (tracing to Crowell v. Benson) that administrative agencies are "adjuncts" to Article III courts, is there any sound reason why adjudication by other non-Article III decision-makers could not be justified on the same theory? Indeed, in its embrace of historical practices including the approval of agency adjudication on an "adjuncts" rationale, doesn't the "inferior tribunals" theory bear important methodological similarities to the "historical exceptions" approach adopted by the plurality opinion in the Northern Pipeline case?

Page 403. Add a new footnote 11a at the end of the first full paragraph:

11a. See also Note, *Assigning the Judicial Power to International Tribunals: NAFTA Binational Panels and Foreign Affairs Flexibility*, 88 Va.L.Rev. 1529 (2002) (arguing that although the constitutionality of NAFTA's binational panel system would be uncertain under otherwise applicable principles, the scheme should be upheld based upon "separation of powers 'flexibility' unique to the foreign affairs area").

Page 404. Add to Paragraph (3)(a):

In Roell v. Withrow, 538 U.S. 580 (2003), the Court held (5–4) that the required consent to trial of a civil action by a full-time magistrate judge can be implied from a party's conduct during litigation.

Page 410. Add to Paragraph (3)(c)(i):

But see Bryant & Tobias, *Quirin Revisited*, 2003 Wisc.L.Rev. 309, 332–61, arguing that the restriction of habeas inquiries to the question whether an alleged offense came within the jurisdiction of a military tribunal should now be regarded as anachronistic. Although it is often maintained that federal habeas courts were once limited to the narrow question whether a sentencing tribunal possessed jurisdiction, see Fifth Edition pp. 1314–17, the scope of habeas inquiries in other contexts broadened dramatically in the decades after World War II, particularly in cases involving challenges to criminal convictions rendered by state courts. See generally Fifth Edition, Chap. XI, Sec. 2. Against this backdrop, the authors maintain that there is no longer a principled basis on which federal habeas review could be limited to the question whether an alleged offense came within the jurisdiction of a military tribunal. Should federal habeas corpus review of the determinations of military commissions proceed on the same basis as federal habeas inquiries into the lawfulness of state criminal convictions?

Page 410. Add a new Sub–Paragraph (3)(c)(iv):

The Justices jousted over the meaning of Milligan and Quirin in Hamdi v. Rumsfeld, 124 S.Ct. 2633 (2004), also discussed pp. 90–102, *infra*. Hamdi involved the claimed authority of the President to detain as an "enemy combatant" an American citizen who had been captured in Afghanistan but then removed to the United States. In a plurality opinion joined by the Chief Justice and Justices Kennedy and Breyer, Justice O'Connor concluded that Quirin "postdates and clarifies Milligan" (p. 2643) by establishing that an American citizen enjoys no immunity from punishment or detention as an enemy combatant that would otherwise be permissible under the laws and usages of war. The plurality then went on to hold that Hamdi was entitled under the Due Process Clause to challenge his designation as an enemy combatant before a competent tribunal. Justice O'Connor referred without elaboration to "the possibility" that the process to which Hamdi was due could be provided "by an appropriately authorized and properly constituted military tribunal" (p. 2651).

Dissenting, Justice Scalia (joined by Justice Stevens) maintained that the traditions underlying the Constitution's guarantee of the privilege of habeas corpus barred the government from simply detaining an American citizen as an enemy combatant without trying him for any crime. In support of this view, Justice Scalia cited Milligan's assertion that the "laws and usages" of war "can never be applied to citizens in states * * * where the courts are open and their process unobstructed" (pp. 2667–68) (quoting Milligan, 71 U.S. (4 Wall.) at 121). According to Justice Scalia, "if the law of war cannot be applied to citizens where courts are open, then Hamdi's imprisonment without criminal trial is no less unlawful than Milligan's trial by military tribunal" (p. 2668). Quirin, Justice Scalia said, sought "to revise Milligan rather than describe" its holding accurately (p. 2669). Even if the revision were accepted, however, Quirin would still not justify the detention in Hamdi: Whereas the petitioners in Quirin were admitted members of enemy forces, in conceded violation of the laws of war, in Hamdi the "jurisdictional facts" for treating the petitioner as an enemy combatant were "*not* conceded" (p. 2670) (emphasis in original), and Hamdi therefore retained a right either to be set free or to be tried for a crime in a civilian court.

Justice Thomas, whose dissenting opinion would have ordered dismissal of Hamdi's habeas corpus petition, thought that Milligan was distinguishable on the ground that it involved criminal punishment, not non-punitive detention. He added that "Quirin overruled Milligan to the extent that those cases are inconsistent" (p. 2682).

Page 412. Add at the end of Sub–Paragraph (5)(c):

In Rasul v. Bush, 124 S.Ct. 2686 (2004), the Court upheld the jurisdiction of the district court for the District of Columbia to consider challenges to the legality of the detention of foreign nationals captured abroad and held for a protracted period at the United States Naval Base at Guantanamo Bay, Cuba, over which the United States exercises "plenary and exclusive jurisdiction, but not 'ultimate sovereignty'" (p. 2693). Justice Stevens' majority opinion found that the petitioners' presence within the territorial jurisdiction of the District Court was not a strict requirement for § 2241 jurisdiction, that previous cases had upheld a district court's authority to issue the writ based on jurisdiction over the custodian, and that "[n]o party questions the District Court's jurisdiction over petitioners' custodians" (p. 2698).[1] Rejecting an argument that the statutory right to habeas corpus applies only within the United States, the Court said that "[w]hatever traction the presumption against extraterritoriality might have in other contexts, it certainly has no application to the operation of the habeas statute with respect to persons detained within 'the territorial jurisdiction' of the United States" (p. 2696). Concurring in the judgment only, Justice Kennedy would have followed "the framework of Eisentrager", Fifth Edition pp. 411, 412–13, in construing the scope of the statutory right to habeas "against the backdrop of the constitutional command of the separation of powers" (p. 2699). He thought the lower court had jurisdiction in Rasul "[i]n light of the status of Guantanamo Bay and the indefinite pretrial detention of the detainees", but "would avoid creating automatic statutory authority to adjudicate the claims of persons located outside the United States" (p. 2701). In a dissenting opinion joined by the Chief Justice and Justice Thomas, Justice Scalia argued that § 2241 extends no rights to habeas to foreign nationals detained outside the territorial jurisdiction of a United States court. He interpreted the majority opinion as taking the "breathtaking" step of "extend[ing] the scope of the habeas statute to the four corners of the earth" (p. 11) and denounced it as "judicial adventurism of the worst sort" (p. 2706).

If Justice Scalia is correct about the implications of the majority opinion in extending federal habeas corpus jurisdiction to aliens across the globe, why does the Court emphasize the special status of Guantanamo Bay? But if the majority opinion turns on the special status of Guantanamo Bay, why doesn't the majority clearly say so in response to Justice Scalia? Should non-citizens detained abroad have the same statutory rights to habeas as citizens? When habeas is available, should non-citizens detained abroad possess the same substantive constitutional rights as citizens? *Cf.* United States v. Verdugo–Urquidez, Fifth Edition p. 414.

Page 413. Add to footnote 9:

For an argument that President Bush's order would be unconstitutional if it did attempt to bar federal habeas corpus review, see Bryant & Tobias, *Youngstown Revisited*, 29 Hastings Const.L.Q. 373 (2002).

Page 414. Add a new footnote 11a at the end of Paragraph (6)(a):

See also Turley, *Tribunals and Tribulations: The Antithetical Elements of Military Governance in a Madisonian Democracy*, 70 Geo.Wash.L.Rev. 649 (2003) (questioning the President's authority to provide for trial of suspected terrorists in military tribunals); Torruella, *On the Slippery Slopes of Afghanistan: Military Commissions and the Exercise of Presidential Power*, 4 U.Pa.J.Const.L. 648 (2002) (critically examining the President's claim of authority to try suspected terrorists before military tribunals and exploring legal issues that trials before such tribunals would raise).

Page 414: Add at the end of the third paragraph in Sub–Paragraph (6)(b):

Although President Bush's Order contemplates the use of military tribunals only to try non-citizens, Justice O'Connor's plurality opinion in Hamdi v. Rumsfeld, 124 S.Ct. 2633 (2004), also discussed p. 25, *supra*, and pp. 90–102, *infra*—which found that the Authorization for Use of Military Force enacted in

---

1. The question of who counts as the custodian for purposes of habeas corpus jurisdiction, although not put in issue in Hamdi, was much controverted in another habeas corpus case decided the same day, Rumsfeld v. Padilla, which is discussed at pp. 110–13, *infra*.

the aftermath of 9/11 permits the President to detain American citizens who are "enemy combatants"—adverted to "the possibility" that the constitutionally requisite process to establish a citizen's "enemy combatant" status could be provided "by an appropriately authorized and properly constituted military tribunal" (p. 2651). The Court did not, however, issue any square ruling on the point.

Page 415. Add at the end of Sub–Paragraph (6)(b):

In Rasul v. Bush, 124 S.Ct. 2686 (2004), also discussed p. 25–26, *supra*, and pp. 104–108, *infra*, the Court held that aliens detained at the U.S. Naval Base at Guantanamo Bay, Cuba, come within federal habeas corpus jurisdiction under § 2241, but it did not make fully clear how much, if at all, its ruling depended on the status of Guantanamo as "a territory over which the United States exercises plenary and exclusive jurisdiction, but not 'ultimate sovereignty' "(p. 2693). For discussion, see *supra*.

Page 415. Add a new footnote 13a at the end of Paragraph (6)(c):

Note, 89 Va.L.Rev. 2005 (2003), argues that the Uniform Code of Military Justice requires the procedures used in military commissions trying alleged enemy combatants to be the same as those applied in courts martial.

Page 416. Add a new Paragraph (7):

(7) Indefinite Detentions of Enemy Combatants. Practically if not conceptually related to the question whether alleged unlawful combatants may be tried before military commissions is the question whether, without bringing a prosecution, the government may indefinitely detain alleged "enemy combatants" with little or no judicial review of their detentions. For discussion, see pp. 90–102, *infra*.

Page 418. Add at the end of Paragraph (4):

Pfander, *The Tidewater Problem: Article III and Constitutional Change*, 79 Notre Dame L.Rev. 1925 (2004), attempts to rationalize Tidewater as involving congressional legislation enacted under Section 5 of the Fourteenth Amendment to protect the privileges or immunities of national citizens living in federal territories from biased state court law enforcement, rather than as upholding a grant of diversity jurisdiction under Article III. For further discussion of this "Fourteenth Amendment account of protective jurisdiction" (p. 1931), see p. 135, *infra*.

SECTION 3.   FEDERAL AUTHORITY AND
STATE COURT JURISDICTION

Page 426. Add at the end of the carryover paragraph:

For a sympathetic discussion of "multijurisdictional models" and an argument that they should be used more extensively, see Friedman, *Under the Law of Federal Jurisdiction: Allocating Cases Between State and Federal Courts*, 104

Colum.L.Rev. 1211 (2004). Among the possibilities are "reference" models, under which a federal court with principal decision-making responsibility in a case can refer certain issues to a state court for authoritative resolution (as discussed on pp. 1200–03 of the Fifth Edition); "collateral review" models, under which a federal court effectively reviews state court decisions of federal law (as, for example, in the case of federal habeas corpus review of state court decisions, see Fifth Edition pp. 1296–1399); and "sequencing" models, which allow a party to state court litigation to reserve federal issues for subsequent litigation in federal court (as occasionally happens under federal "abstention" doctrine, see Fifth Edition p. 1200). *See* 104 Colum.L.Rev. at 1228–35.

Page 461. Add to Paragraph (3):

Questions of congressional authority to mandate procedural rules applicable in state law actions in state courts arose in two cases decided during the 2002 Term. In Pierce County v. Guillen, 537 U.S. 129 (2003), the Court ruled unanimously that Congress possesses power under the Commerce Clause to enact a federal statute barring, in state as well as federal trials, the discovery or introduction into evidence of information "compiled or collected" in connection with certain federal highway safety programs (p. 132). But the Court declined to decide (because the question had not been addressed by the lower court) whether the challenged statute "violates principles of dual sovereignty embodied in the Tenth Amendment because it prohibits a State from exercising its sovereign powers to establish discovery and admissibility rules to be used in state court for a state cause of action" (p. 148 n.10).

In Jinks v. Richland County, 538 U.S. 456 (2003), the Court unanimously upheld a provision of the supplemental jurisdiction statute, 28 U.S.C. § 1367(d), that (under some circumstances) tolls the statute of limitations on state law claims while they are pending in federal court. As a result of the tolling, state courts can be obliged to hear claims over which a federal court declines to exercise supplemental jurisdiction after the otherwise applicable state limitations period has expired. Justice Scalia's opinion for the Court first found the tolling provision "necessary and proper for carrying into execution Congress's power 'to constitute Tribunals inferior to the supreme Court' "(p. 462), because, he said, it is conducive to the fair and efficient administration of justice by the federal courts. The Court then separately rejected a claim that in light of principles of state sovereignty it could not be "proper" for Congress to prescribe procedural rules for the adjudication of purely state law claims in state courts: "Assuming for the sake of argument that a principled dichotomy can be drawn * * * between federal laws that regulate state-court 'procedure' and laws that change the 'substance' of state-law rights of action, we do not think that state-law limitations periods fall into the category of 'procedure' immune from congressional regulation" (pp. 464–65). The Court cautioned, however, that "[t]o sustain § 1367(d) in this case, we need not (and do not) hold that Congress has unlimited power to regulate practice and procedure in state courts" (p. 465).

CHAPTER V

REVIEW OF STATE COURT DECISIONS BY THE SUPREME COURT

SECTION 2. THE RELATION BETWEEN STATE AND FEDERAL LAW

SUBSECTION A: SUBSTANTIVE LAW

Page 493. Add to footnote 4:

For an argument (stimulated by Bush v. Gore) that Article III permits the Supreme Court to review issues of state law in a case like Murdock, or in a state court case that involves diversity of citizenship, see Harrison, *Federal Appellate Jurisdiction Over Questions of State Law in State Courts*, 7 Green Bag 2d 353 (2004). Harrison relies on a straightforward textual argument like that offered by Justice Curtis, and suggests that the Court's qualms in Murdock derived from outmoded notions of dual federalism, under which state and federal domains did not overlap and regulation of one level of government by another was strongly disfavored. He contends that the Supreme Court, if reviewing a state court decision on state law, should ignore "the application or extension of state law by the state courts in the case actually before it" (p. 358), and that the Court's state law decision could be rejected by the state courts in a subsequent case, which would then establish the authoritative state law that federal courts would thereafter have to follow. That approach, he suggests, would protect against state courts' trying to control the outcome of a case with a federal ground (in federal question cases) or to disfavor out-of-state litigants (in cases with diverse parties), and would allow the Supreme Court to ensure state court neutrality—even at the cost of impairing the uniform application of state law.

Is Harrison's argument convincing? As to federal question cases, what exactly was the risk to federal law and supremacy in Murdock? Isn't Murdock quite different, in this respect, from Bush v. Gore? See, in this regard, the distinction noted at Fifth Edition p. 493, Paragraph (5), between issues of state law that are "antecedent" to federal law (as in Bush v. Gore) and those that are "distinct" from federal law (as in Murdock). See also Fifth Edition pp. 536–40, discussing Bush v. Gore. As to state court litigations that involve diverse parties, is the threat to out-of-staters from misapplication of state substantive law as great as that from biased findings of fact or disadvantageous state procedural rulings, both of which are often extremely difficult for any appellate court effectively to review—and if not, should the Supreme Court review these latter issues as well (and under what standard of review)? As to both sets of cases, would Harrison's approach effectively require state courts either to disable themselves from making any change in existing law (perhaps refraining even from distinguishing a precedent) or to risk Supreme Court reversal?

Page 514. Add to footnote 9:

See also Bunkley v. Florida, 538 U.S. 835 (2003)(per curiam)(6–3)(vacating a state court judgment on the basis that the state court's decision of a state law issue antecedent to a federal claim was unclear).

Page 517. Add to Paragraph (6):

According to Note, 66 Alb.L.Rev. 969, 979–83 (2003), in five of the seventeen cases in which the Supreme Court granted certiorari based on Long and then reversed, the state supreme court on remand reinstated its prior judgment based on the state constitution.

Page 532. Add a new footnote 7a at the end of Paragraph (3)(a):

7a.   While most actions alleging a deprivation of property without due process are filed in federal court, actions alleging a taking of property without just compensation ordinarily must first be filed in state court as inverse condemnation actions. See Williamson County Regional Planning Comm'n v. Hamilton Bank of Johnson City, 473 U.S. 172 (1985), Fifth Edition p. 1185. According to Sterk, *The Federalist Dimension of Regulatory Takings Jurisprudence,* 114 Yale L.J. 203 (2004), Supreme Court review of such state court actions may be of limited value in providing guidance and fostering uniformity, as the Takings Clause protects primarily against changes in background state law.

Page 534. At the end of Paragraph (3), add a new subparagraph (3)(d):

(d) In Town of Castle Rock v. Gonzales, 125 S.Ct. ___ (2005), the Court refused to recognize an unusual claim of a property interest. There, the plaintiff told the police that she suspected her estranged husband had abducted her three children in violation of a restraining order. Even after she later told police that her husband had called and said that he had the children at an amusement park, the police took no action. Early the next morning, the husband drove to the police station; inside his truck were the murdered children.

The plaintiff sued the town in federal court for a due process violation, alleging that the restraining order gave her a state-created property interest, as Colorado law provides that a peace offer *"shall* use every reasonable means to enforce a restraining order". (In DeShaney v. Winnebago County Dept. of Social Services, 489 U.S. 189 (1989), the Court refused to recognize a federally-created substantive due process right to government protection against private violence, but left open whether an individual might have a state-created interest.) The Court, per Scalia, J., held that plaintiff had no entitlement, refusing to believe, in view of "[t]he deep-rooted nature of law enforcement discretion, even in the presence of seemingly mandatory legislative commands", that "Colorado law truly made enforcement of restraining orders *mandatory"* (p. ___). He supported that conclusion by noting the "indeterminacy" of the "precise means of enforcement that the Colorado restraining-order statute assertedly mandated" (p. ___); a right merely to have police seek an arrest warrant "would be an entitlement to nothing but procedure—which we have held inadequate even to support standing; much less can it be the basis for a property interest" (p. ___). Justice Scalia also doubted that the statute, even if mandatory, gave the *plaintiff* an entitlement to enforcement, noting that criminal laws generally serve public rather than private ends, and he stressed that the asserted interest lacks any ascertainable monetary value, a fact that, "although it does not disqualify it from due process protection", makes it untraditional. Finally, and "[p]erhaps most radically, the alleged property interest here arises incidentally, not out of some new species of government benefit" but "out of a function that government actors have always performed" (p. ___).[a]

In dissent, Justice Stevens, joined by Justice Ginsburg, accused the Court of giving "short shrift to the unique case of 'mandatory arrest' statutes in the domestic violence context" (p. ___). He suggested that the word "shall" was used advisedly and that other states have interpreted similar legislation as creating a mandatory duty. Viewing the question of the scope of the police obligation as a "red herring" (p. ___), for him the key point was that "the police * * * *lacked the discretion to do nothing*" (p. ___). Enforcement, he argued, was clearly intended to benefit victims of violence and is a government service as worthy of recognition as education.

The majority and dissent debated which court should decide the meaning of Colorado law. Though the dissent suggested that the court of appeals was closer to, and thus more qualified to interpret, Colorado law (which it had read as creating an entitlement), the majority refused to defer, reasoning that the opinion below "did not draw upon a deep well of state specific expertise but relied primary on the text of statutes and the restraining order and a state legislative transcript", and that these texts "say nothing distinctive to Colorado, but use mandatory language that * * * appears in many state and federal statutes" (p. ___). The Court also rejected the dissent's alternative suggestion that it certify the question to the Colorado Supreme Court, noting that neither party favored that approach.

Page 536. After the second line, add a new subparagraph (c):

(c) Following Sandin v. Conner, most challenges to prison conditions have failed on the basis that they do not involve "atypical and significant hardship". But in Wilkinson v. Austin, 125 S.Ct. 2384 (2005), a unanimous Court recognized a state-created liberty interest in avoiding assignment to Ohio's "supermax" facility. Acknowledging the general difficulty of determining the appropriate baseline against which to measure whether a hardship is "atypical and significant", the Court determined that "under any plausible baseline", assignment to the supermax prison qualified (p. 2394): "[A]lmost all human contact is prohibited, even to the point that conversation is not permitted from cell to cell; the light, though it may be dimmed, is on for 24 hours; exercise is for 1 hour per day, but only in a small indoor room. Save perhaps for the especially severe limitations on all human contact, these conditions likely would apply to most solitary confinement facilities, but here there are two added components. First is the duration. Unlike the 30–day placement in Sandin, placement * * * is indefinite and, after an initial 30–day review, is reviewed just annually. Second is that placement disqualifies an otherwise eligible inmate for parole consideration. While any of these conditions standing alone might not be sufficient to create a liberty interest, taken together they impose an atypical and significant hardship within the correctional context". The Court proceeded to hold that the state's procedures for assigning inmates to the supermax prison satisfied due process requirements.

a.   Concurring, Justice Souter, joined by Justice Breyer, stressed that "process is not an end in itself". Citing the Loudermill decision, Fifth Edition p. 531 note 6, he contended that just as a state cannot diminish a property right by specifying a limited set of procedures that accompany it, it may not create a property right by merely mandating a beneficial procedure absent some underlying substantive guarantee.

Page 539. Add to footnote 15:

See also Schapiro, *Article II as Interpretive Theory: Bush v. Gore and the Retreat from Erie*, 34 Loy.U.Chi.L.J. 89, 109 (2002)(contending that the concurring opinion's implicit reliance on a textualist method of statutory interpretation, which was not based specifically on Florida law, harkens back to the era of Swift v. Tyson, "when federal courts invoked general common law, rather than the law of a particular state, to decide certain nonfederal disputes"); Harrison, *Federal Appellate Jurisdiction Over Questions of State Law in State Courts*, 7 Green Bag 2d 353 (2004) (contending that all cases involving federal office arise under federal law within the meaning of Article III, and that, according to an argument set forth at p. 29, *supra*, the Supreme Court has plenary power to review questions of state law).

Page 540. Add to footnote 17:

In Green Tree Financial Corp. v. Bazzle, 539 U.S. 444 (2003), the state supreme court had held that (i) certain contractual arbitration clauses were silent as to whether class arbitration is permitted, and (ii) when a clause is silent, state law permits class arbitration. A splintered Supreme Court vacated to allow the arbitrator, rather than the state court, to decide whether class arbitration was permitted, viewing that question as one that was itself arbitrable under the contracts. In reaching that decision, Justice Breyer's plurality opinion relied on a Supreme Court precedent (in a case originating in federal court) stating that doubts should be resolved in favor of arbitrability, as well as on his view that the availability of class, as distinguished from individual, arbitration was a question appropriate for resolution by an arbitrator. The state supreme court evidently disagreed and had viewed the question as one for it, rather than the arbitrator, to decide. If arbitrability is a matter of contract and if state law governs the interpretation of a contract, what justifies the plurality's failure to honor the state supreme court's view of arbitrability?

Writing separately, Justice Stevens found no reason to upset the state court's determination that class arbitration was available. Although "[a]rguably" the question of the availability of class arbitration should have been decided by an arbitrator rather than the court, because the question was properly resolved "and because petitioner has merely challenged the merits of that decision without claiming that it was made by the wrong decisionmaker", he would have affirmed (p. 455). However, because voting to affirm would leave no controlling judgment of the Court, he concurred in the judgment to vacate.

In dissent, Chief Justice Rehnquist (joined by Justices O'Connor and Kennedy) would have reversed, viewing the contracts as clearly precluding class arbitration. He justified rejecting the state supreme court's contrary view on the basis that the FAA calls for enforcement of the parties' agreement and the state court "imposed a regime that was contrary to the express agreement of the parties" (p. 459).

It is not obvious why most of the Justices were so much less deferential to the state court here than they were in the Volt case cited in the Fifth Edition—particularly when the state court decision in Volt prevented the arbitration that the FAA is meant to foster, while the state court decision here did not. Justice Breyer said only that the question of the availability of class arbitration "does not concern a state statute or judicial procedures, *cf.* Volt * * *. It concerns contract interpretation and arbitration procedures. Arbitrators are well situated to answer that question" (pp. 452–53).

Justice Breyer indicated that he, unlike the dissenters, thought it not obvious whether the contracts authorized class arbitration, but that he could not automatically accept the state court's resolution of that question. Should the plurality then be viewed as suggesting that when a contract is unclear on an issue like the availability of class arbitration, there is a *federal* presumption (which a state court must respect) that the issue is arbitrable? Why should that be?

Pages 540–41. Add to Paragraph (D):

For a wide-ranging discussion of the problems raised in this Note, see Monaghan, *Supreme Court Review of State–Court Determinations of State Law in Constitutional Cases,* 103 Colum.L.Rev. 1919 (2003). Monaghan stresses the prevalence of what he calls "characterization" issues—*e.g.,* the question, in Sandin v. Conner, Fifth Edition p. 534, whether disciplinary segregation implicates "liberty", or the question, in Webb's Fabulous Pharmacies, Inc. v. Beckwith, Fifth Edition p. 532, whether the interest on an interpleader fund is property. He contends that such questions do not involve redetermination of state law but simply questions of federal constitutional interpretation.

But the heart of his article addresses cases that do involve redetermination of state law—cases in which the Constitution assigns significance to a state's fidelity to state law as it stood at some point in the past. One example of such a case is Brand, where the Contract Clause gives federal significance to the question whether, under Indiana law, there was a contractual right at the time that allegedly impairing legislation was enacted. A second example is Bush v. Gore, where, following the theory of the concurring Justices, Article II gives federal significance to the question of what Florida law provided, at the time the 2000 election was held, with regard to the counting of ballots. In such cases, Monaghan argues that the Supreme Court has power to engage in de novo review to determine for itself what state law was at the critical time, and he finds support for that view in numerous cases, including Fairfax's Devisee (the prelude to Martin v. Hunter's Lessee) and Brand. Though he believes that ordinarily deferential review is the appropriate stance, more intrusive review may be necessary, he suggests, "particularly in times of change, or in certain controversial areas of the law" (p. 1966). Uncertain whether criteria can be articulated to specify when de novo review should be exercised, he would leave it to the Court's sense of the situation, though he adds that de novo review would rarely be appropriate in cases involving federal statutory rather than constitutional provisions. He agrees with the Chief Justice's conclusion, in his concurrence in Bush v. Gore, that de novo review was appropriate, but on the basis that the issue whether Florida's election was conducted in accordance with Article II deserved to be decided by the highest court in the nation.

Is Monaghan's account preferable to having the Supreme Court redetermine state law if, but only if, a state court's decision was unreasonable, motivated by hostility to federal rights, or lacking in fair support? Absent such defects in the state court decision, is a "sense of the situation" an adequate basis for disregarding the state court's view of its own law?

Page 544. Add to Paragraph (3)(b):

In Howell v. Mississippi, 125 S.Ct. 856 (2005), the petitioner argued that he had presented his federal claim in state court by implication, because the state-law rule on which he had relied was identical to the federal rule. The Court assumed without deciding that identical standards might overcome a failure to have identified as federal a claim pressed in state court, but ruled that state and federal law in fact differed and hence dismissed the petition.

SUBSECTION B: PROCEDURAL REQUIREMENTS

Pages 564–65. Add to Paragraph (9):

For a novel account of the inadequate state procedural ground doctrine, see Roosevelt, *Light from Dead Stars: The Procedural Adequate and Independent*

State Ground Reconsidered, 103 Colum.L.Rev. 1888 (2003). Professor Roosevelt argues that the source of the inadequate state ground doctrine is 28 U.S.C. § 1257, which requires that the federal right be "specially set up or claimed". In his view, it is thus federal law that governs whether a state court procedural default bars Supreme Court review. But federal law in general incorporates applicable state law, so as not to interfere with a state's ability to establish its own procedural rules.[a] When, however, the federal statutory standard does not incorporate state rules (because the state ground is inadequate), that decision governs only the Supreme Court's jurisdiction; it does not preclude the state court from continuing to follow the rule in similar cases.[b]

Can the language of § 1257 bear the weight that Roosevelt places upon it?

Note that under Roosevelt's approach, a state court might correctly apply state procedural law to refuse to hear a federal claim, and then the Supreme Court, on review, would correctly reverse the state court on the basis that the state court's application of state procedural law cannot bar Supreme Court consideration of the federal claim. Is it consistent with the broader implications of Murdock and Erie to have the applicable law in a single litigation change as the case moves up the appellate ladder to the Supreme Court? And isn't it a bit odd for the Supreme Court to say to the state court, "Your procedural decision was unimpeachable; the law is unchanged and no new facts have arisen; but your decision is reversed"?

If the Supreme Court reverses a state court's refusal to entertain a federal claim, wouldn't the state court, on remand, be obliged to entertain that claim? If so, doesn't a finding of inadequacy necessarily govern not only the Supreme Court's own proceedings but also state court proceedings? And if a federal rule governing inadequacy applies in state courts upon remand from the Supreme Court, why shouldn't it apply in state court prior to Supreme Court review? (Imagine, in that regard, a case coming up through the state courts identical in every pertinent respect to a case in which the Supreme Court recently found a procedural foreclosure inadequate.)

––––––––––

a. Roosevelt also suggests that his account is compatible with the application of procedural default doctrine in habeas corpus, because habeas review, especially as reshaped by the 1996 amendments to the habeas jurisdiction, focuses on the state judgment, much as Supreme Court review does. (But isn't that claim implausible in precisely the cases that he addresses—those involving procedural default—as by definition there will not be a state court determination of the defaulted claim?)

b. Roosevelt suggests that his account differs from that of commentators who agree that determinations of inadequacy have no binding effect, for those commentators look to multiple sources (including, for example, the substantive federal right in question) in determining whether a state ground is inadequate, whereas he looks only to § 1257. But reconsider Wood v. Georgia, Fifth Edition p. 545, a decision that clearly implicates § 1257 (because the issue was never raised in state court at all). Isn't is clear that the nature of the right involved—an alleged conflict of interest on the part of the lawyer who failed to assert Wood's constitutional claim—figured importantly in that decision?

SUBSECTION C: REVIEW OF FACT AND OF APPLICATION OF LAW TO FACT

———

Page 586. Add a new footnote 19a to the end of Paragraph (5)(c):

19a. In Illinois ex rel. Madigan v. Telemarketing Assocs., 538 U.S. 600 (2003), the Court offered a cryptic reference to Bose. In holding that the First Amendment did not preclude a civil fraud action against a fundraising corporation, the Court noted that state law required proof "by clear and convincing evidence" and, citing New York Times v. Sullivan, observed that exacting proof requirements like these have been held in other contexts to provide sufficient breathing room for free expression. The opinion then said (p. 621): "As an additional safeguard responsive to First Amendment concerns, an appellate court *could* independently review the trial court's findings. *Cf.* Bose Corp. (de novo appellate review of findings regarding actual malice)" (emphasis added).

———

SECTION 3. FINAL JUDGMENTS AND THE HIGHEST STATE COURT

———

Page 596. Add to the end of Paragraph (5):

On the last day of the 2002 Term, the Supreme Court decided two cases implicating the finality requirement, but the issue was addressed by only four Justices in one decision and was ignored in the other.

(a) In Nike, Inc. v. Kasky, 539 U.S. 654 (2003)(per curiam), a California resident sued Nike, alleging that the corporation's public statements about its labor practices abroad violated state unfair competition law. The trial court granted Nike's demurrer, which contended that the lawsuit was barred by the First Amendment, but on an interlocutory appeal, the California Supreme Court reversed, finding that the speech involved was "commercial" and was not constitutionally protected if false or misleading. The U.S. Supreme Court granted certiorari but, after argument, dismissed the writ as improvidently granted.

Justice Stevens wrote a concurring opinion (joined by Justice Ginsburg), advancing, as one of several reasons for the disposition, the conclusion that the state judgment was not final. Nike argued that the case fell within the fourth Cox exception because a determination by the Supreme Court that the speech in question was noncommercial would render it absolutely privileged and thus would preclude further litigation. Justice Stevens responded that although that might be so, "the Court could also take a number of other paths that would neither preclude further proceedings in the state courts, nor finally resolve the First Amendment questions in this case" (p. 660).

Dissenting from dismissal of the writ, Justice Breyer (joined by Justice O'Connor) contended that the case fit within the fourth Cox category. He argued that "outright reversal" of the state supreme court's judgment would preclude further litigation, and he deemed it irrelevant that the Court might take some middle ground. Acknowledging the argument that the fourth Cox exception should not apply when the likelihood of outright reversal was low, he reviewed the merits and concluded that outright reversal was a "serious possibility" (p. 681). Finally, he stressed that the California scheme could seriously chill commercial speech by businesses in California, thereby eroding federal policy.

Justices Stevens and Breyer also disagreed about whether the case or controversy requirement barred Supreme Court review. See p. 4, *supra.* Justice Kennedy dissented from the order of dismissal without explanation.

(b) In Stogner v. California, 539 U.S. 607 (2003), the defendant challenged, as a violation of the Ex Post Facto Clause, his prosecution after the expiration of the limitations periods set forth in previously applicable statutes of limitations. A state law, enacted after those periods had expired, purported to revive otherwise time-barred criminal prosecutions for certain sex-related child abuse offenses. The trial court initially dismissed the charges, but on interlocutory review, a state intermediate appellate court ultimately rejected the defendant's position and thus left the charges standing. The Supreme Court granted certiorari to review that judgment and reversed, 5–4. Neither the majority nor the dissent (nor the briefs) discussed whether the state court judgment was final under § 1257.

Should the Ex Post Facto Clause, like the Double Jeopardy Clause, be viewed as conferring an immunity not merely from conviction but also from prosecution—an immunity that would be seriously eroded if Supreme Court review had to await the defendant's conviction? Does the Stogner decision suggest that whenever a state court's denial of a limitations defense depends on an issue of federal constitutional or statutory law (as might be true, for example, when state courts exercise concurrent jurisdiction over federal civil causes of action), the finality requirement does not stand in the way of a defendant's efforts to obtain immediate Supreme Court review of the federal question?

CHAPTER VI

THE LAW APPLIED IN CIVIL ACTIONS IN THE DISTRICT COURTS

SECTION 2. THE POWERS OF THE FEDERAL COURTS IN DEFINING PRIMARY LEGAL OBLIGATIONS THAT FALL WITHIN THE LEGISLATIVE COMPETENCE OF THE STATES

———

Page 636. Add to footnote 3:

See also Weinberg, *Back to the Future: The New General Common Law*, 35 J.Mar. Law & Commerce 523 (2004)(contending, *inter alia*, that the Erie doctrine is rooted in part in the due process clause because "[t]he chosen sovereign cannot rationally, and therefore cannot constitutionally, 'govern' an issue, if it has no interest in applying its law to that issue on the particular facts" (p. 552)).

———

SECTION 3. ENFORCING STATE-CREATED OBLIGATIONS—EQUITABLE REMEDIES AND PROCEDURE

———

Page 644. Add a new footnote 9 at the end of Paragraph (4):

9. See Nash, *Resuscitating Deference to Lower Federal Court Judges' Interpretations of State Law*, 77 S.Cal.L.Rev. 975 (2004)(contending that federal appellate court deference to lower federal court interpretations of state law is desirable in many circumstances and that the Erie rationale argues against such deference only when it is likely to lead to forum shopping or inequitable administration of the laws).

Page 652. Add to footnote 2:

For a spirited defense of the Southland result, see Drahozal, *In Defense of Southland: Reexamining the Legislative History of the Federal Arbitration Act*, 78 Notre Dame L.Rev. 101 (2002). Professor Drahozal concludes, on the basis of a detailed examination of the legislative history of the Act, that "while the 'primary purpose' of the FAA was to make arbitration agreements enforceable in federal court, a secondary purpose was to make arbitration agreements enforceable in state court" (p. 169).

Page 653. Add to footnote 3:

For eloquent support of the dissents in the Grupo Mexicano and Great–West cases, see Resnik, *Constricting Remedies: The Rehnquist Judiciary, Congress, and Federal Power*, 78 Ind.L.J. 223 (2003). In the course of a broad-ranging analysis of the present majority's approach to the judicial power, Professor Resnik criticizes the decisions in both cases as rejecting a dynamic conception of judicial authority "evolving with new forms of commerce or with statutes calling for judges to use equitable powers"; instead, she concludes, the majority, adopting a "cribbed" approach to its authority under statutes, rules, and the common law tradition, has "insisted that contemporary federal judicial power be limited to those remedies * * * believed to have been available in equity during the constitutional era" (p. 226). See also Meltzer, *The Supreme Court's Judicial Passivity*, 2002 Sup.Ct.Rev. 343, 346–51 (noting that the majority's holding in Great–West—that the subrogation remedy sought was not traditionally available in equity—"required considerable effort", and further noting that this holding, coupled with the preemptive effect of the federal statute in question (ERISA), may well mean that the remedy sought would not be available in *any* forum under *any* law).

CHAPTER VII

FEDERAL COMMON LAW

SECTION 1. DEFINING PRIMARY OBLIGATIONS

Pages 698. Add a new footnote 7 at the end of Paragraph (4):

7. Bellia, *State Courts and the Making of Federal Common Law*, 153 U.Pa.L.Rev. 825 (2005), probes how leading theories of the source of federal common lawmaking power accommodate the recognized power and obligation of *state courts* to fashion federal common law in the same circumstances in which a federal court would do so. With respect to theories based upon delegation, he asks, *inter alia*, whether Congress may delegate authority to the state courts and may oblige state courts to exercise common lawmaking authority. (On the latter point, Bellia notes that Louisiana is a civil code jurisdiction that does not recognize judicial lawmaking.) He also argues that delegation would violate the Supremacy Clause, because state-fashioned common law by its nature cannot be the law of the land. An historical examination leads him to the conclusion that state court authority to fashion federal common law extends only to the application of existing principles, and not to forward-looking, policy-based lawmaking. (Is that an administrable distinction? And doesn't it preclude state courts from making common law in cases of first impression, no matter how clear it is that a federal court would fashion a federal common law rule?)

While Bellia provides an interesting prism through which to consider various theories, are his objections to state common lawmaking convincing? For example, he deems it strange to read the Supremacy Clause as authorizing state judges to create the law to which the Clause dictates they are bound (p. 853). He also contends that state courts cannot make law governing the entire nation (hence doubting they truly can make "federal" law) and that state courts may be less sympathetic to federal interests and less expert than federal courts. But wouldn't those objections apply equally to the recognized obligation of state courts, under the Supremacy Clause, to enforce or interpret federal statutes or the Constitution?

Page 726. Add to footnote 6:

See also Klein, *Independent-Norm Federalism in Criminal Law*, 90 Calif.L.Rev. 1541, 1553–54, 1545–64 (2002) (noting that federal criminal prohibitions are almost never held to preempt parallel or overlapping state criminal prohibitions).

Page 735. Add to Paragraph (3):

Norfolk Southern Ry. Co. v. Kirby, 125 S.Ct. 385 (2004), involved a contract for shipment of goods first by sea and then by rail to their final destination. The Court held unanimously that federal law governed the shipper's damages action against the railroad, on the basis that the contract has "reference to maritime service or maritime transactions" (p. 393). The Court rejected a "spatial approach" under which admiralty jurisdiction does not reach contracts that require maritime and nonmaritime transport unless the nonmaritime portion is "merely incidental" (p. 394), ruling instead that any local interest in applying state law had to yield to the federal interest (especially in uniformity) in regulating maritime commerce.

Page 735. Add to footnote 7:

See also the discussion at p. 70, *infra*, of Robertson & Sturley, *The Admiralty Extension Act Solution*, 34 J.Mar.L. & Comm. 209 (2003).

Page 738. Add a new footnote 10a:

For criticism of Professor Gutoff's argument that congressional grants of jurisdiction delegated lawmaking authority to the federal courts, see Young, *It's Just Water: Toward the Normalization of Admiralty*, 35 J. Mar. L & Comm. 469, 485–507 (2004).

Page 743. Add a new Subsection E, before Banco Nacional de Cuba v. Sabbatino:

E. The Alien Tort Statute

For a recent decision suggesting that the federal courts' lawmaking authority in an entirely different area arises from a congressional grant of jurisdiction, one enacted on the understanding that the courts would apply judge-made law (in this case under the law of nations), see Sosa v. Alvarez–Machain, 124 S.Ct. 2739 (2004), p. 42, *infra*, interpreting the Alien Tort Statute, 28 U.S.C. § 1350.

Page 753. Add a new Paragraph (4a):

(4a) The American Insurance Association Decision. The Supreme Court's latest decision concerning federal preemption of state laws bearing on foreign affairs came in American Ins. Ass'n v. Garamendi, 539 U.S. 396 (2003), where the Court, dividing 5–4, invalidated California's Holocaust Victim Insurance Relief Act (HVIRA). That Act, a response to the widespread confiscation of, or refusal to honor, life insurance policies held by Jews in Europe before and during the Second World War, required insurance companies, as a condition of doing business in California, to disclose information about all insurance policies sold in Europe from 1920–45. The Supreme Court's decision, like its decision in Crosby (Fifth Edition p. 751), can be viewed as exhibiting less hesitation about preempting state laws when they touch on international relations.

Justice Souter's majority opinion sketched the history of the U.S. Government's engagement with Germany concerning restitution to victims of Nazi persecution. He noted that a flood of Holocaust-related class actions in American courts in the 1990s generated protests by foreign insurers and their governments, and in turn led the U.S. Government to take action. "From the beginning the Government's position * * * stressed mediated settlement 'as an alternative to endless litigation' promising little relief to aging Holocaust survivors" (p. 389). Subsequent negotiations resulted in the German Foundation Agreement, signed in 2000 by President Clinton and German Chancellor Schröder, in which Germany agreed to create a foundation to compensate victims of Nazi persecution, funded with 10 billion Deutsche marks contributed equally by the German Government and German companies. In response to German desires for security from American lawsuits, the Foundation Agreement called for the U.S. Government to submit, in any Holocaust-era claim against a German company in an American court, a statement that "it would be in the foreign policy interests of the United States for the Foundation to be the exclusive forum and remedy for the resolution of all asserted claims against German companies" arising from the Nazi regime and World War II and "that U.S. policy interests favor dismissal on any valid legal ground" (p. 390). The

United States subsequently formed similar agreements with France and Austria.

Turning to the argument that federal law preempts the California disclosure provision, Justice Souter emphasized, *inter alia,* that a concern for uniformity undergirded the Constitution's allocation of foreign affairs power to the national government. Acknowledging, however, that the executive agreements here at issue contain no express preemption provision, Justice Souter stated that the argument for preemption relied heavily on Zschernig v. Miller (Fifth Edition p. 750). Justice Souter discussed Zschernig at some length, describing the majority as endorsing "field preemption" as to matters concerning foreign affairs, while Justice Harlan's concurrence rested more narrowly on "conflict preemption" (specifically, a conflict between the Oregon statute at issue in Zschernig and a federal treaty). Justice Souter found it unnecessary to resolve which view was correct, reasoning that HVIRA was preempted even under Justice Harlan's more limited approach in view of the "clear conflict" between the policies adopted by the President and those adopted by California. Presidential policy had encouraged European governments and companies to volunteer settlement funds in preference to litigation. California's approach called for more disclosure than would occur under the consensual international procedures on which the Foundation would rely and more than is viewed as appropriate under privacy notions of many European nations. To permit California to require such disclosure would "undercut[] the President's diplomatic discretion and the choice he has made exercising it" (p. 401) and would make it more difficult to obtain practical results in negotiations. "The basic fact is that California seeks to use an iron fist where the President has consistently chosen kid gloves" (p. 403).[a]

Justice Ginsburg's dissent (joined by Justices Stevens, Scalia, and Thomas) stressed that "no executive agreement or other formal expression of foreign policy disapproves state disclosure laws like the HVIRA" (p. 405) and pointed to language in the Foundation Agreement stating that "[t]he United States does not suggest that its policy interests concerning the Foundation in themselves provide an independent legal basis for dismissal" (p. 409). The agreement, she said, does not clearly preempt even litigation of Holocaust-era claims, much less a mere regime of disclosure. And she objected to the majority's treating statements by high executive officials as if they represented *presidential* policy. (The majority responded that "there is no suggestion that these high-level executive officials were not faithfully representing the President's chosen policy" and that there is no reason for adopting a "nondelegation" rule within the Executive Branch (p. 401 n. 13).)

Justice Ginsburg also criticized the majority's invocation of Zschernig, noting that the Court had not relied on it since it was decided. Stating that the strongest basis for the notion of dormant foreign affairs preemption with which Zschernig is associated is to prohibit states from criticizing foreign governments or sitting in judgment on them, she contended that HVIRA does not judge any contemporary foreign government but merely regulates private insurers doing business in California, and said that she would not "extend Zschernig into this dissimilar domain" (p. 412).

---

a. The Court added the suggestion that in preemption cases, as under the dormant commerce clause, it is reasonable to consider the strength of the state interest, and found that California's interests as regulator of insurance were weak in the present context.

For detailed criticism of Garamendi, arguing that the Court gave preemptive effect not to a statute, treaty, or even an executive agreement, but rather to an executive policy that (unlike the policy in *Crosby*) was not an exercise of power delegated by Congress, and that in doing so the Court disserved both federalism and separation of powers, see Denning & Ramsey, *American Insurance Association v. Garamendi and Executive Preemption in Foreign Affairs*, 46 Wm. & Mary L.Rev. 825 (2004).

Page 755. Add to footnote 8:

See also Stephan, *Courts, The Constitution, and Customary International Law: The Intellectual Origins of the Restatement (Third) of the Foreign Relations Law of the United States*, 44 Va.J.Int'l L. 33 (2003) (suggesting (i) that the Third Restatement's embrace of the "modern" position fit both with scholars' perception that the Supreme Court of the 1970s was not inclined to question governmental authority and with declining faith in the executive branch, and (ii) that the "modern" position may fit less well in the contemporary world after the waning of authoritarian regimes and the challenges faced after 9/11).

Page 755. Add to Paragraph (5):

In Roper v. Simmons, 125 S.Ct. 1183 (2005), the Supreme Court held that the Constitution prohibits imposition of a death sentence on an offender who was under 18 at the time of the crime. While not mentioning CIL as such, the Court said that its interpretation of the Cruel and Unusual Punishment Clause "finds confirmation" in the "stark reality" that the United States was the only nation in the world "to give official sanction to the juvenile death penalty" (p. 1198).

Page 758. Add a new Paragraph (6)(e):

(e) Many of the uncertainties surrounding the Alien Tort Statute (ATS) were resolved in Sosa v. Alvarez–Machain, 124 S.Ct. 2739 (2004), where Alvarez–Machain, a Mexican citizen, alleged that he had been abducted from Mexico and taken, in violation of the law of nations, to the United States by Sosa (also a citizen of Mexico) and others, under a plan developed by the U.S. Drug Enforcement Authority. The plaintiff prevailed in the lower courts on his ATS claim of arbitrary arrest and detention. The Supreme Court unanimously reversed, but in doing so it gave the statute a significant though restricted scope and rebuffed efforts to repudiate wholesale the approach of the Filartiga decision and subsequent lower court cases.

In a portion of his opinion joined by all members of the Court, Justice Souter rejected the view that the ATS was "authority for creation of a new cause of action for torts in violation of international law" (p. 2755). Instead, he found that the ATS was merely a grant of subject matter jurisdiction. As support for the jurisdictional nature of the statute, he noted that the language "bespoke a grant of jurisdiction, not power to mold substantive law", and added that its placement as one section "of the Judiciary Act, a statute otherwise exclusively concerned with federal-court jurisdiction, is itself support for its strictly jurisdictional nature" (p. 2755).

"But holding the ATS jurisdictional raises a new question," Justice Souter noted, "this one about the interaction between the ATS at the time of its enactment and the ambient law of the era. Sosa would have it that the ATS was stillborn because there could be no claim for relief without a further statute expressly authorizing adoption of causes of action. *Amici* professors of federal jurisdiction and legal history take a different tack, that federal courts could entertain claims once the jurisdictional grant was on the books, because torts in violation of the law of nations would have been recognized within the common law of the time. We think history and practice give the edge to this latter position" (p. 2755). After reviewing the historical materials, the Court identified a "sphere in which * * * rules [of the law of nations] binding individuals for the benefit of other individuals overlapped with the norms of state relationships. * * * It was this narrow set of violations of the law of nations, admitting of a judicial remedy and at the same time threatening serious consequences in international affairs, that was probably on minds of the men who drafted the ATS" (p. 2756). Justice Souter mentioned in particular three examples given by Blackstone of offenses against the law of nations that were criminal in England: violation of safe conducts, infringement of the rights of ambassadors, and piracy. The Court read the ATS as having been enacted "on the understanding that the common law would provide a cause of action for the modest number of international law violations with a potential for personal liability at the time" (p. 2761).

In the final portion of the Court's opinion (joined by five other Justices), Justice Souter said that while no evidence indicated that Congress had in mind any torts beyond those corresponding to Blackstone's three offenses, no development between 1789 and the Filartiga decision in 1980 "has categorically precluded federal courts from recognizing a claim under the law of nations as an element of common law" (p. 2761). However, he listed five reasons "for a restrained conception of the discretion a federal court should exercise in considering a new cause of action of this kind" (p. 2761): (i) the modern conception of the common law as made, rather than found, which highlights the substantial discretion involved when a judge recognizes an international norm; (ii) the decision in Erie, which sharply limits the range of federal judicial lawmaking; (iii) the Court's general reluctance to create a private right of action; (iv) the risk of adverse foreign policy consequences, especially regarding modern international law norms that regulate the power of foreign governments over their own citizens; and (v) the lack of a congressional mandate for recognizing "new and debatable violations of the law of nations" (p. 2763). Refusing, however, to "close the door to further independent judicial recognition of actionable international norms", Justice Souter explained why he thought "the door is still ajar subject to vigilant doorkeeping" (p. 2764): post–Erie decisions recognize limited enclaves of judge made law; "[f]or two centuries we have affirmed that the domestic law of the United States recognizes the law of nations"; ever since the Filartiga decision, the federal courts have agreed with that position; and Congress has expressed no disagreement (p. 2764).

Turning to Alvarez–Machain's claim, the Court said that "federal courts should not recognize private claims under federal common law for violations of any international law norm with less definite content and acceptance among civilized nations than the historical paradigms familiar when § 1350 was enacted" (p. 2765). He cited decisions, including Filartiga, holding that a norm must be specific, universal, and obligatory to sustain an action under § 1350. Measured by these standards, the plaintiff's claim of an arbitrary arrest and detention, in violation of the Universal Declaration of Human Rights and the International Covenant on Civil and Political Rights, fell short. "[T]he Declaration does not of its own force impose obligations as a matter of international law" (p. 2767). While the Covenant does bind the United States as a matter of international law, "the United States ratified [it] on the express understanding that it was not self-executing and so did not itself create obligations enforceable in the federal courts" (p. 2767). More generally, Alvarez's claim that his arrest and abduction were unauthorized by positive law (here of the United States) was far broader than "any binding customary rule having the specificity we require" (p. 2769).[b]

Justice Scalia, joined by the Chief Justice and Justice Thomas, concurring in part and in the judgment, would have closed the door altogether on the recognition of new causes of action, and viewed the last part of the Court's opinion as "commit[ting] the Federal Judiciary to a task it is neither authorized nor suited to perform" (pp. 2769–70). He stressed that after Erie, a grant of jurisdiction does not ordinarily carry with it lawmaking authority, and " 'the fact that a rule has been recognized as [customary international law], by itself, is not an adequate basis for viewing that rule as part of federal common law.' Meltzer, *Customary International Law, Foreign Affairs, and Federal Common Law*, 42 Va. J. Int'l L. 513, 519 (2002)" (p. 2772). The Court, he said, focused too much on whether Congress had precluded federal courts from recognizing new claims under § 1350, when the real question was what authorizes the federal courts to recognize such claims in the first place. He added that post-Erie federal common lawmaking is so different from the general common law adjudication through which the law of nations was thought to apply in 1789 that "it would be anachronistic to find authorization to do the former in a statutory grant of jurisdiction that was thought to enable the latter" (p. 2773). Finally, he expressed concern that the Court bestowed too much latitude upon lower federal courts, noting that the decision below, which the Court unanimously reversed, rested on a verbal formulation very similar to that endorsed by the last part of the Court's opinion.

While resolving many questions, the opinion leaves a number of others unanswered. The Court holds that § 1350 is entirely jurisdictional, which suggests that the substantive law applied in actions properly brought under that statute is federal common law. (Were it otherwise, would the statute comport with Article III, at least absent diversity of citizenship?) But the profound shift in jurisprudential assumptions occasioned by Erie raises some difficult issues about the nature of that federal common law. The ATS appears to have assumed the existence of a body of customary international law (CIL) that would be part of "the common law" as applied by the federal courts before Erie. By contrast, modern, post-Erie premises about federal common lawmaking—particularly the association of common law rules with the lawmaking authority of a particular jurisdiction (*e.g.,* the federal government, or one of the

---

b. For a narrow interpretation of the kinds of CIL claims that qualify under the majority's approach, see Kontorovich, *Implementing Sosa v. Alvarez–Machain: What Piracy Reveals About the Limits of the Alien Tort Statute,* 80 Notre Dame L.Rev. 111 (2004), who argues that the Court's eighteenth century examples are quite different from modern human rights claims. The first two Blackstonian examples—violation of safe conducts and infringement of the rights of ambassadors—involved conduct by citizens of the forum state that threatened their country's interests. The third, piracy, was directed against foreigners, but modern human rights claims do not share its six characteristics: it was universally condemned, narrowly defined, uniformly punished (by death) so as to avoid double jeopardy problems, committed by private actors who (unlike privateers) rejected sovereign protection, difficult to prohibit without universal jurisdiction, and threatening to many nations.

How clear is the Sosa opinion about the extent or nature of resemblance that a new CIL claim must have to the historical examples given by the Court?

fifty states)—make the appropriateness of absorbing CIL into federal common law quite uncertain.

Consider, in this regard, whether a CIL norm that is sufficiently specific, universal, and obligatory to sustain an ATS action in federal court would also apply (as is typical of modern federal common law) were a similar action brought in a state court. Would a state court have to treat as invalid, under the Supremacy Clause, any state law that would stand in the way of such a state court action? Or should § 1350 be interpreted as a relic that preserves, in the domain in which it operates, a pre-Erie approach under which federal courts recognize a "spurious" federal common law applicable only in the federal courts? Is there any adequate "translation" of a statute written on pre-Erie assumptions into the jurisprudential framework of a post-Erie world? See generally Lessig, *Fidelity in Translation*, 71 Tex.L.Rev. 1165 (1993).

With respect to the set of claims appropriately brought under the ATS, the Sosa decision appears to reject the position of Bradley and Goldsmith, Fifth Edition pp. 754–55, that CIL is not federal common law. But does the decision lay the ground for even broader acceptance of CIL as federal common law? Imagine, for example, that a U.S. citizen brought suit in federal court for a tort committed in violation of the law of nations. That case would fall outside the ambit of the ATS, because the plaintiff is not an alien. But would a federal court nonetheless have the same range of power approved in the Sosa decision to recognize and apply CIL norms that are sufficiently specific, universal, and obligatory—with jurisdiction provided by the grant of federal question jurisdiction in § 1331?

On the one hand, if a federal court could entertain such an action, then at least today, when (unlike in 1789) there is a general grant of federal question jurisdiction, the ATS may appear to be superfluous, as any actions falling under it could also be brought under § 1331. On the other hand, perhaps the absorption of CIL norms into federal common law, as approved by Sosa, is limited to actions under the ATS, and is explainable on the special ground that Congress apparently contemplated it in actions under that provision. The latter, more limited position finds support in a footnote in the majority opinion: "Our position does not, as Justice Scalia suggests, imply that every grant of jurisdiction carries with it an opportunity to develop common law (so that the grant of federal-question jurisdiction would be equally as good for our purposes as § 1350). Section 1350 was enacted on the congressional understanding that courts would exercise jurisdiction by entertaining some common law crimes derived from the law of nations; and we know of no reason to think that federal-question jurisdiction was extended subject to any comparable congressional assumption" (p. 2765 n. 19). But if CIL must count as federal law for purposes of Article III (for if it doesn't, then, absent diversity, the ATS may be unconstitutional), and if § 1331 extends to actions arising under federal law, then doesn't the limited approach suggested by the Court create some tension with its insistence that the ATS is merely jurisdictional? See Dodge, *Bridging Erie: Customary International Law in the U.S. Legal System After Sosa v. Alvarez–Machain*, 12 Tulsa J.Comp. & Int. L. 87 (2004).[c]

---

c. For a critique of Sosa along some-what different lines, see Ku & Yoo, *Beyond* *Formalism in Foreign Affairs: A Functional Approach to the Alien Tort Statute*, 2004 Sup.

SECTION 2.   ENFORCING PRIMARY OBLIGATIONS

SUBSECTION A: CIVIL ACTIONS

Page 759. Add to footnote 1:

In Jones v. R.R. Donnelley & Sons Co., 541 U.S. 369 (2004), the Court unanimously held that § 1658's four-year period governed a cause of action under a statute enacted prior to 1990 but amended thereafter. Plaintiffs' civil rights claim under 42 U.S.C. § 1981 would have lacked merit prior to 1991, when § 1981 was amended to extend to such a claim. In Jones, the Court, after finding § 1658's text to be unclear about the statute's application in such a situation, stressed that § 1658 was adopted in part to eliminate the complexities involved in borrowing state limitations periods: "The history that led to the enactment of § 1658 strongly supports an interpretation that fills more rather than less of the void that has created so much unnecessary work for federal judges" (p. 380). Therefore, the Court concluded, a cause of action "aris[es] under an Act of Congress enacted after December 1, 1990 * * * if the plaintiff's claim * * * was made possible by a post–1990 enactment" (p. 382).

Would the same result obtain if a post–1990 enactment increased the available damages on a claim that was viable prior to 1990?

Page 763. Add a new footnote 8a at the end of Paragraph (6):

8a.   In Graham County Soil & Water Conservation Dist. v. United States ex rel. Wilson, 125 S.Ct. 2444 (2005), the Court, per Thomas, J., again borrowed state law, refusing to apply a limitations period found elsewhere in the same federal statute. The False Claims Act authorizes both actions to recover on false claims submitted to the United States and actions by employees who suffer retaliation from their employer for having helped to pursue a false claim action. The focus of both the Court and the dissenters was whether the False Claims Act's express limitations period (not more than six years after the violation or more than three years after the facts were or should have been known) applies to retaliation actions; the Court held that it did not. But in a more general vein, the Court stated that borrowing an analogous federal limitations period is rare and is undertaken only when good reasons are presented, while Justice Breyer (joined in dissent by Justice Ginsburg) complained that the majority's decision substituted for a uniform six-year period "a crazy-quilt" drawn from 51 jurisdictions, some of whose periods are as short as 90 or 180 days (p. 40).

Ct.Rev. 153. Like some other critics of ATS litigation, the authors believe that modern CIL should be treated as state common law and thus that claims based on violations of CIL should be cognizable under the ATS only when there is diversity of citizenship. But in assessing the contrary conclusion of Sosa, Ku and Yoo assert that the most plausible purpose to attribute to the decision is to permit federal courts to promote the development and enforcement of international law. Relying on a comparative institutional analysis, they contend that in pursuing that purpose, the executive branch has numerous advantages over the federal courts, including greater expertise, access to better information, greater unity and speed, the capacity to revisit decisions as circumstances change, and more effective tools to enforce compliance. Although recognizing that their preferred regime creates the potential for divergent state understandings of CIL, they suggest that the dangers are not great and can be adequately dealt with by exercise of the President's power to preempt state law (and thus CIL)—a power recognized in the Garamendi decision, p. 40, *supra*.

Page 783. Add to Paragraph (2) and footnote 7:

Stephenson, *Public Regulation of Private Enforcement: The Case for Expanding the Role of Administrative Agencies,* 91 Va.L.Rev. 93 (2005), elaborates the benefits and costs of private enforcement in achieving appropriate deterrence of violations, and argues that the desirability of private enforcement in a particular domain is a complex question requiring evaluation of context-specific information. While decided cases have focused on whether Congress or the judiciary is better situated to make that evaluation, he argues that a responsible federal administrative agency (where there is one) may be better equipped than either, that it would often be desirable for Congress to delegate to agencies the authority to determine the reach of private enforcement, and that "the *Chevron* presumption—that ambiguous statutes implicitly delegate decisionmaking authority to administrative agencies"—should be extended to private enforcement questions (p. 172).

Pages 785–86. Add a new footnote 8a to the end of Paragraph (3):

8a. For a thoughtful discussion criticizing recent Supreme Court decisions that have narrowly construed statutory grants of equity jurisdiction, see Resnik, *Constricting Remedies: The Rehnquist Judiciary, Congress, and Federal Power,* 78 Ind.L.J. 223 (2003). Resnik links those decisions not only to the Court's restrictiveness in implying private rights of action but also to lobbying positions taken by the Judicial Conference urging congressional hesitation in creating federal rights enforceable in federal court.

Page 786, Add a new footnote 8a at the end of Paragraph (3):

8a. Consider the questions raised in the Fifth Edition in light of Jackson v. Birmingham Bd. of Educ., 125 S.Ct. 1497 (2005), where the Court held that Title IX's implied right of action embraces a suit by a male teacher alleging discrimination on the basis of the school board's retaliation against him for protesting sex discrimination in the high school's athletic program. Justice O'Connor's majority opinion noted that Title IX did not define specific discriminatory practices and that prior decisions (notably those barring sexual harassment) had interpreted Title IX broadly. She proceeded to conclude that the complaint's averment of an intentional response by the board to the teacher's protest constituted discrimination "on the basis of sex". She stressed, *inter alia,* that Title IX was enacted against a background of other statutory prohibitions on retaliation and that Title IX's purposes could not be achieved were recipients of federal funds free to retaliate against those who complain about noncompliance. Justice Thomas' dissent, joined by the Chief Justice and Justices Scalia and Kennedy, objected that (a) Title IX, unlike many other civil rights statutes, does not itself prohibit retaliation, (b) the male teacher was not discriminated against because of *his* sex, (c) obligations imposed under the conditional spending power must be clear, and (d) Title IX does not clearly confer any rights on those who are not direct victims of discrimination but who merely complain of retaliation. He accused the majority of returning to the days when implied rights were crafted out of the Court's vision of congressional purpose.

Is Justice Thomas correct that the approach in Jackson is hard to square with Sandoval and other recent decisions? If so, does Jackson herald a new approach? Or is it only the recognition of the continuing effects of a decision from an earlier era, with the majority simply delineating the scope of the right of action recognized in Cannon—a right of action that might not have been recognized at all had the question first arisen in 2005 rather than in 1979?

Page 787. Add to Paragraph (5):

For thorough discussion of the questions raised in this Paragraph, see Sloss, *Constitutional Remedies for Statutory Violations,* 89 Iowa L.Rev. 355 (2004). Sloss notes that in nine decisions over the 1996–2002 Terms, the Supreme Court, following Shaw v. Delta Air Lines, reached the merits of suits to enjoin state officials from enforcing state *statutes* that were allegedly preempted by federal law, all without discussing whether the private plaintiff had an implied right of action for injunctive relief. He also notes that in *Verizon Maryland, Inc. v. Public Service Comm'n of Maryland,* 535 U.S. 635 (2002), the Court upheld subject matter jurisdiction over a suit to enjoin enforcement, on statutory preemption grounds, of a state administrative agency's adjudicative order—an order that, Sloss suggests, was neither legislative nor executive in character. He contrasts these decisions with several others, including Sandoval, in which the Court refused to recognize an implied right of action to enjoin state *executive* action alleged to violate federal law.[a] (Sloss acknowledges that, strictly speaking, the holdings in Shaw and similar cases, and in Verizon, merely affirmed subject matter jurisdiction rather than expressly recognizing an implied right of action.)

Would (should) it have mattered in Sandoval if the complaint, instead of alleging that state executive officials *violated* plaintiffs' federal rights, had instead alleged that federal law *preempted* the challenged state action? Would it have mattered if the challenged English-only policy for driver's license examinations had been embodied in a state statute instead of an executive decision? Recall that that policy was adopted only after enactment of a state constitutional amendment declaring English to be the official language of Alabama. Should the plaintiffs have brought suit alleging that federal law preempted both that amendment and state legislation vesting authority in officials of the Alabama Department of Public Safety, insofar as those constitutional and statutory provisions directed or authorized executive officials to adopt the English-only policy?

Sloss argues that the Court should recognize an implied right of action, under the Supremacy Clause, that would embrace "all claims in which plaintiffs seek prospective relief to remedy an ongoing or threatened violation of federal law" (p. 433), whether by state legislative, executive, or administrative action. (For an argument that the Supremacy Clause is merely a rule of priority when federal and state law conflict, rather than a source of substantive federal rights, see Meltzer, *The Supreme Court's Judicial Passivity*, 2002 Sup.Ct.Rev. 343, 366–67.)

SUBSECTION B: REMEDIES FOR CONSTITUTIONAL VIOLATIONS

Page 804. Add to footnote 14:

For an argument that constitutional violations should sometimes be redressed by the award of damages *ex post* but not by injunctive relief *ex ante*, see Kontorovich, *Liability Rules for Constitutional Rights: The Case of Mass Detentions*, 56 Stan.L.Rev. 755 (2004). The author

---

a. Sloss notes that although Sandoval involved statutory conditions on a federal spending program, a context in which the Court has shown particular reluctance to imply rights of action, the Court reached the merits of the preemption issue in Pharmaceutical Rsch. & Mfrs. of America v. Walsh, 538 U.S. 644 (2003), which also involved a spending clause claim. Indeed, Justice Scalia's separate opinion in that case would have denied relief on the ground that the private plaintiffs could not bring suit alleging that the state had violated spending conditions under the Medicaid Act. That Act, he argued, provided as the exclusive remedy a fund cutoff by the federal Secretary of Health and Human Services.

draws on the distinction in private law between liability rules (under which rightholders cannot prevent unconsented violations of their entitlements but may obtain compensation) and property rules (under which rightholders can prevent unconsented violations of entitlements). The Just Compensation Clause is an example of an explicit constitutional liability rule, but most other constitutional rights are protected by property rules—*i.e.*, the presumption is that injunctive relief is available. Seeking to qualify that presumption, Kontorovich illustrates his argument with mass detentions during emergencies, reasoning that "[b]ecause the Court is reluctant to impose or be blamed for the social costs that might result from an injunction—namely, an enemy attack—one should not be surprised if it avoids finding detentions unconstitutional in the first place" (p. 779). He suggests that if redress were limited to *ex post* compensation, "detainees would have a greater chance of receiving meaningful redress . . . , [s]ociety would receive the security advantages of mass detentions while being spared some of the social discord caused by uncompensated detentions[, and] the Supreme Court would be able to call constitutional shots as it sees them, without having its substantive reasoning clouded by the massive social costs that might ensue from an injunction ordering the release of detainees" (pp. 797–98). *Cf.* Stewart and Sunstein, Fifth Edition p. 783 n.7.

CHAPTER VIII

THE FEDERAL QUESTION
JURISDICTION OF THE
DISTRICT COURTS

SECTION 1.   INTRODUCTION

———

Page 829. Add to footnote 29:

See also Breuer v. Jim's Concrete of Brevard, 538 U.S. 691 (2003)(holding that a provision in the Fair Labor Standards Act that an action "may be *maintained* * * * in any Federal or State court of competent jurisdiction" does not preclude removal of a state court action, in view of 28 U.S.C. § 1441(a)'s general authorization of removal "[e]xcept as otherwise *expressly* provided by Act of Congress") (emphasis added).

———

———

SECTION 2.   THE SCOPE OF THE CONSTITUTIONAL
GRANT OF FEDERAL QUESTION JURISDICTION

———

Page 847. Add to Paragraph (3)(a):

Bellia, *Article III and the Cause of Action*, 89 Iowa L.Rev. 777 (2004), argues that at the time Osborn was decided, a litigant had a cause of action "only if one could show that a set of legal determinants entitling one to judicial relief under a particular form of proceeding resolved themselves in one's favor"; the plaintiff had to identify not merely a right but also an entitlement to a particular remedy under a particular legal form (p. 801). An "ingredient" of the cause, as that term was used by Chief Justice Marshall, was one of the legal determinants bearing on the case that the plaintiff had the burden of pleading or proving. Bellia thus views contentions like that of Justice Frankfurter in his Lincoln Mills dissent—that Osborn extends to any case in which a federal issue might possibly arise—as a misreading of Osborn; whether or not federal question jurisdiction should attach on this broader basis, it cannot do so based merely on Osborn's reasoning.

———

SECTION 3. THE SCOPE OF THE STATUTORY GRANT OF FEDERAL QUESTION JURISDICTION

SUBSECTION A: THE STRUCTURE OF ARISING UNDER JURISDICTION UNDER THE FEDERAL QUESTION STATUTE

Pages 862–63. Add to footnote 9:

With respect to the citation of tentative drafts of the ALI's Federal Judicial Code Project, both here and elsewhere in this Chapter (see Fifth Edition pp. 909 n.9, 924 n.2, 928 n.8, and 930 n.11), note that the Project was ultimately approved by the American Law Institute and published in 2004.

Page 869. Add to the end of Paragraph (4):

See also footnote 5 of Grable & Sons Metal Prods., Inc. v. Darue Engineering & Mfg., immediately following, which echoes Merrell Dow's understanding of Shoshone.

Pages 870–86. Substitute, for the principal case of Merrell Dow Pharmaceuticals Inc. v. Thompson on pp. 870–80, and for the "Note on the Scope of 'Arising Under' Jurisdiction under 28 U.S.C. § 1331" on pp. 880–86, the following principal case and revised "Note on the Scope of 'Arising Under' Jurisdiction Under 28 U.S.C. § 1331":

Grable & Sons Metal Prods., Inc. v. Darue Engineering & Mfg.

___ U.S. ___, 125 S.Ct. 2363, L.Ed.2d ___ (2005).
Certiorari to the United States Court of Appeals for the Sixth Circuit.

■ JUSTICE SOUTER delivered the opinion of the Court.

The question is whether want of a federal cause of action to try claims of title to land obtained at a federal tax sale precludes removal to federal court of a state action with non-diverse parties raising a disputed issue of federal title law. We answer no, and hold that the national interest in providing a federal forum for federal tax litigation is sufficiently substantial to support the exercise of federal question jurisdiction over the disputed issue on removal, which would not distort any division of labor between the state and federal courts, provided or assumed by Congress.

I

[The Internal Revenue Service seized real property belonging to Grable to satisfy a federal tax delinquency. Grable received notice, by certified mail, of the seizure before the IRS sold the property to Darue. Grable also received notice of the sale but did not exercise its statutory right to redeem the property within 180 days of the sale, and after that period had passed, the Government gave Darue a quitclaim deed.]

Five years later, Grable brought a quiet title action in state court, claiming that Darue's record title was invalid because the IRS had failed to notify Grable of its seizure of the property in the exact manner required by [26 U.S.C.] § 6335(a), which provides that written notice must be "given * * * to the owner of the property [or] left at his usual place of abode or business." Grable said that the statute required personal service, not service by certified mail.

Darue removed the case to Federal District Court as presenting a federal question, because the claim of title depended on the interpretation of the notice statute in the federal tax law. The District Court declined to remand the case * * *. On the merits, the court granted summary judgment to Darue, holding that although § 6335 by its terms required personal service, substantial compliance with the statute was enough.

The Court of Appeals for the Sixth Circuit affirmed. * * * We granted certiorari on the jurisdictional question alone, to resolve a split within the Courts of Appeals on whether Merrell Dow Pharmaceuticals Inc. v. Thompson, 478 U.S. 804 (1986), always requires a federal cause of action as a condition for exercising federal-question jurisdiction. We now affirm.

II

Darue was entitled to remove the quiet title action if Grable could have brought it in federal district court originally, 28 U.S.C. § 1441(a), as a civil action "arising under the Constitution, laws, or treaties of the United States," § 1331. This provision for federal-question jurisdiction is invoked by and large by plaintiffs pleading a cause of action created by federal law (*e.g.,* claims under 42 U.S.C. § 1983). There is, however, another longstanding, if less frequently encountered, variety of federal "arising under" jurisdiction, this Court having recognized for nearly 100 years that in certain cases federal question jurisdiction will lie over state-law claims that implicate significant federal issues. *E.g.,* Hopkins v. Walker, 244 U.S. 486, 490–491 (1917). The doctrine captures the commonsense notion that a federal court ought to be able to hear claims recognized under state law that nonetheless turn on substantial questions of federal law, and thus justify resort to the experience, solicitude, and hope of uniformity that a federal forum offers on federal issues, see ALI, Study of the Division of Jurisdiction Between State and Federal Courts 164–166 (1968).

The classic example is Smith v. Kansas City Title & Trust Co., 255 U.S. 180 (1921), a suit by a shareholder claiming that the defendant corporation could not lawfully buy certain bonds of the National Government because their issuance was unconstitutional. Although Missouri law provided the cause of action, the Court recognized federal-question jurisdiction because the principal issue in the case was the federal constitutionality of the bond issue. Smith thus held, in a somewhat generous statement of the scope of the doctrine, that a state-law claim could give rise to federal-question jurisdiction so long as it "appears from the [complaint] that the right to relief depends upon the construction or application of [federal law]." *Id.,* at 199.

The Smith statement has been subject to some trimming to fit earlier and later cases recognizing the vitality of the basic doctrine, but shying away from the expansive view that mere need to apply federal law in a state-law claim will suffice to open the "arising under" door. As early as 1912, this Court had confined federal-question jurisdiction over state-law claims to those that "really and substantially involv[e] a dispute or controversy respecting the validity, construction or effect of [federal] law." Shulthis v. McDougal, 225 U.S. 561, 569 (1912). This limitation was the ancestor of Justice Cardozo's later explanation that a request to exercise federal-question jurisdiction over a state action calls for a "common-sense accommodation of judgment to [the] kaleidoscopic situations" that present a federal issue, in "a selective process which picks the substantial causes out of the web and lays the other ones aside." Gully v. First Nat. Bank in Meridian, 299 U.S. 109, 117–118 (1936). It has in fact become a constant refrain in such cases that federal jurisdiction demands not only a contested federal issue, but a substantial one, indicating a serious federal interest in claiming the advantages thought to be inherent in a federal forum. E.g., Chicago v. International College of Surgeons, 522 U.S. 156, 164 (1997); Merrell Dow, supra, at 814, and n. 12; Franchise Tax Bd. of Cal. v. Construction Laborers Vacation Trust for Southern Cal., 463 U.S. 1, 28 (1983).

But even when the state action discloses a contested and substantial federal question, the exercise of federal jurisdiction is subject to a possible veto. For the federal issue will ultimately qualify for a federal forum only if federal jurisdiction is consistent with congressional judgment about the sound division of labor between state and federal courts governing the application of § 1331. Thus, Franchise Tax Bd. explained that the appropriateness of a federal forum to hear an embedded issue could be evaluated only after considering the "welter of issues regarding the interrelation of federal and state authority and the proper management of the federal judicial system." Id., at 8. Because arising-under jurisdiction to hear a state-law claim always raises the possibility of upsetting the state-federal line drawn (or at least assumed) by Congress, the presence of a disputed federal issue and the ostensible importance of a federal forum are never necessarily dispositive; there must always be an assessment of any disruptive portent in exercising federal jurisdiction.

These considerations have kept us from stating a "single, precise, all-embracing" test for jurisdiction over federal issues embedded in state-law claims between nondiverse parties. Christianson v. Colt Industries Operating Corp., 486 U.S. 800, 821 (1988) (Stevens, J., concurring). We have not kept them out simply because they appeared in state raiment, as Justice Holmes would have done, see Smith, supra, at 214 (dissenting opinion), but neither have we treated "federal issue" as a password opening federal courts to any state action embracing a point of federal law. Instead, the question is, does a state-law claim necessarily raise a stated federal issue, actually disputed and substantial, which a federal forum may entertain without disturbing any congressionally approved balance of federal and state judicial responsibilities.

III

A

This case warrants federal jurisdiction. Grable's state complaint must specify "the facts establishing the superiority of [its] claim," Mich. Ct. Rule 3.411(B)(2)(c) (West 2005), and Grable has premised its superior title claim on a failure by the IRS to give it adequate notice, as defined by federal law. Whether Grable was given notice within the meaning of the federal statute is thus an essential element of its quiet title claim, and the meaning of the federal statute is actually in dispute; it appears to be the only legal or factual issue contested in the case. The meaning of the federal tax provision is an important issue of federal law that sensibly belongs in a federal court. The Government has a strong interest in the "prompt and certain collection of delinquent taxes," United States v. Rodgers, 461 U.S. 677, 709 (1983), and the ability of the IRS to satisfy its claims from the property of delinquents requires clear terms of notice to allow buyers like Darue to satisfy themselves that the Service has touched the bases necessary for good title. The Government thus has a direct interest in the availability of a federal forum to vindicate its own administrative action, and buyers (as well as tax delinquents) may find it valuable to come before judges used to federal tax matters. Finally, because it will be the rare state title case that raises a contested matter of federal law, federal jurisdiction to resolve genuine disagreement over federal tax title provisions will portend only a microscopic effect on the federal-state division of labor. See n. 3, *infra*.

This conclusion puts us in venerable company, quiet title actions having been the subject of some of the earliest exercises of federal-question jurisdiction over state-law claims. In Hopkins, the question was federal jurisdiction over a quiet title action based on the plaintiffs' allegation that federal mining law gave them the superior claim. Just as in this case, "the facts showing the plaintiffs' title and the existence and invalidity of the instrument or record sought to be eliminated as a cloud upon the title are essential parts of the plaintiffs' cause of action."[3] [244 U.S.] at 490. As in this case again, "it is plain that a controversy respecting the construction and effect of the [federal] laws is involved and is sufficiently real and substantial." *Id.*, at 489. This Court therefore upheld federal jurisdiction in Hopkins, as well as in * * * similar quiet title matters * * *. Consistent with those cases, the recognition of federal jurisdiction is in order here.

B

Merrell Dow Pharmaceuticals Inc. v. Thompson, 478 U.S. 804 (1986), on which Grable rests its position, is not to the contrary. Merrell Dow considered a state tort claim resting in part on the allegation that the defendant drug company had violated a federal misbranding prohibition, and was thus presumptively negligent under Ohio law. The Court assumed that federal law would have to be applied to resolve the claim, but after closely examining the strength of the federal interest at stake and the implications of opening the federal forum, held federal jurisdiction unavailable. Congress had not provided a private federal cause of action for violation of the federal branding requirement, and the Court found "it would ... flout, or at least undermine, congressional intent to conclude that federal courts might nevertheless exercise federal-question jurisdiction and provide remedies for violations of that federal

---

3. The quiet title cases also show the limiting effect of the requirement that the federal issue in a state-law claim must actually be in dispute to justify federal-question jurisdiction. In Shulthis v. McDougal, 225 U.S. 561 (1912), this Court found that there was no federal question jurisdiction to hear a plaintiff's quiet title claim in part because the federal statutes on which title depended were not subject to "any controversy respecting their validity, construction, or effect." *Id.,* at 570. As the Court put it, the requirement of an actual dispute about federal law was "especially" important in "suit[s] involving rights to land acquired under a law of the United States," because otherwise "every suit to establish title to land in the central and western states would so arise [under federal law], as all titles in those States are traceable back to those laws." *Id.,* at 569–570.

statute solely because the violation ... is said to be a ... 'proximate cause' under state law." *Id.*, at 812.

Because federal law provides for no quiet title action that could be brought against Darue, Grable argues that there can be no federal jurisdiction here, stressing some broad language in Merrell Dow (including the passage just quoted) that on its face supports Grable's position, see Note, *Mr. Smith Goes to Federal Court: Federal Question Jurisdiction over State Law Claims Post– Merrell Dow*, 115 Harv. L.Rev. 2272, 2280–2282 (2002) (discussing split in Circuit Courts over private right of action requirement after Merrell Dow). But an opinion is to be read as a whole, and Merrell Dow cannot be read whole as overturning decades of precedent, as it would have done by effectively adopting the Holmes dissent in Smith, see *supra*, at 5, and converting a federal cause of action from a sufficient condition for federal-question jurisdiction[5] into a necessary one.

In the first place, Merrell Dow disclaimed the adoption of any bright-line rule, as when the Court reiterated that "in exploring the outer reaches of § 1331, determinations about federal jurisdiction require sensitive judgments about congressional intent, judicial power, and the federal system." 478 U.S., at 810. The opinion included a lengthy footnote explaining that questions of jurisdiction over state-law claims require "careful judgments," *id.*, at 814, about the "nature of the federal interest at stake," *id.*, at 814, n. 12 (emphasis deleted). And as a final indication that it did not mean to make a federal right of action mandatory, it expressly approved the exercise of jurisdiction sustained in Smith, despite the want of any federal cause of action available to Smith's shareholder plaintiff. Merrell Dow then, did not toss out, but specifically retained the contextual enquiry that had been Smith's hallmark for over 60 years. At the end of Merrell Dow, Justice Holmes was still dissenting.

Accordingly, Merrell Dow should be read in its entirety as treating the absence of a federal private right of action as evidence relevant to, but not dispositive of, the "sensitive judgments about congressional intent" that § 1331 requires. The absence of any federal cause of action affected Merrell Dow's result two ways. The Court saw the fact as worth some consideration in the assessment of substantiality. But its primary importance emerged when the Court treated the combination of no federal cause of action and no preemption of state remedies for misbranding as an important clue to Congress's conception of the scope of jurisdiction to be exercised under § 1331. The Court saw the missing cause of action not as a missing federal door key, always required, but as a missing welcome mat, required in the circumstances, when exercising federal jurisdiction over a state misbranding action would have attracted a horde of original filings and removal cases raising other state claims with embedded federal issues. For if the federal labeling standard without a federal cause of action could get a state claim into federal court, so could any other federal standard without a federal cause of action. And that would have meant a tremendous number of cases.

One only needed to consider the treatment of federal violations generally in garden variety state tort law. "The violation of federal statutes and regulations is commonly given negligence per se effect in state tort proceedings."[6] Restate-

---

5. For an extremely rare exception to the sufficiency of a federal right of action, see Shoshone Mining Co. v. Rutter, 177 U.S. 505, 507 (1900).

6. Other jurisdictions treat a violation of a federal statute as evidence of negligence or, like Ohio itself in Merrell Dow Pharma-

ment (Third) of Torts (proposed final draft) § 14, Comment *a*. A general rule of exercising federal jurisdiction over state claims resting on federal mislabeling and other statutory violations would thus have heralded a potentially enormous shift of traditionally state cases into federal courts. Expressing concern over the "increased volume of federal litigation," and noting the importance of adhering to "legislative intent," Merrell Dow thought it improbable that the Congress, having made no provision for a federal cause of action, would have meant to welcome any state-law tort case implicating federal law "solely because the violation of the federal statute is said to [create] a rebuttable presumption [of negligence] . . . under state law." 478 U.S., at 811–812 (internal quotation marks omitted). In this situation, no welcome mat meant keep out. Merrell Dow 's analysis thus fits within the framework of examining the importance of having a federal forum for the issue, and the consistency of such a forum with Congress's intended division of labor between state and federal courts.

As already indicated, however, a comparable analysis yields a different jurisdictional conclusion in this case. Although Congress also indicated ambivalence in this case by providing no private right of action to Grable, it is the rare state quiet title action that involves contested issues of federal law, see n. 3, *supra*. Consequently, jurisdiction over actions like Grable's would not materially affect, or threaten to affect, the normal currents of litigation. Given the absence of threatening structural consequences and the clear interest the Government, its buyers, and its delinquents have in the availability of a federal forum, there is no good reason to shirk from federal jurisdiction over the dispositive and contested federal issue at the heart of the state-law title claim.[7]

IV

The judgment of the Court of Appeals, upholding federal jurisdiction over Grable's quiet title action, is affirmed.

It is so ordered.

■ JUSTICE THOMAS, concurring.

The Court faithfully applies our precedents interpreting 28 U.S.C. § 1331 * * *. In this case, no one has asked us to overrule those precedents and adopt the rule Justice Holmes set forth in American Well Works Co. v. Layne & Bowler Co., 241 U.S. 257 (1916), limiting § 1331 jurisdiction to cases in which federal law creates the cause of action * * *. In an appropriate case, and perhaps with the benefit of better evidence as to the original meaning of § 1331's text, I would be willing to consider that course.

Jurisdictional rules should be clear. Whatever the virtues of the Smith standard, it is anything but clear. *Ante*, at 4 (the standard "calls for a 'common-sense accommodation of judgment to [the] kaleidoscopic situations' that pres-

---

ceuticals Inc. v. Thompson, 478 U.S. 804 (1986), as creating a rebuttable presumption of negligence. Restatement (Third) of Torts (proposed final draft) § 14, Comment *c*. Either approach could still implicate issues of federal law.

7. * * * Grable's counsel espoused the position that after Merrell Dow, federal-question jurisdiction over state-law claims absent a federal right of action, could be recognized

only where a constitutional issue was at stake. There is, however, no reason in text or otherwise to draw such a rough line. As Merrell Dow itself suggested, constitutional questions may be the more likely ones to reach the level of substantiality that can justify federal jurisdiction. But a flat ban on statutory questions would mechanically exclude significant questions of federal law like the one this case presents.

ent a federal issue, in 'a selective process which picks the substantial causes out of the web and lays the other ones aside' " (quoting Gully v. First Nat. Bank in Meridian, 299 U.S. 109, 117–118 (1936))); *ante,* at 5 ("[T]he question is, does a state-law claim necessarily raise a stated federal issue, actually disputed and substantial, which a federal forum may entertain without disturbing any congressionally approved balance of federal and state judicial responsibilities"); *ante,* at 9 (" '[D]eterminations about federal jurisdiction require sensitive judgments about congressional intent, judicial power, and the federal system' "; "the absence of a federal private right of action [is] evidence relevant to, but not dispositive of, the 'sensitive judgments about congressional intent' that § 1331 requires" (quoting Merrell Dow, *supra,* at 810)).

Whatever the vices of the American Well Works rule, it is clear. Moreover, it accounts for the " 'vast majority' " of cases that come within § 1331 under our current case law, Merrell Dow, *supra,* at 808 (quoting Franchise Tax Bd. of Cal. v. Construction Laborers Vacation Trust for Southern Cal., 463 U.S. 1, 9 (1983))—further indication that trying to sort out which cases fall within the smaller Smith category may not be worth the effort it entails. See R. Fallon, D. Meltzer, & D. Shapiro, Hart and Wechsler's The Federal Courts and the Federal System 885–886 (5th ed.2003). Accordingly, I would be willing in appropriate circumstances to reconsider our interpretation of § 1331.

————

NOTE ON THE SCOPE OF "ARISING UNDER" JURISDICTION UNDER 28 U.S.C. § 1331

(1) Cases Involving Disputes Over Land Originally Owned by the United States. Grable is the most recent decision on the reach of § 1331 with respect to state law causes of action that incorporate a federal ingredient. Some of the very oldest decisions addressing this question also involved disputes about real property rights in which one or more of the chains of title included a grant or patent from the United States. Very occasionally, the cause of action governing a real property dispute is (or at least might be understood to be) created by federal law; the Grable opinion reads the Shoshone decision, discussed in the Fifth Edition p. 867, that way. But in the great majority of real property disputes, state law creates the plaintiff's right of action, and thus federal jurisdiction cannot be justified under the Holmes cause of action test.

An earlier example of such a dispute, noted in Grable, is Hopkins v. Walker, 244 U.S. 486 (1917). There, the Court upheld jurisdiction, after finding that under both "general" and Montana law, "the facts showing the plaintiff's title and the existence and invalidity of the instrument or record sought to be eliminated as a cloud upon the title are essential parts of the plaintiff's cause of action" (p. 490). It is noteworthy that the complaint in Hopkins left no doubt that the validity of the competing federal grants was in dispute, and thus the case was not one in which the federal grant was merely an old and uncontested link in the plaintiff's title.

As the Grable Court notes, however, other decisions have refused to recognize federal question jurisdiction over land disputes that involve some federal ingredient. Thus, five years before Hopkins, jurisdiction was denied in Shulthis v. McDougal, 225 U.S. 561 (1912), an action to quiet title. The Court in Grable (see footnote 3) explains Shulthis on the basis that although the complainant's claim of right was derived from federal law, his averments made no reference to "any controversy respecting [the] validity, construction, or effect" of federal statutes. Thus, for all that one could tell, the dispute might have had nothing to do with the fact that the complainant derived his title from federal law.

Jurisdiction was also denied in Joy v. St. Louis, 201 U.S. 332 (1906), an action for ejectment by a plaintiff not in possession. In Joy too, the Court noted that although the plaintiff claimed title from a federal patent or an Act of Congress, there might be no dispute about federal law. But in reaching that conclusion, Joy also rested in part on pleading conventions: in an ejectment action, it is not necessary to allege the source of plaintiff's title or that there is a dispute about the validity of that title. It is possible that Shulthis also rested in part on what was viewed as a necessary allegation in an action to quiet title. (Although the Court in Grable describes Hopkins as a quiet title action, the case was actually one *to remove a cloud on title*.)

Joy and possibly Shulthis illustrate a distinct aspect of the well-pleaded complaint rule: a plaintiff may not unlock the door to federal court by including allegations concerning issues of federal law not required by pleading rules. This aspect of the rule is beside the point when the claim states a federal cause of action, but the rule still bites in cases that incorporate a federal element in a state law claim; there, whether a complaint is "well-pleaded" depends on the niceties of pleading requirements.

While the decisions in Hopkins, Shulthis, and Joy all predate Erie R.R. v. Tompkins, today it is clear that state law generally governs allocation of the burden of pleading with respect to a state law claim in federal court.[1] (Note that in Part III(A) of the Grable opinion, the Court begins by noting that under Michigan law, "Grable's state complaint must specify 'the facts establishing the superiority of [its] claim'", and that those facts included the failure of the IRS to provide the kind of notice alleged to be required by statute.) It surely makes sense to distinguish cases where a claim of title based on federal law is in the background but not in controversy, as may have been true in Shulthis, from those in which there is a genuine dispute about the existence or validity of a claim of title under federal law, as in Grable and Hopkins. But can a convincing case be made that the appropriateness of federal adjudication depends on whether pleading conventions require the plaintiff to include allegations about a dispute respecting the federal title claimed by one of the disputants? If, in a case like Grable, a different state did not require a plaintiff seeking to quiet title to allege the invalidity of the competing title, would federal jurisdiction be lacking? Should it?

(2) The Merrell Dow Decision. The Grable decision suggests that there is longstanding authority, in decisions like Hopkins and Smith, for the exercise of federal question jurisdiction in the absence of a federal cause of action, and the Court's unanimity may suggest a degree of clarity and stability in the law. But that authority had been thrown into question by the Court's 5–4 decision in Merrell Dow Pharmaceuticals Inc. v. Thompson, 478 U.S. 804 (1986), which featured a lengthy debate between majority and dissent about the proper

---

1. However, federal statutes or rules that prescribe pleading requirements on particular issues arising in a state law cause of action (*e.g.*, Fed. R. Civ. Proc. 8(c)) may override state law. *Cf.* Palmer v. Hoffman, 318 U.S. 109 (1943).

understanding of federal question jurisdiction and which generated considerable confusion in the lower courts.

At issue in Merrell Dow were tort actions in which the plaintiffs, some residents of Canada and some of Scotland, alleged that children were born with deformities as a result of their mothers' use during pregnancy of the drug Bendectin. One count in the complaint alleged that the company's failure, in labeling the drug, adequately to warn of its dangers constituted "misbranding" in violation of the Federal Food, Drug, and Cosmetic Act (FDCA) and that this violation created a rebuttable presumption of negligence under Ohio law. Thus, embedded within a state law tort claim was a federal issue about the meaning and application of the FDCA.

The actions were filed in state court, but the defendant removed them to federal court, alleging that they were "founded, in part, on an alleged claim arising under the laws of the United States" (p. 806). The Supreme Court held that the district court lacked federal question jurisdiction over the removed actions and should have remanded them to state court.

(a) The Majority's Opinion. Justice Stevens' opinion for the Court acknowledged (pp. 808–12) that "a case may arise under federal law 'where the vindication of a right under state law necessarily turned on some construction of federal law'", but he stressed that "this statement must be read with caution * * * . [T]he phrase 'arising under' masks a welter of issues regarding the interrelation of federal and state authority and the proper management of the federal judicial system" and "in exploring the outer reaches of § 1331, determinations about federal jurisdiction require sensitive judgments about congressional intent, judicial power, and the federal system. * * *

"In this case, both parties agree with the Court of Appeals' conclusion that there is no federal cause of action for FDCA violations. For purposes of our decision, we assume that * * * Congress did not intend a private federal remedy for violations of the statute that it enacted. Thus * * * it is appropriate to assume that * * * some combination of the following factors is present: (1) the plaintiffs are not part of the class for whose special benefit the statute was passed; (2) the indicia of legislative intent reveal no congressional purpose to provide a private cause of action; (3) a federal cause of action would not further the underlying purposes of the legislative scheme; and (4) the respondents' cause of action is a subject traditionally relegated to state law.

" * * * [T]he very reasons for the development of the modern implied remedy doctrine—the 'increased complexity of federal legislation and the increased volume of federal litigation,' as well as 'the desirability of a more careful scrutiny of legislative intent,' Merrill Lynch, Pierce, Fenner & Smith, Inc., v. Curran, 456 U.S. 353, 377 (1982)(footnote omitted)—are precisely the kind of considerations that should inform the concern for 'practicality and necessity' * * * when jurisdiction is asserted because of the presence of a federal issue in a state cause of action.

"The significance of the necessary assumption that there is no federal private cause of action thus cannot be overstated. For the ultimate import of such a conclusion * * * is that it would flout congressional intent to provide a private federal remedy for the violation of the federal statute. We think it would similarly flout, or at least undermine, congressional intent to conclude that the federal courts might nevertheless exercise federal-question jurisdiction and provide remedies for violations of that federal statute solely because the violation of the federal statute is said to be a 'rebuttable presumption' or a 'proximate cause' under state law, rather than a federal action under federal law.''

In an important footnote (p. 814 n. 12), the Court added: "Several commentators have suggested that our § 1331 decisions can best be understood as an evaluation of the *nature* of the federal interest at stake. See, *e.g.*, Shapiro, *Jurisdiction and Discretion*, 60 N.Y.U.L.Rev. 543, 568 (1985); Cohen, *The Broken Compass: The Requirement That A Case Arise 'Directly' Under Federal Law*, 115 U.Pa.L.Rev. 890, 916 (1967). * * *

"Focusing on the nature of the federal interest, moreover, suggests that the widely perceived * * * conflict between the finding of federal jurisdiction in Smith v. Kansas City Title & Trust Co., 255 U.S. 180 (1921), and the finding of no jurisdiction in Moore v. Chesapeake & Ohio R. Co., 291 U.S. 205 (1934), is far from clear. For the difference in results can be seen as manifestations of the differences in the nature of the federal issues at stake. In Smith, * * * the issue was the constitutionality of an important federal statute. In Moore, in contrast, the Court emphasized that the violation of the federal standard as an element of state tort recovery did not fundamentally change the state tort nature of the action.

"The importance of the nature of the federal issue in federal question jurisdiction is highlighted by the fact that, despite the usual reliability of the Holmes test as an inclusionary principle, this Court has sometimes found that formally federal causes of action were not properly brought under federal-question jurisdiction because of the overwhelming predominance of state-law issues. * * * See * * * Shoshone Mining Co. v. Rutter, 177 U.S. 505, 507 (1900) ('We pointed out in the former opinion that it was well settled that a suit to enforce a right which takes its origin in the laws of the United States is not necessarily one arising under the Constitution or laws of the United States, within the meaning of the jurisdiction clauses, for if it did every action to establish title to real estate (at least in the newer States) would be such a one, as all titles in those States come from the United States or by virtue of its laws')''.

In Merrell Dow, the defendant had offered two arguments that there was a federal interest in federal court adjudication. First, it suggested that uniform interpretation of the FDCA was important and that federal adjudication would help to achieve uniformity. The Court responded that if state court interpretation of the FDCA threatens the regulatory regime the Act creates, the defendant should be arguing not for federal jurisdiction over state FDCA–based causes of action but for FDCA preemption of state court jurisdiction over the dispute. Justice Stevens added that the concern about uniformity was "considerably mitigated" by the existence of Supreme Court review of any state court decision (p. 816).

The defendant also argued that the case presented a novel question about whether the FDCA applies to extraterritorial sales in Canada and Scotland. The court rejected that argument, stating that whether a claim arises under federal law does not depend on the novelty of the federal issue and that the system of federal jurisdiction would be "ill served" by required case-by-case appraisal of novelty (p. 817).

Thus, the Court concluded that "a complaint alleging a violation of a federal statute as an element of a state cause of action, when Congress has determined that there should be no private, federal cause of action for the violation, does not state a claim 'arising under the Constitution, laws, or treaties of the United States' " (*id.*).

(b) Justice Brennan's Dissent. Joined by Justices White, Marshall, and Blackmun, Justice Brennan wrote a vigorous dissent. His starting point was Smith v. Kansas City Title & Trust Co. "The continuing vitality of Smith is beyond challenge. We have cited it approvingly on numerous occasions, and reaffirmed its holding several times—most recently just three Terms ago by a unanimous Court in Franchise Tax Board v. Construction Laborers Vacation Trust, 463 U.S. [1,] 9 [1983]. * * * Moreover, * * * Smith has been widely cited and followed in the lower federal courts. * * * Furthermore, the principle of the Smith case has been recognized and endorsed by most commentators as well" (pp. 820–21). Because the plaintiff's " 'right to relief depend[ed] upon the construction or application of the Constitution or laws of the United States,' " Smith, 255 U.S., at 199, and was not frivolous, Justice Brennan concluded that the claim arises under federal law.

In a footnote, he objected to the majority's approach of evaluating the nature of the federal interest (p. 821 n. 1):

"The Court suggests that Smith and Moore may be reconciled if one views the question whether there is jurisdiction under § 1331 as turning upon 'an evaluation of the *nature* of the federal interest at stake.' *Ante,* n. 12 (emphasis in original). * * *

"In one sense, the Court is correct in asserting that we can reconcile Smith and Moore on the ground that the 'nature' of the federal interest was more significant in Smith than in Moore. * * * But this is so only because a test based upon an ad hoc evaluation of the importance of the federal issue is infinitely malleable: at what point does a federal interest become strong enough to create jurisdiction? * * * Why, for instance, was the statute in Smith so 'important' that direct review of a state court decision (under our mandatory appellate jurisdiction) would have been inadequate? Would the result in Moore have been different if the federal issue had been a more important element of the tort claim? The point is that if one makes the test sufficiently vague and general, virtually any set of results can be 'reconciled.' However, the inevitable—and undesirable—result of [such] a test * * * is that federal jurisdiction turns in every case on an appraisal of the federal issue, its importance and its relation to state law issues. Yet it is precisely because the Court believes that federal jurisdiction would be 'ill served' by such a case-by-case appraisal that it rejects petitioner's claim that the difficulty and importance of the statutory issue presented by its claim suffices to confer jurisdiction under § 1331. The Court cannot have it both ways.

"My own view is in accord with those commentators who view the results in Smith and Moore as irreconcilable. That fact does not trouble me greatly, however, for I view Moore as having been a 'sport' at the time it was decided and having long been in a state of innocuous desuetude * * * ".[2]

2. [Ed.] In Moore, a railroad employee, sought recovery under a Kentucky statute for injuries suffered. The state statute provided that no employee should be held to be contributorily negligent, or to have assumed the risk, when the violation of any federal safety standard contributed to the injury, and Moore's complaint asserted violations of the Federal Safety Appliance Act. The Court held that the case did not arise under federal law (pp. 214–17):

Justice Brennan proceeded to argue that Congress' failure to create under the FDCA a private right of action for damages did not imply that federal jurisdiction should not be exercised over a state cause of action incorporating an issue under the FDCA. He stressed the expertise, sympathy to federal purposes, and capacity to generate uniformity of federal courts when interpreting and applying federal law, and he declared that his 30 years' experience as a Justice convinced him that Supreme Court review of state court decisions cannot come close to doing the job of assuring correct and uniform interpretation of federal law. He added that interpretation of the FDCA, even when incorporated in a state law cause of action, will shape behavior and thus "implicates the concerns that led Congress to grant the district courts power to adjudicate cases involving federal questions in precisely the same way as if it was federal law that 'created' the cause of action" (p. 828).

Finally, Justice Brennan contended that the reasons identified by the majority as underlying the Court's stringent approach to implying private rights of action—the increased complexity of federal legislation, the growing volume of federal litigation, and the desirability of careful examination of legislative intent—argued for rather than against the exercise of federal jurisdiction. Greater complexity of federal law made the greater expertise of federal courts especially important. And "while the increased volume of litigation may appropriately be considered in connection with reasoned arguments that justify limiting the reach of § 1331, I do not believe that the day has yet arrived when this Court may trim a statute solely because it thinks that Congress made it too broad" (p. 829). As for examination of legislative intent, Justice Brennan stressed that the FDCA regime is typical of regulatory schemes, in which an administrative agency like the FDA has authority to seek a broad range of remedies to combat violations. As all of those remedies are provided by the federal courts, "it seems rather strange to conclude that it either 'flout[s]' or 'undermine[s]' congressional intent for the federal courts to adjudicate a private state law remedy that is based upon violating the FDCA" (p. 831). If Congress has not preempted state provision of a private remedy for violation of

"Questions arising in actions in state courts to recover for injuries sustained by employees in intrastate commerce and relating to the scope or construction of the Federal Safety Appliance Acts are, of course, federal questions which may appropriately be reviewed in this Court. * * * But it does not follow that a suit brought under the state statute which defines liability to employees who are injured while engaged in intrastate commerce, and brings within the purview of the statute a breach of the duty imposed by the federal statute, should be regarded as a suit arising under the laws of the United States * * *.

"[N]othing in the Safety Appliance Acts precluded the State from incorporating in its legislation applicable to local transportation the paramount duty which the Safety Appliance Acts imposed as to the equipment of cars used on interstate railroads. As this Court said in Minneapolis, St. Paul & Sault Ste. Marie R. Co. v. Popplar, [237 U.S. 369], as to an action for injuries sustained in intrastate commerce: 'The action fell within the familiar category of cases involving the duty of a master to his servant. This duty is defined by the common law, except as it may be modified by legislation. The federal statute, in the present case, touched the duty of the master at a single point and, save as provided in the statute, the right of the plaintiff to recover was left to be determined by the law of the State.' "

Isn't reconciliation of Moore and Smith easier than either opinion in Merrell Dow suggested? Under the Kentucky statute in Moore, a violation of the FSAA merely negated defenses of contributory negligence and assumption of risk. Because the federal issue came in, as in Mottley, only by way of reply to a defense, Moore failed the well-pleaded complaint rule.

the FDCA, it should not be understood to have foreclosed federal jurisdiction over that state law remedy.

(c) The Meaning and Impact of Merrell Dow. After Merrell Dow, there was considerable uncertainty about when § 1331 conferred jurisdiction in the absence of a federal cause of action. On the one hand, the majority had carefully refrained from overruling Smith.[3] Rather, it purported to find, in Congress' (hypothesized) decision not to create a federal cause of action for violations of the FDCA, special reasons militating against jurisdiction.

But in virtually all cases in which a plaintiff seeks to rely on the Smith rule (rather than on the Holmes test), no federal right of action is available. Thus, it was arguable that the Merrell Dow analysis—that federal court adjudication would undermine the policy that animated the decision not to have a substantive federal cause of action—would usually apply. On this view, little would be left of the Smith approach—except in the unusual situation in which a federal right of action exists but the plaintiff chooses to sue only on a state cause of action with a federal ingredient.[4]

3. Two years after Merrell Dow, in Christianson v. Colt Industries Operating Corp., 486 U.S. 800, 808 (1988), the Court, per Brennan, J., said that a case arises under federal law if "the plaintiff's right to relief necessarily depends on resolution of a substantial question of federal law". The case was an antitrust action alleging that the defendant had driven plaintiffs out of business. One of plaintiffs' theories was that the defendant told plaintiffs' customers that plaintiffs were misappropriating defendant's trade secrets; the plaintiffs denied misappropriation on the ground that defendant's patents were invalid. After the plaintiffs prevailed in the district court, the defendant appealed to the Court of Appeals for the Federal Circuit, which, under 28 U.S.C. § 1295(a)(1), has exclusive appellate jurisdiction when the district court's jurisdiction is based in whole or in part on 28 U.S.C. § 1338's grant of jurisdiction over cases "arising under" the patent laws. Thus, if the case arose under the patent laws, the appeal was proper; if instead it arose under the antitrust laws, the regional court of appeals (the Seventh Circuit) had appellate jurisdiction. The Supreme Court unanimously ruled that the case did not arise under the patent laws. The Court stressed that the multiplicity of antitrust theories pleaded in the complaint gave rise to many reasons, wholly unrelated to the question of patent validity, why the plaintiffs might or might not be entitled to relief under the antitrust laws: "a claim supported by alternative theories in the complaint may not form the basis for § 1338(a) jurisdiction unless patent law is essential to each of those theories" (p. 810).

On § 1295(a)(1) and its relationship to § 1338, see Holmes Group, Inc. v. Vornado Air Circulation Sys., 535 U.S. 826 (2002), Fifth Edition p. 862 & n. 9.

4. That unusual situation seems to have been present in City of Chicago v. International College of Surgeons, 522 U.S. 156 (1997), where the Court upheld district court jurisdiction over a state-created cause of action that incorporated a federal ingredient. The plaintiff had filed a state court action under Illinois' Administrative Review Law, seeking judicial review of a municipal agency's unfavorable land use decision. The plaintiff claimed that both the municipal law and the manner in which certain proceedings had been conducted violated the Fourteenth Amendment of the U.S. Constitution; the plaintiff also alleged various violations of state law.

The Court, per O'Connor, J., ruled that the case had been properly removed to federal court under §§ 1331 and 1441. The Court's discussion of the issue was brief: it did not even mention Smith, and it cited Merrell Dow only for an unrelated point (that insubstantial claims do not confer federal jurisdiction). The Court noted "that the federal constitutional claims were raised by way of a cause of action created by state law, namely the Illinois Administrative Review Law" (p. 164). Then, the Court stated that " '[e]ven though state law creates [a party's] cause of action, its case might still 'arise under' the laws of the United States if a well-pleaded complaint established that its right to relief under state law requires resolution of a substantial question of federal law' " (p. 164,

As the Grable opinion notes, some lower courts had read Merrell Dow as taking this highly restrictive view of § 1331; others had viewed the approach of Smith as more vital and broadly important. Grable resolves this conflict by endorsing the second approach, viewing Smith and Hopkins as generative cases and Merrell Dow as a limited exception.

(3) Discretion and Federal Interests. While the Court upheld jurisdiction in Grable and refused it in Merrell Dow, in both cases the Court sought to reserve discretion to tailor the "arising under" jurisdiction to the practical needs of the particular situation. What is the proper role of discretion in determining the appropriate reach of § 1331?

(a) In Merrell Dow, Justice Stevens cited Cohen, *The Broken Compass: The Requirement That a Case Arise "Directly" Under Federal Law,* 115 U.Pa.L.Rev. 890 (1967), which argued against the use of any analytic formula for determining when a case "arises under" federal law for purposes of § 1331 and in favor of "pragmatic standards for a pragmatic problem". Cohen suggests that the relevant "pragmatic" considerations include "the extent of the caseload increase * * * if jurisdiction is recognized"; the extent to which cases "of this class" turn on federal versus state law; "the extent of the necessity for an expert federal tribunal"; and "the extent of the necessity for a sympathetic federal tribunal" (p. 916). His position appears to be that *district* courts should exercise a case-by-case discretion, unguided by any "formulation", in determining whether jurisdiction is justified by "pragmatic" factors. Would such a regime be tolerable? (Note that it would both narrow and complicate Supreme Court supervision of this area.)

(b) Justice Stevens' opinion in Merrell Dow also cited Shapiro, *Jurisdiction and Discretion,* 60 N.Y.U.L.Rev. 543, 568–70 (1985). Professor Shapiro disassociates himself from the *ad hoc* approach of Professor Cohen, stressing that the range of discretion under § 1331, "though extremely broad at the outset, has been significantly narrowed by the course of decisions since the jurisdictional statute was enacted" (p. 568 n. 149). He explains: "The discretion I advocate relates primarily to the existence of a range of permissible choices under the relevant grants of jurisdiction. It is entirely consistent with this view for judicial precedent to narrow the scope of discretion and even to generate predictable rules" (pp. 588–89). In Shapiro's view, "no formulation can possibly explain or even begin to account for the variety of outcomes unless it accords sufficient room for the federal courts to make a range of choices based on considerations of judicial administration and the degree of federal concern." He continues:

"[The] cases suggest that the Court's authority, but not its obligation, is very broad indeed. In Smith, the presence of a federal ingredient made relevant by state law was sufficient to confer jurisdiction, but in Shoshone [Fifth Edition p. 867], a federally created claim that turned on issues of state law was not. Both cases, however, may be better understood if viewed in terms of the federal interest at stake and the effect on the federal docket. Cases like Smith arise

quoting Franchise Tax Bd. of Cal. v. Construction Laborers Vacation Trust, 463 U.S. 1, 13 (1983), Fifth Edition p. 891).

The Court appeared to acknowledge that the plaintiff, instead of filing a state administrative review proceeding, could have filed a federal cause of action under 42 U.S.C. § 1983 against the local agency and its officials for the alleged violations of federal constitutional rights, but did not rely on that observation in upholding federal question jurisdiction.

infrequently, but the issue—the ability of a party to invest in federally authorized securities—was a matter of great federal moment. Cases like Shoshone must have arisen with monotonous regularity at the turn of the century, but the degree of federal interest in an outcome dependent on local custom was marginal at best" (pp. 568–70).

Doesn't the Court's analysis in Grable rather closely track the approach advocated by Professor Shapiro?

(c) How determinate is the pattern established by Hopkins, Smith, Merrell Dow, and Grable? In seeking to explain the differing outcomes in Smith and Merrell Dow, some observers noted that the issue in Smith was one of constitutional law.[5] Recall that the Grable opinion notes that "[a]s Merrell Dow itself suggested, constitutional questions may be the more likely ones to reach the level of substantiality that can justify federal jurisdiction. But a flat ban on statutory questions would mechanically exclude significant questions of federal law like the one this case presents".

Can Merrell Dow and Smith be distinguished on a different basis? If the failure of Congress to provide an express private remedy in the FDCA argues against "arising under" jurisdiction in Merrell Dow, is the parallel argument about the lack of such a private remedy in the statute at issue in Smith less forceful, given the absence of a comprehensive scheme of federal enforcement? Put differently, it is conceivable that Congress might have enacted a private right of action under the FDCA (and thus Congress' assumed failure to do so is significant); but it is difficult to imagine that Congress would have considered enacting a statute authorizing shareholders to sue a corporation for having purchased bonds issued under an invalid federal statute (and hence the failure to do so has little significance). Do Merrell Dow, and the Grable Court's discussion of Merrell Dow, perhaps suggest this distinction?

(d) Are you persuaded that the statutory issue in Grable is more appropriate for federal adjudication than the statutory issue in Merrell Dow?

(i) Grable says that upholding federal jurisdiction in Merrell Dow would have opened the federal courthouse to a horde of cases—all those in which a federal regulatory standard is embedded in a state cause of action. (While that concern may in fact have motivated the majority in Merrell Dow, the Court's opinion there had barely adverted to it.) And the problem is broader than state negligence actions like Merrell Dow; consider, for examples, disputes about a state's "piggyback" income tax, which incorporates a federal definition of taxable income. Could a persuasive response be made that the mere fact that a set of cases is numerous does not show that any individual member of that set is inappropriate for federal adjudication?

(ii) The issue in Grable appears to be close to a pure issue of law that could be settled once and for all and thereafter would govern numerous tax sale cases. The issue in Merrell Dow, by contrast, involved the application of law to fact; a determination whether Bendectin was misbranded might provide little guidance about the meaning of FDCA labeling requirements as applied to other products. (Compare, in this regard, the Note on Control of Factfinding and on Application of Law to Fact, Fifth Edition p. 571.) But on this dimension, was Justice Brennan right in Merrell Dow that the majority did not do justice to the

---

5. So, too, was the issue in the College of Surgeons case, note 4, *supra*, where the Court also upheld jurisdiction.

argument that a different question about the FDCA, whether it applies extra-territorially, merited federal adjudication—not because of its novelty but because it, too, was a relatively pure legal issue whose resolution would thereafter govern many cases? If federal jurisdiction is ill-served by case-by-case assessment of novelty, as the Merrell Dow majority suggested, is it ill-served by case-by-case assessment of the federal interest, as is called for by the Grable decision? Or is such an assessment necessary if the Court is to avoid two undesirable poles: (A) providing that § 1331 reaches no state law cause of action, no matter how great the federal interest in adjudication of a federal ingredient in that action (an approach that would require overruling Hopkins, Smith, and Grable), or (B) accepting jurisdiction over every case in which a federal issue must be alleged as part of a well-pleaded complaint, no matter how unimportant or uncontested that issue may be (a position that Justice Brennan's dissent in Merrell Dow can be viewed as taking)?[6]

(iii) While the government was not a party to Grable, the Solicitor General filed an amicus brief urging the Court to uphold jurisdiction, and, as the opinion noted, the government has an obvious interest in its ability to satisfy its tax claims and to confer secure title upon purchasers at tax sales. In other cases, when the government is less directly interested in a federal issue that arises in a state law action between private parties, will (should) the federal courts be less likely to recognize jurisdiction under Smith?

(iv) In Grable, the Solicitor General argued that in Merrell Dow, "the State voluntarily decided to incorporate the federal misbranding standard as evidence of negligence under state law. That voluntary absorption of a federal standard did not fundamentally change the state law character of the plaintiff's tort action * * *. In contrast, in resolving a state quiet title action challenging a federal tax deed, a state court is required by the Supremacy Clause to apply federal standards in deciding whether title is validly transferred". Brief for the United States as Amicus Curiae at 9. The Court in Grable did not rest on that distinction. Should it have? Wouldn't endorsing that distinction have cast doubt on Smith?

(5) Simple vs. Refined Jurisdictional Rules. The question whether § 1331 should be understood to include some cases in which no federal cause of action is alleged does not often arise. Only a very few Supreme Court decisions—Hopkins and similar cases, Smith, Grable, and College of Surgeons, note 4, *supra*—clearly uphold jurisdiction in the absence of a federal cause of action.[7] Lower federal court decisions upholding jurisdiction in such cases, though obviously more numerous, remain relatively infrequent.

---

6. See also Yackle, Reclaiming the Federal Courts 114–16 (1994), urging that general federal question jurisdiction should exist whenever a substantial question of federal law is an essential element of the plaintiff's case. Professor Yackle also proposes, *inter alia*, that original jurisdiction should extend to a case in which the plaintiff "alleges that a substantial federal question that may resolve the dispute will appear in an answer or other allowable pre-trial proceeding or motion." *Id.*

7. See also De Sylva v. Ballentine, 351 U.S. 570 (1956), Fifth Edition p. 724, where the Court decided on the merits—without discussing any jurisdictional question—a federal court action involving a state law claim to partial ownership of copyright renewal terms. "Since there was no diversity of citizenship, and no infringement, the only, and a sufficient, explanation for the taking of jurisdiction was the existence of two major questions of construction of the Copyright Act." T.B. Harms Co. v. Eliscu, 339 F.2d 823, 827 (2d Cir.1964).

Justice Thomas' concurrence cites the Fifth Edition as raising this question: assuming that in some cases (like Grable and Smith) the exercise of federal question jurisdiction over state law causes of action is desirable, is the game worth the candle? Powerful arguments have been made that rules of subject matter jurisdiction should be subject to a "bright line" test. See Chafee, Some Problems of Equity 1–102 (1950).[8] Justice Holmes' cause of action test is simpler and clearer—and while excluding cases like Smith or Grable, it avoids the need in a much larger number of cases to engage in what can be a refined and uncertain analysis—an analysis that some courts may not handle successfully. See Meltzer, *Jurisdiction and Discretion Revisited*, 79 Notre Dame L.Rev. 1891, 1913 (2004) (suggesting that the lower court decisions after Merrell Dow and before Grable contain "some surprising statements" and, overall, raise a question "whether federal judges, as intelligent and dedicated as most of them are, can in fact establish a coherent framework for the boundaries of subject matter jurisdiction predicated not upon a federal claim for relief but instead upon a federal ingredient in a state law claim for relief"). Thus, the law review note cited by Justice Thomas found that since 1994, the courts of appeals had discussed Smith jurisdiction in 69 reported cases and in 45 of them had reversed the district court. See Note, 115 Harv.L.Rev. 2272, 2280 (2002).

To be sure, Meltzer's assessment, and a reversal rate of 65%, may have been the product of the unusual uncertainty generated by Merrell Dow—and reported appeals may be an unrepresentative sample of cases discussing jurisdiction under Smith. Will Grable lead to a more consistent understanding of the reach of § 1331 than existed after Merrell Dow? If so, does that argue in favor of the Court's approach? If not, does that argue in favor of confronting the question raised by Justice Thomas?

SUBSECTION B: STATUTORY JURISDICTION OVER DECLARATORY JUDGMENT ACTIONS

Pages 901–04. Add to Paragraph (3):

For thorough discussion of many of the issues raised in this Paragraph, see Sloss, *Constitutional Remedies for Statutory Violations*, 89 Iowa L.Rev. 355 (2004), discussed at p. 47, *supra*.

SECTION 4. FEDERAL QUESTION REMOVAL

Page 907. Add to the end of Paragraph (2):

The Court reaffirmed the "complete preemption" doctrine, and found that it authorized removal, in Beneficial Nat'l Bank v. Anderson, 539 U.S. 1 (2003).

---

8. See also Hirshman, *Whose Law Is It Anyway? A Reconsideration of Federal Question Jurisdiction Over Cases of Mixed State and Federal Law*, 60 Ind.L.J. 17 (1984)(supporting a return to the Holmes test).

There, plaintiffs' state court action alleged that a bank chartered under the National Bank Act had violated state usury law; the complaint alleged no federal violation. The Court, with Justice Stevens writing, upheld removal. The majority relied upon Avco (which it described as "resting on the unusually 'powerful' preemptive force of § 301" of the LMRA) (p. 6) and Metropolitan Life (which it described as resting on (1) ERISA's provision of not only an express federal remedy but also a jurisdictional subsection using language similar to that of § 301, and (2) the unambiguous expression, in ERISA's legislative history, of an intent to treat actions under ERISA similarly to those under § 301). The Court summarized those two decisions as permitting removal "when a federal statute wholly displaces the state-law cause of action through complete pre-emption" (p. 7), and noted that in both instances "the federal statutes at issue provided the exclusive cause of action for the claim asserted and also set forth procedures and remedies governing that cause of action" (*id.*).

The Court found that the National Bank Act "unquestionably pre-empts any [state-law] rule that would treat * * * as usurious" rates that were lawful under the Act (p. 9). But a federal preemption defense would not alone justify removal; "[o]nly if Congress intended [the pertinent provision of the federal Act] to provide the exclusive cause of action for usury claims against national banks would the statute be comparable to the provisions" in Avco and Metropolitan Life (*id.*). Analyzing the federal scheme, the Court found that provisions of the National Bank Act "supersede both the substantive and the remedial provisions of state usury laws and create a federal remedy for overcharges that is exclusive" (p. 11)—and that therefore the claim in this case could arise only under federal law. A footnote added that "the proper inquiry focuses on whether Congress intended the federal cause of action to be exclusive rather than on whether Congress intended that the cause of action be removable" (p. 9 n. 5).

This last sentence directly answers the question posed in the first full paragraph on page 907 of the Fifth Edition, since the majority states that the complete preemption doctrine does not depend on showing a special legislative intent to permit removal. Indeed, the opinion suggests that any federal statute that both preempts state law and provides a substitute federal remedy creates an "exclusive cause of action" that falls within the complete preemption doctrine.

Justice Scalia's dissent (joined by Justice Thomas) took issue with the foundations of the complete preemption doctrine, characterizing Avco as a radical departure from the well-pleaded complaint rule and Metropolitan Life simply as following suit because ERISA was modeled on § 301 of the LMRA. Criticizing the entire doctrine as illogical, he urged that it be confined to cases under the LMRA or statutes modeled on it.

Do you agree with Justice Scalia that the complete preemption cases depart from the well-pleaded complaint rule?[i] Is it an answer that in these cases is the only possible "well-pleaded" complaint one that arises under federal law?

---

i. The following Term, in Aetna Health Inc. v. Davila, 542 U.S. 200 (2004), a decision involving ERISA, Justice Thomas, writing for a unanimous Court in upholding removal un-

If Justice Scalia's criticism is correct, isn't his intermediate position—to retain the doctrine but confine it to cases under the LMRA or statutes modeled on it—an odd resting point? On the one hand, given the procedural character of the issue and the absence of any significant reliance interests, stare decisis concerns don't appear to militate strongly against scrapping the doctrine altogether. On the other hand, if Avco and Metropolitan Life are to be retained, it is surely difficult to distinguish cases under the National Bank Act.

———

———

SECTION 5. SUPPLEMENTAL (PENDENT) JURISDICTION

———

Page 927. Add, after the second line on the page:

(For a summary and analysis of the Court's important decision in Exxon Mobil Corp. v. Allapattah Services, Inc., 125 S.Ct. ___ (2005), dealing with the intersection between § 1367 and the jurisdictional amount requirement in diversity litigation, see p. 139, *infra.*)

Page 927. Add to Paragraph 6(a):

For a recent decision holding that § 1367 "has displaced, rather than codified, whatever validity inhered in the earlier view that a permissive counterclaim requires independent jurisdiction (in the sense of federal question or diversity jurisdiction)", see Jones v. Ford Motor Credit Co., 358 F.3d 205, 213 (2d Cir.2004).

Pages 929–30. Add to footnote 10:

In Jinks v. Richland County, 538 U.S. 456 (2003), the Court unanimously reversed the decision of the South Carolina Supreme Court discussed in the Fifth Edition, and upheld the constitutionality of § 1367(d)'s tolling provision as applied to an action against a political subdivision of the state. There, a federal district court declined, under § 1367(c)(3), to exercise supplemental jurisdiction over a tort claim against a county and dismissed that claim without prejudice. The plaintiff re-filed in state court, where the claim would have been time-barred but for § 1367(d)'s tolling provision. Justice Scalia's opinion upheld that provision as "necessary and proper" for carrying out Congress' power to establish inferior federal courts in a fair and efficient manner. Absent such a provision, district courts would face unsatisfactory options: (1) they could condition dismissal on the defendant's waiver of a limitations defense, but the defendant might refuse to waive; (2) they could continue to exercise supplemental jurisdiction over the state claim, but state-court adjudication of that claim might be more appropriate; or (3) they could dismiss while permitting the plaintiff to re-open the federal case should the state court hold the claim to be time-barred. The Court concluded that § 1367(d) provides a preferable, more efficient alternative to these options and ensures that plaintiffs with related federal and state law claims can avail themselves of federal court jurisdiction without risking the dismissal of supplemental state law claims as time-barred.

The county objected to the application of § 1367(d) on the ground that Congress had infringed state sovereignty both by regulating the procedures that state courts use to

der the complete preemption doctrine, described that doctrine as "an exception" to the well-pleaded complaint rule (p. ___).

adjudicate state law claims and by extending the liability of a political subdivision. For discussion of the Court's rejection of those objections, see p. 28, *supra*, p. 73, *infra*.

———

SECTION 6.   ADMIRALTY JURISDICTION

———

Page 937. Add a new footnote 8a to the end of the second full paragraph on the page:

8a.   For a discussion stressing the need for clear guidelines for admiralty jurisdiction and bemoaning both the departure in Executive Jet from the principle that admiralty jurisdiction depends on the location of the wrong and the erosion of the earlier principle that with admiralty jurisdiction comes the application of substantive federal admiralty law, see Robertson & Sturley, *The Admiralty Extension Act Solution*, 34 J.Mar.L. & Comm. 209 (2003). The authors propose adoption of an interpretation of the Admiralty Extension Act (see Fifth Edition p. 935) "as a stand-alone basis for admiralty jurisdiction"—*i.e.*, as a basis for jurisdiction independent of the satisfaction of the requirements of Executive Jet and subsequent decisions (p. 238). They also propose that substantive federal admiralty law (rather than state law) should apply "to the full range of cases within [the Extension Act's] coverage" (p. 243).

———

CHAPTER IX

SUITS CHALLENGING OFFICIAL ACTION

SECTION 1. SUITS CHALLENGING FEDERAL OFFICIAL ACTION

SUBSECTION A: REMEDIES

Page 939. Add a new footnote 2a at the end of the first paragraph of Paragraph (1):

2a. For an informative historical study of the development of official accountability in England, with emphasis on the period from the thirteenth century through the seventeenth, see Seidman, *The Origins of Accountability: Everything I Know About the Sovereign's Immunity, I Learned from King Henry III*, 49 St.Louis U.L.J. 393 (2004). Professor Seidman concludes that "[c]ommon law jurists and parliamentarians rejected the idea of divine rights of kings in favor of popular sovereignty and the more balanced regime of a constitutional monarchy" (p. 399).

SUBSECTION B: THE SOVEREIGN IMMUNITY OF THE UNITED STATES AND ASSOCIATED REMEDIAL PROBLEMS

Page 945. Add a new footnote a at the end of the carry-over paragraph at the top of the page:

a. See generally Jackson, *Suing the Federal Government: Sovereignty, Immunity, and Judicial Independence*, 35 Geo.Wash.Int'l L.Rev. 521 (2003)(criticizing the doctrine of federal sovereign immunity as at odds with the spirit of Marbury v. Madison and with the implications of the text of Article III, and contending that the doctrine is not justified by a need to protect the primacy of Congress over the appropriation of money or by concern for the maintenance of judicial independence).

Page 970. Add to footnote 17:

As part of an exhaustive analysis of statutory waivers of federal sovereign immunity, Professor Sisk criticizes the Bowen decision as having "sown jurisdictional chaos" and urges *that it be repudiated. Sisk, The Tapestry Unravels: Statutory Waivers of Sovereign Immunity and Money Claims Against the United States, 71 Geo.Wash.L.Rev. 602, 706 (2003).*

SECTION 2.   SUITS CHALLENGING STATE OFFICIAL ACTION

SUBSECTION A: THE ELEVENTH AMENDMENT AND STATE SOVEREIGN IMMUNITY

Page 982. Substitute the following for the last sentence of footnote 6:

Professor Purcell, in *The Particularly Dubious Case of Hans v. Louisiana: An Essay on Law, Race, History, and "Federal Courts"*, 81 N.C.L.Rev. 1927 (2003), argues that Hans should not be given weight as precedent precisely because the result was so influenced by the nature of the Court's response to the context in which it was rendered. First, the case was "the product of * * * judicial instrumentalism, a result of the Court's shifting and pragmatic efforts to shape the jurisdiction of the federal courts to serve its evolving ideas of desirable national policy" (p. 2057). Second, the decision was "an integral part of the nation's surrender to southern intransigence and racial oppression" (p. 1954). Finally, and as a result of these contextual factors, the decision was "a rejection of both established Eleventh Amendment doctrine and the principles of the new post-Civil War Constitution" (p. 1954).

Page 982. Add a new footnote 6a after the citation to Monaco v. Mississippi:

6a. Lee, *The Supreme Court of the United States as Quasi–International Tribunal: Reclaiming the Court's Original and Exclusive Jurisdiction over Treaty–Based Suits by Foreign States Against States*, 104 Colum.L.Rev. 1765 (2004), criticizes the rationale of the Monaco case and argues that it should at least be limited to its facts (involving jurisdiction based solely on diversity) because the states, in ratifying the Constitution, gave up their immunity to suits against them by foreign states, particularly those based on alleged treaty violations. Such suits, however, must in his view be confined to the original and exclusive jurisdiction of the Supreme Court.

Page 995. Add a new footnote 3 at the end of Paragraph (3)(c):

3. In Frew v. Hawkins, 540 U.S. 431 (2004), private plaintiffs had obtained a consent decree, approved by the federal district court, in their action against state officials to remedy claimed federal law violations of its federally supported Medicaid program. Two years later, the plaintiffs sought enforcement of the decree—which contained a number of requirements that were more specific than the general mandates of the relevant federal statute—in a proceeding against state officials in their official capacity. On review of a district court decision in favor of plaintiffs, the court of appeals ruled that the Eleventh Amendment barred enforcement of the decree to the extent that it imposed obligations that went beyond the general statutory mandates.

A unanimous Supreme Court, in an opinion by Justice Kennedy, reversed. The Court held that under the doctrine of Ex parte Young, "a remedy the state officials themselves had accepted when they asked the District Court to approve the decree" could be enforced without violating the Eleventh Amendment (p. 439). Recognizing the special obligation of a federal court to modify a consent decree that significantly affects a state program when reason to do so has been shown, the Court concluded that in the absence of such a modification, "the decree should be enforced according to its terms" (p. 442).

Page 995. Add a new footnote 4 at the end of Paragraph (3)(c):

4. Despite the Court's continued adherence to Ex parte Young, the case still has its critics. In one exhaustive, and exhausting (150 page), essay, the author argues that the Young doctrine is not constitutionally viable both because it usurps congressional authority and because it violates the sovereign immunity of the states by interfering with their political decision-making authority. Leonard, *Ubi Remedium, Ibi Jus, or, Where There's a Remedy, There's a Right: A Skeptic's Critique of Ex Parte Young*, 54 Syracuse L.Rev. 215 (2004). Professor Leonard suggests as an alternative the use of relator actions (see Fifth Edition pp. 1032–33), supervised by politically accountable federal officials.

Page 1003. Add a new footnote 1 at the end of Paragraph (2)(b):

1. Babcock, *The Effect of the Supreme Court's Eleventh Amendment Jurisprudence on Clean Water Act Citizen's Suits*, 83 Or.L.Rev. 47 (2004), echoes the concern expressed in this Paragraph—about the potential impact of Pennhurst on the enforceability of federal requirements in cooperative state-federal programs—in the context of clean water regulation. Noting that the Clean Water Act gives the states primary responsibility for implementing certain federal policies, Professor Babcock suggests that the Pennhurst rule may effectively thwart use of the Act's citizen suit provision, in either state or federal court, to remedy state violations of federal policies.

Page 1027. Add to footnote 4:

For consideration of the relation between the Treaty Power and state sovereign immunity as an aspect of broader questions of American federalism, see Swayne, *Does Federalism Constrain the Treaty Power?*, 103 Colum.L.Rev. 403, 433–41, 487–92, 524–32 (2003). Professor Swayne concludes that, although the Court is unlikely to hold that the Treaty Power can serve as a basis for abrogating state immunity, there are significant "arcane loopholes" (*e.g.* the doctrine of Ex parte Young) that are relevant to effective implementation of international agreements, and perhaps more significantly, that practical solutions to the problem may be found through creative use of state and national authority relating to foreign and interstate compacts.

Despite the broad language of Florida Prepaid, quoted in text (Fifth Edition p. 1027), questions continue to be raised about the authority of Congress to abrogate state sovereign immunity under specific clauses of Article I. Thus the Court in the Hood case (see p. 78, *infra*), explicitly declined to consider the question of congressional authority to abrogate under the Bankruptcy Clause, and one recent comment has argued that the states have surrendered their immunity with regard to congressional exercise of the war power, see Hirsch, *Can Congress Use Its War Powers To Protect Military Employees from State Sovereign Immunity?*, 34 Seton Hall L.Rev. 999 (2004).

Page 1032. Add to Paragraph (5):

In the 2002 Term of the Supreme Court, as the Fifth Edition went to press, there were two pending Supreme Court cases (cited in footnote 8) that raised questions of congressional power to abrogate state sovereign immunity in the exercise of its authority under § 5 of the Fourteenth Amendment.

(i) In one of these cases, Nevada Dep't of Human Resources v. Hibbs, 538 U.S. 721 (2003), the Court, by a vote of 6–3, upheld the abrogation of state sovereign immunity in the Family and Medical Leave Act of 1993 (FMLA). This Act, *inter alia*, entitles eligible employees (including certain employees of public agencies) to up to 12 work weeks of unpaid leave annually for any of several reasons, including the onset of a "serious health condition" in the employee's spouse, child, or parent, and creates a private right of action "against any employer (including a public agency)" for equitable and monetary relief. The Court, per Chief Justice Rehnquist, held that Congress had met its burden under § 5: it had satisfied the requirement that the statement of abrogation be clearly made and, in light of the relevant evidence of gender-based discrimination in the legislative record, had sufficient evidence of a "pattern of constitutional violations on the part of the States in this area" to warrant the provision of the FMLA's private rights and remedies as "appropriate prophylactic legislation"; moreover, the challenged provisions were "congruent and proportional to the targeted violation" (pp. 728, 729, 737). The Court noted particularly the evidence that women had been disadvantaged in both private and public employment because of mutually enforcing, prevailing stereotypes that women are responsible for family care-giving and that men lack domestic responsibilities. Decisions discussed in this Paragraph in the Fifth Edition, especially the Kimel and Garrett cases, were distinguished on the basis of the stronger legislative record in Hibbs, the narrower targeting of the provisions of the FMLA, and (with respect to the sufficiency of the legislative record) the fact that classifications based on gender (rather than age or disability) are subject to heightened scrutiny.

Justice Souter, joined by Justices Ginsburg and Breyer, concurred on the ground that the validity of the challenged provisions followed a fortiori from his understanding of § 5 as expressed in prior dissents, and also noted that he continued to adhere to the dissenting views expressed in Seminole. Justice Stevens, concurring only in the judgment, expressed doubt that the legislation could be justified under § 5, but agreed with the result on the ground stated in his dissent in Seminole—that when a state is sued by one of its own citizens, "Congress may abrogate [the] common-law defense [of state sovereign immunity] pursuant to its power to regulate commerce 'among the several states' " (p. 741).

Justice Kennedy, joined by Justices Scalia and Thomas, dissented. He strongly disagreed with the majority's conclusion that the legislative record justified the challenged provisions, arguing, *inter alia*, that much of the evidence was general in nature and out-of-date, that evidence relating only to practices with respect to "parenting leave" was not adequate to warrant any conclusions with respect to the broader issue of "family leave", that there was little or no evidence of discriminatory application of non-discriminatory laws by a state (as distinguished from a private) employer, and that, for these and other reasons, Congress had exceeded its powers under § 5 by designing "an entitlement program, not a remedial statute" (p. 756). Justice Scalia, also dissenting separately, stressed his conviction that in order to justify the application of "prophylactic legislation" to a particular state, it was insufficient to rely on a notion of collective guilt; the question must be "whether the State has itself engaged in discrimination sufficient to support the exercise of Congress's prophylactic power" (p. 743).

(ii) The other pending case cited in the Fifth Edition, Medical Bd. v. Hason, 538 U.S. 958 (2003)(dismissed without opinion), involved congressional power to abrogate state immunity in Title II of the ADA, which prohibits exclusion of the disabled from participation in, or denial of the benefits of, "programs or activities of a public agency", or subjection of the disabled to discrimination by any such entity. But the issue in the Hason case was (in part) resolved the following Term in Tennessee v. Lane, 541 U.S. 509 (2004). In Lane, the plaintiffs (two paraplegics, one a criminal defendant and the other a court reporter) claimed in a federal court action that the state and several of its counties had denied them physical access to the state's courts in violation of Title II, and sought both damages and injunctive relief. In a 5–4 decision, the

Supreme Court, per Justice Stevens, upheld the refusal of the lower courts to grant the state's motion to dismiss on Eleventh Amendment grounds. The Court first concluded that Congress had plainly intended to abrogate immunity in such a case. It then held that Congress had the authority to abrogate immunity and provide a prophylactic remedy under § 5, at least when, as here, there was ample evidence of "pervasive unequal treatment" (p. 524) of the disabled in the administration of state and local services and programs generally, and with respect to access to courthouses in particular, and when the constitutional claim asserted—the due process right of access to courts— triggered an elevated standard of review. In this latter respect, the Court stated, the case was analogous to the Court's treatment of sex-based classifications in Hibbs.[a]

The Court, over vigorous objection in the Chief Justice's dissent, relied, *inter alia*, on evidence relating to the conduct of local entities. "To operate on that premise [that only the action of the states themselves should be considered] would be particularly inappropriate", the Court said, "because this case concerns the provision of judicial services, an area in which local governments are typically treated as 'arms of the State' for Eleventh Amendment purposes [citing cases]" (p. 527 n. 16). Compare the Court's refusal to consider the actions of local entities as relevant to the § 5 power in the Kimel case, discussed and criticized in Fifth Edition pp. 1031–32.[b]

In his dissent, Chief Justice Rehnquist, who authored the opinion in Hibbs, was joined by Justices Kennedy and Thomas. His opinion included a detailed discussion of the evidence before Congress and concluded that a " 'history and pattern' of violations of these constitutional rights [access to courthouses] by the States with respect to the disabled" had not been established (p. 541). Moreover, he asserted, even if the record did establish the existence of "inaccessible courthouses", "[w]e have never held that a person has a constitutional right to make his way into a courtroom without any external assistance" (p. 546). Finally, he contended, the remedies imposed by Title II, applying to far more than access to courthouses, failed the "congruence and proportionality" requirement test of congressional authority to enact prophylactic legislation under § 5.

Justice Scalia, dissenting separately, argued for abandonment of the "flabby" congruence and proportionality test for the validity of prophylactic legislation, except in matters of racial discrimination, and even there, he urged, the legislation should be confined to "those particular States in which there has been an identified history of relevant constitutional violations" (pp. 557,564).

a. Thus, the Court put to one side such questions as whether Title II could be used to "subject the States to private suits for money damages for failing to provide reasonable access to hockey rinks, or even to voting booths" (p. 842). On the Court's refusal to consider the validity of the statute on its face, a refusal strongly criticized in the Chief Justice's dissent, see p. 11, *supra*.

b. In a concurring opinion, Justice Souter, joined by Justice Ginsburg, explicitly adhered to his prior objections to the Court's Eleventh Amendment jurisprudence and also cited instances in which the "judiciary itself has endorsed the basis for some of the very discrimination subject to congressional remedy under § 5" (p. 534, citing Buck v. Bell, 274 U.S. 200 (1927)(upholding court-approved sterilization of a retarded person)). Justice Ginsburg, joined by Justices Souter and Breyer, also wrote a concurrence, emphasizing her view that the record of denial to the disabled of access to public facilities and services fully warranted legislation applicable to *all* government actors. (In this respect, her concurrence was specifically aimed at Justice Scalia's dissent.)

In all other areas, Congress' § 5 authority should be limited to facilitating "enforcement" (*e.g.*, by imposing reporting requirements on the states) of actual violations of the amendment's prohibitions.

(iii) The Hibbs and Lane cases are among several in recent Terms in which the Court rejected, or managed to avoid passing on, a claim of state sovereign immunity. (Some of these cases are discussed below.) None of these decisions purported to modify or overrule any existing precedent, and indeed several presented entirely novel issues. Moreover, the Court during this period extended state sovereign immunity to federal administrative adjudications (FMC, Fifth Edition p. 1061). Nevertheless, do these decisions, taken together, suggest that a majority of the Court is beginning to develop limits to the capacity of the concept of state sovereign immunity to impede the implementation of federal law—even in situations where such traditional approaches as that recognized in Ex parte Young are not available? Or should each decision be considered and explained as resting on its special circumstances? For example, the decision in Hibbs might be explained as resting in large part on the applicability of "heightened scrutiny" to issues of gender discrimination. And the Lane decision might be seen as resting both on the fundamental due process right of access to courthouses and on facts that put the state in a particularly unfavorable light.

Page 1033. Add a new footnote 8a at the end of Paragraph (6):

8a. As in other instances where the Court has distinguished between a state and its political subdivisions (see, *e.g.*, Lincoln County v. Luning, Fifth Edition p. 985; Jinks v. Richland County, discussed below), the Court held unanimously, in Cook County v. United States ex rel. Chandler, 538 U.S. 119 (2003), that local governments are "persons" subject to *qui tam* actions under the False Claims Act. Citing precedent and other historical materials for the proposition that municipal corporations should generally be treated like private ones for statutory and constitutional purposes, the Court went on to hold that "quasi-corporations" like counties should be similarly treated (p. 127 n. 7).

Page 1033. Add a new Paragraph (8):

(8) Options After Seminole (vi): In Rem Proceedings. The Court's willingness to allow the use of in rem proceedings in admiralty to determine a state's interest in property not in its possession was established in California v. Deep Sea Research, Inc., Fifth Edition p. 982, n. 7. For discussion of the Court's extension of this approach to bankruptcy proceedings, see p. 78, *infra*. Are there are other situations in which the approach is available?

Page 1034. Add to footnote 10:

See also Lee, *The Dubious Concept of Jurisdiction*, 54 Hastings L.J. 1613, 1632–35 (2003)(suggesting that understanding subject matter jurisdiction not as referring to a court's physical "power" but to its legal authority may help to explain several doctrinal anomalies, including the waivability of a state's Eleventh Amendment immunity).

Page 1037. Add to footnote 14:

The view that Congress has no authority to abrogate state sovereign immunity with respect to bankruptcy proceedings has been followed by at least five federal courts of appeals, but was rejected by the Sixth Circuit in Hood v. Tennessee Student Assistance Corp., 319 F.3d 755 (6th Cir.2003). Arguing on the basis of both the text of the Bankruptcy Clause in Article I and historical evidence, the court of appeals in Hood concluded that the states have ceded both legislative power and immunity from suit in bankruptcy matters. On review of the judgment, the Supreme Court did not resolve this conflict, relying instead on the in rem nature of a bankruptcy proceeding to hold only that a state's sovereign immunity did not preclude the discharge in bankruptcy of a debt owed by the bankrupt to the state. 541 U.S. 440 (2004). For full discussion of the Hood decision, see p. 78, *infra*.

On the specific issue raised in this footnote and in the accompanying text—whether a state's voluntary appearance as a plaintiff in federal court (including appearance as a claimant in bankruptcy) waives the state's sovereign immunity with respect to compulsory (or permissive) counterclaims, and if so whether the relief sought must be of the same kind and not in an amount greater than that sought by the state—the circuits are currently divided. See 71 U.S.L.W. 2592 (2003).

Page 1039. Add a new footnote 19 at the end of Paragraph(3)(b):

19.   Does the Lapides holding imply that even in a case coming squarely within the text of the Eleventh Amendment (*e.g.*, a state sued on a non-federal claim by a citizen of another state), Congress could provide for original federal subject-matter jurisdiction, which could be exercised by the court unless the state asserted a sovereign immunity defense? For an interesting discussion of this and related questions, see Horton, *Lapides v. Board of Regents and the Untrustworthiness of Unanimous Supreme Court Decisions*, 41 San Diego L.Rev. 1057 (2004).

Page 1039. Add a new footnote 20 at the end of Paragraph (3)(b):

20.   For an in-depth discussion of the history of the Court's waiver doctrine, including an analysis of what actions (and by whom) give rise to a waiver, see Siegel, *Waivers of State Sovereign Immunity and the Ideology of the Eleventh Amendment*, 52 Duke L.J. 1167 (2003). Professor Siegel argues, *inter alia*, that until 1945 the Court was more willing to find a waiver than during later years, when the Court gave increasing strength to the doctrine of state sovereign immunity, but that recently he has shown what he sees as encouraging signs (as in such decisions as Lapides and Schmidt—both discussed in the text of this Paragraph) of a return to the pre–1945 view. This fluctuation, he concludes, suggests that the waiver doctrine has "ebbed and flowed with the overall ideological tide of the Eleventh Amendment" (p. 1212). Professor Siegel also distinguishes between "waiver"—which can arise by implication from conduct, can occur without regard to the intent of the state or its officers, and is irrevocable—and "consent"—which requires a clear statement, is voluntary and subject to conditions imposed by the state, and may be withdrawn (pp. 1188–96).

Page 1060. Add to footnote 2:

In Franchise Tax Board of California [CFTB] v. Hyatt, 538 U.S. 488 (2003), the Supreme Court explicitly declined to reexamine the holding of Nevada v. Hall that the Constitution does not confer sovereign immunity on the states in the courts of sister states. In the CFTB case, Hyatt, a Nevada resident at the time of filing, brought an action against CFTB in a Nevada state court, alleging that the defendant had committed negligent and intentional torts in the course of auditing Hyatt's California state tax returns. Holding that California's sovereign interests warranted recognition of CFTB's claim of immunity with respect to negligence but that they did not outweigh Nevada's interests with respect to intentional torts, the Nevada Supreme Court rejected CFTB's claim of immunity with respect to the latter aspect of the complaint, and the U.S. Supreme Court unanimously affirmed.

The Court stated that petitioner CFTB "does not ask us to reexamine [the holding of Hall summarized above] and we therefore decline the invitation of petitioner's amici States * * * to do so" (p. 497). The Court then went on to consider CFTB's claim, said to implicate "Hall's second holding: that the Full Faith and Credit Clause did not require California to apply Nevada's sovereign immunity statutes where such application would violate California's own legitimate public policy" (*id.*). Relying heavily on both the ruling of Hall on this issue and on Sun Oil Co. v. Wortman, Fifth Edition p. 641, the Court rejected CFTB's claim that the Full Faith and Credit Clause required a determination that California's sovereign interest in enforcing its tax laws outweighed Nevada's interests in providing a remedy for an intentional tort allegedly injuring one of its citizens within its borders. After noting that "[t]he Nevada Supreme Court sensitively applied principles of comity with a healthy regard for California's sovereign status," the Court "decline[d] to embark on the constitutional course of balancing coordinate States' competing sovereign interests to resolve conflicts of laws under the Full Faith and Credit Clause'' (p. 499).

The Court has not always been loath to reconsider a decision when no party has asked it to (see, *e.g.*, Erie RR v. Tompkins, 304 U.S. 64 (1938)), especially when it does not find an alternative ground for reaching the result that overruling the prior decision would achieve. Does the CFTB case thus suggest that despite the difficulty of reconciling Hall's rationale with that of Alden v. Maine, Hall is not likely to be overruled?

Page 1064. Add a new footnote 8a at the end of the second paragraph of Paragraph (7):

8a.   Even after Alden, may a state employee sue an unconsenting state in a state court for injuries incurred as a result of the state's alleged violation of the Jones Act (creating a federal cause of action for injuries resulting from an employer's negligence during work on a maritime vessel)? Professor Pfander makes what is by his own admission a surprising argument that the state's claim of immunity may fail. See Pfander, *Jones Act Claims Against the States After Alden v. Maine: The Surprisingly Strong Case for a Compulsory State Court Forum*, 36 J.Mar.L. & Com. 1 (2005). He relies in significant part on (a) the Court's failure in Alden to overrule the Hilton case (see Fifth Edition p. 1043), which allowed a private FELA suit to be brought against a state in a state court, and (b) the inadequacy—indeed, unavailability—of alternative means of achieving compliance with federal law. (But didn't the Court in Alden, at least implicitly, reject the view that the Hilton decision could be invoked to override a state's sovereign immunity claim?)

Pages 1064–1065. Substitute the following for the last paragraph of Paragraph (7):

What of the ability of a bankrupt to obtain a discharge of any debts owing to a state? To the surprise of many observers, including members of the bankruptcy bar, the Court held, 7–2, that such a discharge may be obtained because the exercise of a federal court's in rem jurisdiction over the bankrupt's estate to effect the discharge does not infringe the sovereignty of the state. Tennessee Student Assistance Corp. (TSAC) v. Hood, 541 U.S. 440 (2004). The Hood case involved a student who had signed promissory notes for student loans made by a federal lender and guaranteed by TSAC. The student later filed a ''no asset'' Chapter 7 bankruptcy proceeding in federal court. The federal lender assigned its claim to TSAC, and Hood, following federal law making such loans non-dischargeable in the absence of a showing of ''undue hardship'', did not list the loans in the proceeding. Therefore, the general discharge Hood obtained did not cover those loans. Hood later reopened the proceeding, however, to seek a discharge from the loans on the grounds of undue hardship, and served her complaint and amended complaint on several parties, including TSAC. TSAC moved to dismiss on sovereign immunity grounds, and the motion was denied, the court of appeals holding (in conflict with every other circuit to consider the question) that the states had ceded their sovereign immunity from private suits in bankruptcy in the Constitutional Convention, and that Congress therefore had authority to abrogate that immunity when acting under the Bankruptcy Clause of Article I.

On review, Chief Justice Rehnquist, for the majority, declined to reach the question decided below on the ground that the in rem nature of the bankruptcy court's discharge of a bankrupt's debts ''does not implicate a State's Eleventh Amendment immunity'' (p. 445). Relying on the Court's prior holdings relating to the power of a federal court to determine the nature of a state's interest in property in an in rem proceeding in admiralty (see Fifth Edition p. 982, n. 7), as well as on several pre-Seminole bankruptcy decisions and on Moore's treatise on Federal Practice, the Chief Justice wrote that ''the [bankruptcy] court's jurisdiction is premised on the debtor and his estate, and not on the creditors" (p. 447). (In distinguishing an earlier decision refusing to allow an injunction against a state court action in which the state sought to establish ownership of property that conflicted with an earlier federal court determination, the Chief Justice said that even though a bankruptcy discharge operates by federal law as an injunction against creditors seeking to collect a discharged debt, "the enforcement of such an injunction against the State by a federal court is not before us" (p. 449 n. 4)). Finally, the Court rejected the argument that the in rem rationale was unavailable because the Bankruptcy Rules require the debtor to file an "adversary proceeding" against the State in order to discharge a student loan debt. Regardless of the particular provisions of the Bankruptcy Rules, the Court stated, the proceeding was in substance a proceeding in rem to determine the status of property under the control of the bankruptcy court, not to obtain property in the hands of the State.[c]

Justice Thomas, joined by Justice Scalia, dissented. He argued first that the in rem rationale should not be considered because the procedure actually used was an adversary one against the state, and because in any event, Hood's failure to raise the in rem argument constituted a waiver. (The in rem argument had apparently been made only in an amicus brief in the Supreme Court.)

Justice Thomas went on to argue that the in rem approach was in itself sufficiently troublesome that its appropriateness in the bankruptcy context should not be resolved without full briefing and consideration by the court of appeals. The admiralty decisions invoked by the majority were, in his view, not determinative because the scope of those rulings is uncertain and because they "reveal no clear principle to govern which, if any, bankruptcy suits are exempt from the Eleventh Amendment's bar" (p. 461). Indeed, he stated, "we have never applied an in rem exception to the sovereign-immunity bar against monetary recovery, and have suggested that no such exception exists" (p. 462, quoting United States v. Nordic Village Inc., 503 U.S. 30, 38 (1992)). Finally, Justice Thomas rejected the rationale of the court below, stating that the Bankruptcy Clause creates no exception to the inability of Congress to abrogate state immunity in the exercise of its Article I powers.

Although the Hood case settles a question of basic importance in bankruptcy law, it leaves some difficult issues unresolved. For example, what if, after discharge, the state nevertheless brings a state court proceeding to collect the discharged debt? What remedy, if any, does the debtor have in federal court? And what if the bankrupt's estate seeks to recover from the state a payment to it that is regarded under federal bankruptcy law as a voidable preference? Or to collect from the state money or property otherwise claimed to be owing to the bankrupt, including money or property simply taken by the state through self-help while the bankruptcy proceeding was pending? Under the Court's approach, is possession 10/10ths of the law?

Page 1065. Add to footnote 9:

In Jinks v. Richland County, 538 U.S. 456 (2003), referred to in this footnote as pending in the Supreme Court, the Court held unanimously (a) that the tolling provision of § 1367(d) was not facially unconstitutional because it was "necessary and proper" to the effective administration of justice in the federal courts (see p. 69, *supra*), and (b) that the provision

---

c. Concurring for himself and Justice Ginsburg, Justice Souter said that he joined in the Court's opinion, save for "any implicit approval" of the holding in Seminole (p. 455).

operated to toll a state statute of limitations for 30 days in order to allow a claim against a state political division to be filed in a state court following dismissal of that claim in a federal court. Such subdivisions, the Court reasoned, do not enjoy constitutional immunity from suit and thus may be subjected by Congress to suit in state court pursuant to a valid exercise of congressional authority.

Page 1066. Add to Paragraph (8):

The wealth of legal commentary on the Eleventh Amendment and state sovereign immunity continues to increase. Since the Fifth Edition went to press, significant commentary—in addition to that cited elsewhere in this Supplement—has included:

- General discussion of the issues presented by the line of Supreme Court decisions taken as a whole, see, *e.g.*, Choper & Yoo, *Who's So Afraid of the Eleventh Amendment: The Limited Impact of the Courts Sovereign Immunity Rulings?*, 105 Colum.L.Rev. ___ (2005)(contending (a) that in view of the available alternatives, critics have exaggerated the importance of the Court's Eleventh Amendment decisions, and (b) that the decisions are rooted less in federalism concerns than in separation of powers issues, *e.g.*, increasing the role of the Executive Branch in the enforcement of federal law); Gey, *The Myth of State Sovereignty*, 63 Ohio St.L.J. 1601 (2002)(criticizing the Court for lack of a coherent rationale for its decisions, suggesting that there would be "little downside" to "outright recognition that the states lost their sovereignty with the adoption of the Constitution", and maintaining that granting the states "true sovereignty" would lead to a "Yugoslavian-style battle among parochial sovereign entities" (p. 1681)); Lee, *Making Sense of the Eleventh Amendment: International Law and State Sovereignty*, 96 Nw. U.L.Rev. 1027 (2002)(advocating a renewed focus on the literal language of the Eleventh Amendment in the light of international law principles existing—and well-known to lawyers and statesmen—at the time the Amendment was adopted); Manning, *The Eleventh Amendment and the Reading of Precise Constitutional Texts*, 113 Yale L.J. 1663, 1669–70 (2004) (arguing that "at least where the Constitution speaks in precise, rule-like terms, as the Eleventh Amendment does," the Court should apply the method used to interpret unambiguous statutory texts, rather than the current, "strongly purposive" approach); Randall, *Sovereign Immunity and the Uses of History*, 81 Neb.L.Rev. 1 (2002)(concluding that the Framers did not intend any governmental entity, state or federal, to enjoy immunity from suit in Article III courts); Solimine, *Formalism, Pragmatism, and the Conservative Critique of the Eleventh Amendment*, 101 Mich.L.Rev. 1463 (2003)(urging—in a book review of Noonan, Narrowing the Court's Power: The Supreme Court Sides with the States (2002)(see Fifth Edition p. 1067 note 12)—that the Court "struggle toward a middle ground * * * encompass[ing], say, more benign views of Congressional power under [§ 5] or under the Conditional Spending Power"); Young, *Is the Sky Falling on the Federal Government? State Sovereign Immunity, the Section Five Power, and the Federal Balance*, 81 Tex.L.Rev. 1551, 1552 (2003)(reviewing Noonan's book and agreeing with Noonan's conclusion that the Court has erred, but criticizing the book for its lack of balance and "feverish" tone); *Symposium: The Eleventh Amendment, Federalism, and Judicial Activism: Questions and Answers*, 2002 Geo.J.L. & Pub.Pol. 7, especially 7–39.

- Discussion of one or more of the Court's decisions involving Congress's authority under § 5 of the Fourteenth Amendment, see, *e.g.*, Bandes, *Fear and Degradation in Alabama: The Emotional Subtext of University of Alabama v. Garrett*, 5 U.Pa.J.Const.L. 520 (2003)(focusing on "the emotive cast of the majority's language about the states" in the Court's opinion in Garrett as suggestive of the majority's "emotional commitments and blind spots: toward Congress, toward civil rights plaintiffs and civil rights statutes, and toward its own prerogatives"); Beck, *The Heart of Federalism: Pretext Review of Means–Ends Relationships*, 36 U.C. Davis L.Rev. 407 (2003)(defending the Court's use of means-end limitations "such as proportionality and proximity"—in both § 5 cases and cases relating to the Commerce Power—as comporting with the Court's approach in McCulloch v. Maryland); Kaczorowski, *Congress's Power To Enforce Fourteenth Amendment Rights: Lessons from Federal Remedies the Framers Enacted*, 42 Harv.J. on Legis. 187 (2005)(supporting with historical evidence the author's criticism of the Supreme Court's § 5 jurisprudence as insufficiently sensitive to the framers' intent to endow Congress with broad remedial powers); Post & Siegel, *Legislative Constitutionalism and Section Five Power: Policentric Interpretation of the Family and Medical Leave Act*, 112 Yale L.J. 1943 (2003)(contrasting the Court's "enforcement model" view of the § 5 power with the authors' proposed "policentric model", in which Congress—within limits believed by the Court to be needed to protect individual rights and such structural values as separation of powers and federalism—may exercise its § 5 power to enact legislation based on its own interpretation of constitutional rights); Symposium, *The Eleventh Amendment, Garrett, and Protection for Civil Rights*, 53 Ala.L.Rev. 1183 (2002).

- Discussion of the authority of Congress to induce a "waiver" of state sovereign immunity through use of the conditional spending and (possibly) other powers, see, *e.g.*, Baker & Berman, *Getting off the Dole: Why the Court Should Abandon Its Spending Doctrine, and How a Too–Clever Congress Could Provoke It To Do So*, 78 Ind.L.J. 459, 461 (2003)(arguing that the "Dole test" for judging Congress's power to condition aid to the states on waiver of various sovereign rights is "substantively and conceptually infirm" and suggesting that the Court is unlikely to tolerate legislative efforts to exploit that test as a means of circumventing the Court's federalism decisions); Childers, *State Sovereign Immunity and the Protection of Intellectual Property: Do Recent Congressional Attempts to "Level the Playing Field" Run Afoul of Current Eleventh Amendment Jurisprudence and Other Constitutional Doctrines?*, 82 N.C.L.Rev. 1067 (2004)(questioning the constitutionality of recently proposed legislation designed to protect against state infringement of intellectual property rights and suggesting more moderate measures that he believes would pass muster); Gibson, *Congressional Authority To Induce Waivers of State Sovereign Immunity: The Conditional Spending Power (and Beyond)*, 29 Hastings Const.L.Q. 439 (2002)(analyzing the availability of the spending power as a basis for inducing waiver and suggesting the use of other powers for that purpose, especially the power to limit access to the jurisdiction of the lower federal courts).

- Discussion (mostly critical) of the Court's reliance on the concept of "dignity" as a basis for state immunity from suit, see *e.g.*, Resnik & Suk,

Adding Insult to Injury: Questioning the Role of Dignity in Conceptions of Sovereignty, 55 Stan.L.Rev. 1921, 1962 (2003)(arguing that although the concept of "institutional dignity" has value in many contexts, it should not be used as a justification for immunizing states from accounting for their behavior: "requiring governments to participate in litigation * * * enhanc[es], rather than diminish[es] the role-dignity appropriate to sovereignty"); Smith, *States as Nations: Dignity in Cross–Doctrinal Perspective*, 89 Va.L.Rev. 1, 7 (2003)(suggesting that the "dignity" rationale is implicitly drawn from the Court's long recognition of the dignity of foreign nations and urging that (1) this notion should not apply to the constituent states of our federal union, and (2) to the extent that it is applied, "the doctrinal consequence ought to be that Congress has authority [as it does with respect to foreign nations] to abrogate the states' immunity").

SUBSECTION C: FEDERAL STATUTORY PROTECTION AGAINST STATE OFFICIAL ACTION: HEREIN OF 42 U.S.C. § 1983

Page 1081. Add to footnote 5:

For analysis and critique of the Brentwood decision, as well as thoughtful discussion of other issues relating to the liability of private entities under § 1983, see *Symposium, Private Parties as Defendants in Civil Rights Litigation*, 26 Cardozo L.Rev. 1 (2004).

Page 1087. Add to footnote 3:

See also Achtenberg, *Taking History Seriously: Municipal Liability Under 42 U.S.C. § 1983 and the Debate over Respondeat Superior*, 73 Fordham L.Rev. 2183 (2005)(contending that an understanding of 19th century principles of the common law, and of the methods of implementing those principles, supports the respondeat superior liability of municipalities in § 1983 actions).

Page 1089. Add a new footnote 5a at the end of Paragraph (5)(b):

5a.   For an eloquent argument in favor of a broader interpretation of "custom or usage" in § 1983—one including "fusion of both pervasive private practices and official acquiescence"—as well as a similar broadening of the interpretation of congressional authority under § 5 of the Fourteenth Amendment, see Rutherglen, *Custom and Usage as Action Under Color of State Law: An Essay on the Forgotten Terms of Section 1983*, 89 Va.L.Rev. 925, 927, 967 (2003).

Page 1091. Add to footnote 6:

See also Bandes, *Not Enough Blame To Go Around: Reflections on Requiring Purposeful Government Conduct*, 68 Brook.L.Rev. 1195 (2003). Professor Bandes criticizes—as a misguided approach requiring a search for a malevolent state of mind on the part of an artificial entity—the Court's emphasis on something akin to a mens rea requirement as a basis for finding municipal liability. She adds: "There is far too little information on the ways in which governmental entities make decisions, and the sorts of incentives, legal or otherwise, that would best promote accountability. Thus the misuse of blame is not the sole culprit * * * "(p. 1210).

Page 1092. Add a new Paragraph (8a):

(8a) Indian Tribes as Plaintiffs and Defendants. In Inyo County v. Paiute–Shoshone Indians, 538 U.S. 701 (2003), an Indian Tribe sought injunctive and declaratory relief under § 1983 against a county and certain county officials seeking injunctive and declaratory relief. The complaint asserted that because of its sovereign status, it was immune from the processes of the county—in particular, from execution of search warrants against the Tribe and tribal property. The Supreme Court assumed without deciding "that Native American tribes, like States of the Union, are not subject to suit under § 1983" (p. 707). The Court then held that "in the situation here presented [in which the Tribe was not complaining of any conduct that would have violated the federal rights of a private individual or entity but rather was objecting to an interference with its sovereign status], the Tribe does not qualify as a 'person' who may sue under § 1983" (p. 704). "Section 1983", the Court said, "was designed to secure private rights against government encroachment, not to advance a sovereign's prerogative to withhold evidence relevant to a criminal investigation" (p. 711). Justice Stevens, concurring in the judgment, contended that a Tribe is always a "person" for purposes of defining who may sue under § 1983, but stated that a claim "based entirely on the Tribe's sovereign status [] is not one for which the § 1983 remedy was enacted" (p. 714).

Prior to this decision, the Court had held that § 1983 was available to protect commercial or taxpayer interests against state regulation in violation of the "dormant Commerce Clause" or against otherwise valid state regulation preempted by federal statutory law. See Fifth Edition pp. 1095–96. Is there a valid distinction between resorting to § 1983 to assure such protection under federal law and resorting to it to protect the sovereign interests claimed under federal law in this case? And if you believe that there is, is there a material difference—given the majority's careful limitation of its holding to the circumstances presented—between the majority's approach and that of Justice Stevens? Does the result in the case make more sense if phrased in terms of what constitutes a cause of action under § 1983 or in terms of when a plaintiff should be considered a "person" for purposes of the particular action?

Page 1095. Add a new footnote 2a at the end of the first paragraph on this page:

2a. For a painstaking and thorough effort to work through the implications of Gonzaga and its predecessors in the context of federal Medicaid legislation, see Clayworth v. Bonta, 295 F.Supp.2d 1110 (E.D.Cal. 2003). In this case, providers and beneficiaries under California's Medi–Cal program (the state program supported by federal Medicaid funds) brought a federal court § 1983 suit against a state officer, challenging the validity under federal law of a reduction in the reimbursement rate paid to providers. On the basis of a full analysis of the relevant cases and statutes the court found itself compelled to reach an almost Byzantine set of conclusions: "Medi–Cal beneficiaries have both standing and a cause of action and * * * Medi–Cal providers have third party standing to assert claims for beneficiaries concerning fee-for-service rates. However, the court does not find that either beneficiaries or providers have a claim under § 1983 to enforce the provisions of the Medicaid statute relating to managed care plans" (p. 1112).

Page 1095. Add to footnote 3:

For a holding that a § 1983 action does not lie for a violation of a federal *regulation*, see Save Our Valley v. Sound Transit, 335 F.3d 932 (9th Cir.2003). The decision is criticized in Note, 117 Harv.L.Rev. 735 (2003) (relying in part on the existence of congressional authority to delegate to agencies the ability to promulgate regulations with the force of law, and also reporting a circuit split on the issue).

Page 1096. Add to Paragraph(3)(b):

In City of Rancho Palos Verdes v. Abrams, 125 S.Ct. 1453 (2005), the Court apparently went one step beyond the rationale of the Sea Clammers case in barring a § 1983 action for violation of a federal statute. The Abrams case involved an attempt to use that section as a means of enforcing a provision of the federal Telecommunications Act limiting the authority of state and local governments to impede the installation of facilities for wireless communications. The Act itself authorizes a private remedy for violation of this provision, and the Court held that this private remedy superseded any remedy under § 1983. Noting that the statutory remedy was in several respects more restrictive than that provided by § 1983, Justice Scalia, in an opinion for the Court, first rejected the Government's argument that such a specific statutory remedy should *conclusively* establish an intent to preclude § 1983 relief. But he then stated that "[t]he provision of an express, private means of redress in the statute itself is *ordinarily* an indication that Congress did not intend to leave open a more expansive remedy under § 1983" (p. 1458)(emphasis added)—an inference that can be overcome "by textual indication, express or implicit, that the remedy is to complement, rather than supplant, § 1983" (p. 1459). Justice Breyer, concurring in an opinion joined by Justices O'Connor, Souter, and Ginsburg, agreed with the creation of an "ordinary inference" of remedial exclusivity resulting from a specific private remedy in the governing statute and praised the Court for "wisely reject[ing]" the conclusive presumption urged by the Government (p. 1462). But he added that the inference should in his view be rebuttable not only on the basis of the text but of the overall context. Justice Stevens, concurring only in the judgment, criticized the Court's opinion on two grounds: its assumption "that the legislative history of the statute is totally irrelevant" and its failure to "properly acknowledge[] the strength of our normal presumption that Congress intended to preserve, rather than preclude, the availability of § 1983 as a remedy for the enforcement of federal statutory rights" (pp. 1464–65).

SECTION 3.   OFFICIAL IMMUNITY

Page 1130. Add to footnote 10:

In Groh v. Ramirez, 540 U.S. 551 (2004), a Bivens action complaining of a violation of the Fourth Amendment, plaintiffs managed to persuade a bare majority of the Court that, at least at the pretrial stage, the two-step requirement laid down in the Anderson and Saucier cases had been met. In this case, Groh, a federal agent, had obtained a search warrant for plaintiffs' premises on the basis of an admittedly proper application, but the warrant itself, as drafted by Groh and approved by the magistrate, failed to specify any of the items to be searched for and seized. (In the actual search, no items were seized.) Writing for a majority of five, Justice Stevens concluded that granting summary judgment in Groh's favor was improper because (a) the failure of the warrant to describe the items to be seized violated the Fourth Amendment, and (b) Groh was not entitled to the defense of qualified immunity since "no reasonable officer could believe that a warrant that did not comply with the [particularity requirement of the Fourth Amendment] was valid" (p. 563). (Groh's assertion that the particularity requirement was satisfied by his *oral* statement to the plaintiffs at the time of the search involved, the

Court said, a disputed question of fact that was not before it on review of the grant of a motion for summary judgment.)

Justice Kennedy, joined by the Chief Justice, dissented. Conceding that the conduct alleged violated the Fourth Amendment, Justice Kennedy contended that the defense of qualified immunity should be upheld. He argued that since Groh was unaware of his "clerical error" (of not describing the property to be seized) when he drafted the warrant, his "mistaken belief that the warrant contained the proper language was a reasonable belief" (p. 567). Justice Thomas, joined by Justice Scalia, also dissented. He argued first that there was no Fourth Amendment violation because this particular search on the basis of a defective warrant was not unreasonable. He then argued (in a discussion also joined by the Chief Justice) that in the specific circumstances, Groh was in any event entitled to qualified immunity because his failure to notice the defect in the warrant was no more than a failure to proofread adequately and was not objectively unreasonable.

Groh and its predecessors underscore both the sharp division in the Court about the proper interpretation of the Fourth Amendment and the even sharper division about what constitutes an objectively reasonable mistake as to whether particular conduct violates that amendment. Do they also raise a question about the wisdom of the two-step process itself, at least in the Fourth Amendment context? *Cf.* Fifth Edition p. 1335, Paragraph (2)(e). That question came to the fore the following Term, in Brosseau v. Haugen, 125 S.Ct. 596 (2004)(per curiam), a § 1983 case alleging unconstitutional use of excessive force. In rejecting a court of appeals ruling on the issue of qualified immunity, a divided Court held that under the proper "more particularized" standard, it was not "clearly established" that the defendant was acting unconstitutionally (p. 599). In the course of its opinion, the Court refused to reconsider its requirement that in such cases, lower courts should decide the constitutional question *prior* to deciding the qualified immunity question; rather the Court exercised its summary reversal power "simply to correct a clear misapprehension of the qualified immunity standard" (p. 598 n.3). Justice Breyer, in a concurrence joined by Justices Scalia and Ginsburg, urged that the two step requirement imposed on lower courts should be reconsidered because "a rigid 'order of battle' makes little administrative sense and can sometimes lead to a constitutional decision that is effectively insulated from review" (p. 601). (Justice Stevens, dissenting, contended that the defendant's action was unconstitutional and that the qualified immunity issue should be left to the jury.)

Page 1140. Add to footnote 3:

The 50th anniversary of the Youngstown decision, in 2002, served as the occasion both for revisiting the case and for examining its significance with respect to the scope of executive power to deal with contemporary problems relating to foreign affairs, the conduct of war, and the threat of terrorism here and abroad. See, *e.g,* Bryant & Tobias, *Youngstown Revisited*, 29 Hastings Const.L.Q. 373 (2002); Symposium, *Youngstown at Fifty*, 19 Const. Comment. 1 (2002); Symposium, *President Truman and the Steel Seizure Case*, 41 Duq.L.Rev. 667 (2003). (The Youngstown decision was in fact cited in several of the opinions in Hamdi v. Rumsfeld, 124 S.Ct. 2633 (2004), one of the cases involving the availability of habeas corpus jurisdiction to test the lawfulness of executive detention of persons designated by the executive as enemy combatants, discussed at pp. 90–102, *infra*. Of particular significance is its citation in Justice O'Connor's plurality opinion for the proposition that "a state of war is not a blank check for the President when it comes to the rights of the Nation's citizens" (124 S.Ct. at 2650).)

Page 1141. Add to Section D:

Important questions in addition to those discussed above in this section are whether and to what extent federal officers should be immune from prosecution for violations of *state* criminal law. For a survey and critique of the doctrinal landscape on this question, see Waxman & Morrison, *What Kind of Immunity? Federal Officers, State Criminal Law, and the Supremacy Clause*, 112 Yale L.J. 2195 (2003). Noting the paucity of cases, the authors contend that federal officers should be immune from state criminal liability for actions they believed reasonably necessary in the performance of their federal duties—a standard essentially coextensive with that for qualified immunity in private civil actions.

CHAPTER X

JUDICIAL FEDERALISM: LIMITATIONS ON DISTRICT COURT JURISDICTION OR ITS EXERCISE

SECTION 1.   STATUTORY LIMITATIONS ON FEDERAL COURT JURISDICTION

SUBSECTION B: OTHER STATUTORY RESTRICTIONS ON FEDERAL COURT JURISDICTION

Page 1167. Add to footnote 13.

The circuits appear to be split on the question whether the Anti–Injunction Act bars injunctions against state court litigation commenced subsequent to the filing of a federal action. *See* Denny's, Inc. v. Cake, 364 F.3d 521, 529 (4th Cir.2004).

Page 1173. Add to Paragraph (C)(1):

In Hibbs v. Winn, 124 S.Ct. 2276 (2004), the Court held, 5–4, that the Tax Injunction Act (TIA) did not bar an action seeking to enjoin the continuation of a tax credit that, the plaintiffs alleged, violated the Establishment Clause. (Taxpayers received credits for contributions to organizations that in turn could disburse funds to religious schools.) Justice Ginsburg's majority opinion noted that several Supreme Court decisions had reached the merits of civil rights actions challenging state tax credits, and that federal restrictions on tax-related injunctions, on which the TIA was modeled, do not bar actions that, rather than challenging taxes imposed on a plaintiff, instead contest the constitutionality of tax benefits bestowed upon others. The TIA, she argued, was not, as the defendant suggested, "a sweeping congressional direction to prevent 'federal-court interference with all aspects of state tax administration'" (p. 2279, quoting the Brief for Petitioner), but was directed at taxpayers seeking to avoid paying their taxes; broader characterizations of the TIA in prior decisions could not be detached from the facts presented in those cases, which involved taxpayer-plaintiffs seeking to reduce their tax liabilities and thereby potentially diminishing state tax revenue.

Justice Kennedy, joined by the Chief Justice and Justices Scalia and Thomas, dissented, accusing the majority of misreading the statutory text and legislative history because of skepticism about the capacity of state courts to vindicate constitutional rights. He acknowledged that "unexamined custom" supports the inapplicability of the TIA but contended that the statutory text points the other way. Examining the use of the word "assessment" in the Act and in dictionaries dating from the time of the TIA's enactment, he contended that at a minimum, the text bars restraining "a State's recording of taxpayer liability on its tax rolls, whether the recordings are made by self-reported taxpayer filing forms or by a State's calculation of taxpayer liability" (p. 2295), and he found that the instant suit ran afoul of that prohibition. Federal cases permitting actions otherwise similar to the present one were distinguishable, he argued, because there was no alternative forum for the taxpayers' claims; here, the plaintiffs were free to file in state court. He also stressed that one purpose of the Act was to ensure that state tax law was interpreted by state courts.

SECTION 2.   JUDICIALLY-DEVELOPED LIMITATIONS ON FEDERAL COURT JURISDICTION: DOCTRINES OF EQUITY, COMITY, AND FEDERALISM

SUBSECTION A: EXHAUSTION OF NONJUDICIAL REMEDIES

Page 1184. Add at the end of the second paragraph in Paragraph 5(b):

Roosevelt, *Exhaustion Under the Prison Litigation Reform Act: The Consequence of Procedural Error*, 52 Emory L.J.1771 (2003), argues that treating section 1983 claims as forfeited whenever a prisoner fails to bring a timely complaint within an administrative grievance system is unnecessarily harsh, especially because state prison officials typically have the power to entertain prisoner complaints even when they are not timely filed (p. 1810 & n.192). Arguing that "a failure to observe procedural niceties should not * * * have any effect on a state prisoner's subsequent section 1983 suit" (p. 1808), Roosevelt would apparently treat the exhaustion requirement as satisfied whenever a prisoner has pursued administrative remedies for a grievance, even if in an untimely fashion.

SUBSECTION B: ABSTENTION: PULLMAN AND RELATED DOCTRINES

Page 1200. Add to Paragraph (4):

In San Remo Hotel, L.P. v. City and County of San Francisco, 125 S. Ct. 2491 (2005), the Supreme Court gave a limiting definition to the scope of the England "reservation" procedure. The plaintiff hotel operators initiated litigation in both state and federal court asserting both facial and as-applied challenges to a city ordinance requiring them to pay a $567,000 fee for converting residential rooms to tourist rooms. After the Ninth Circuit held the as-applied challenge unripe and abstained under Pullman from ruling on the facial claims, the plaintiffs sought to reserve their federal constitutional claims under England, then returned to state court, where they advanced various claims that the ordinance was unconstitutional both on its face and as-applied under California law. When the state courts ruled against the plaintiffs on the merits, the plaintiffs sought to revive their federal claims in federal court, but the Supreme Court held that preclusion doctrine barred them from doing so, despite their efforts to reserve their federal claims under England. The Court, in an opinion by Justice Stevens, began by observing that " '[t]ypical' England cases generally involve federal constitutional challenges to a state statute that can be avoided if a state court construes the statute in a particular manner. In such cases, the purpose of abstention is not to afford state courts an opportunity to adjudicate an issue that is functionally identical to the federal question." (p. ___).

Having described the purpose of the England reservation procedure in these terms, the Court reasoned that although the plaintiffs "were entitled to insulate from preclusive effect one federal issue—their facial constitutional challenge to the [city ordinance]"—they had advanced broad state law claims that could have led to facial invalidation of the ordinance under the California constitution on the same legal theory that supported their challenge under the federal Constitution (p. ___). By doing so, "petitioners effectively asked the state court to resolve the same federal issues they asked it to reserve. England does not support the exercise of any such right" (p. ___). Nor had the plaintiffs successfully reserved their as-applied takings claims. Because unripe, those claims "were never properly before the District Court, and there was no reason to expect that they could be relitigated in full if advanced in the state proceedings" (p. ___). Chief Justice Rehnquist, joined by Justices O'Connor, Kennedy, and Thomas, concurring in the judgment, did not discuss the pertinence of England.

Could the plaintiffs have successfully reserved their facial challenge under the federal Constitution if they had asked the state court to rule the ordinance facially invalid under the state constitution, but on a different legal theory from that supporting their federal claim (due to relevant differences between state and federal constitutional law)?[1]

Page 1201. Add to footnote 6:

See also Calabresi, *Federal Courts and State Courts: Restoring a Workable Balance*, 78 N.Y.U.L.Rev. 1293 (2003) (arguing, *inter alia*, for increased use of certification and suggesting congressional authorization of state court appellate review of federal appellate decisions on issues of state law); *but cf.* Nash, *Examining the Power of Federal Courts to Certify Questions of State Law*, 88 Corn.L.Rev. 1672, 1749 (2003) (objecting that "certification conflicts with the fundamental purpose of diversity jurisdiction" to provide a neutral forum for out-of-state litigants).

SUBSECTION C: EQUITABLE RESTRAINT

———

Page 1228. Add a new footnote 16a at the end of Paragraph (7)(c):

16a. A number of courts of appeals have recognized an exception to Younger principles for cases in which plaintiffs seek to enjoin state prosecutions on double jeopardy grounds. See,

---

1. If pressing in state court a state law claim identical in substance to a federal claim counts as presenting the federal claim to a state court for purposes of Pullman abstention, should such action count equally as having presented a federal claim to a state court for other purposes—for example, when a criminal defendant explicitly raises a federal claim for the first time in the Supreme Court or in federal habeas proceedings, but had raised a substantively identical claim in state court? Cf. Howell v. Mississippi, 125 S.Ct. 856 (2005), p. 33, *supra*.

e.g., Gilliam v. Foster, 75 F.3d 881, 903–05 (4th Cir.1996) (en banc); Mannes v. Gillespie, 967 F.2d 1310, 1312 (9th Cir.1992). Beginning with the well-settled premise that the Double Jeopardy Clause prohibits not merely subsequent convictions but also subsequent prosecutions, the decisions reason that because the Clause's "full protection would be irretrievably lost if it could not be asserted before the occurrence of the subsequent prosecution that it prohibits, the comity concerns behind Younger must yield to the paramount right of the individual." Carter v. Medlock, No. 93–7221, 1994 WL 687287, at *3 n.9 (4th Cir. Dec. 9, 1994) (unpublished opinion). Is this reasoning consistent with Younger? Even if the premise is granted that the Double Jeopardy Clause creates a special right to be free from trial and not just conviction (could the same not be said of other constitutional rights?), why should state courts be viewed as less competent to vindicate rights under the Double Jeopardy Clause than under other constitutional provisions? (Note, however, that the Supreme Court allows appeal before trial of denial of motions to dismiss indictments on double jeopardy grounds. See Abney v. United States, Fifth Edition p. 1562.)

Page 1239. Add at the end of Paragraph (2)(a):

Friedman, *Under the Law of Federal Jurisdiction: Allocating Cases Between State and Federal Courts,* 104 Colum.L.Rev. 1211, 1248–54 (2004), argues that litigants who have not yet violated a state statute, but wish to do so and believe that the Constitution would protect them, have a stronger claim to federal adjudication of their constitutional challenges than litigants who have already committed violations under a "don't break the law" principle. Do you agree?

Page 1250. Add to footnote 7:

But cf. Kowalski v. Tesmer, 125 S.Ct. 564 (2004), p. 8, *supra* (holding that plaintiffs challenging a state statute in federal court lacked third-party standing to assert the rights of defendants in state court criminal actions who would have been unable to appear as parties in the federal litigation on account of the *Younger* doctrine).

CHAPTER XI

FEDERAL HABEAS CORPUS

SECTION 1. INTRODUCTION

Page 1286. Add, before the "Note on the Jurisdictional Statutes," the following new Note:

NOTE ON THE AVAILABILITY OF HABEAS CORPUS TO CHALLENGE DETENTION ARISING FROM THE "WAR ON TERROR"

---

(1) Introduction. At the end of the 2003 Term, the Supreme Court decided three important cases involving the use of habeas corpus to challenge executive detention outside of the criminal process. All three cases had their origins in the terrorist attacks of September 11, 2001 and the government's response to those attacks.

Two of the decisions, Rasul v. Bush, 124 S.Ct. 2686 (2004), and Rumsfeld v. Padilla, 124 S.Ct. 2711 (2004), are discussed in detail at pp. 104–13, *infra*. The Padilla decision turned on a rather narrow, venue-like question whether an American citizen detained as an alleged enemy combatant could file a habeas corpus petition in the Southern District of New York (where he was initially held) or only in the District of South Carolina (where he was detained at the time of filing). The Rasul decision is far more significant, for it recognizes that aliens detained at the U.S. Naval Base at Guantanamo Bay, Cuba may avail themselves of the writ of habeas corpus to test the legality of their detention by the Executive, rejecting the government's claim that the federal courts lack jurisdiction to review detentions of non-citizens held outside the borders of the United States. However, the Court expressly reserved the question of exactly what kind of review had to be provided to the Guantanamo detainees.

The third of these decisions, Hamdi v. Rumsfeld, 124 S.Ct. 2633 (2004), most fully discusses both (a) the historic role of the writ of habeas corpus in providing a means of testing the legality of executive detention and thereby protecting personal liberty, and (b) the appropriate scope of inquiry when a habeas court is asked to examine the legality of detaining an alleged enemy combatant. The decision is summarized below, both to illustrate the purposes of the writ and to examine its application to the difficult problems posed by the war against terror.

(2) The Facts and the Decisions Below. Yaser Hamdi, an American citizen who resided in Afghanistan in 2001, was seized by members of the Northern

Alliance (a coalition of military groups opposed to the Taliban government), and eventually was turned over to the United States military. He was transferred to the U.S. Naval Base at Guantanamo Bay in 2002 and, when authorities later learned that he was an American citizen, to the naval brigs in Norfolk, Virginia and Charleston, South Carolina, where he was subjected to interrogation. The government designated Hamdi as an "enemy combatant" and took the position that Hamdi could be held indefinitely, without formal charges or proceedings.

Hamdi's father filed a petition for a writ of habeas corpus in the Eastern District of Virginia, naming various federal officials as respondents. The petition alleged that the government held his son without legal authorization, and that his son, as an American citizen, was entitled to access to an impartial tribunal, the assistance of counsel, and the full protections of the Constitution. The petition alleged that Hamdi went to Afghanistan to do relief work and had received no military training, and it requested, should the government contest those factual allegations, that the court schedule an evidentiary hearing.

After various proceedings in the lower courts, the government filed a response and a motion to dismiss the petition, supported by a declaration from Michael Mobbs, an official in the Department of Defense. Mobbs stated that he was generally familiar with the war against al Qaeda and the Taliban, and with American policies and procedures applicable to detention of al Qaeda and Taliban personnel, and that "based upon my review of the relevant records and reports, I am also familiar with the facts and circumstances related to the capture of . . . Hamdi and his detention by U.S. military forces" (p. 2637). In the only evidentiary support for Hamdi's detention that the government submitted to the courts, Mobbs stated that after Hamdi traveled to Afghanistan in July or August of 2001, he "affiliated with a Taliban military unit and received weapons training", that he remained with his Taliban unit following September 11, that his Taliban unit surrendered in battle to the Northern Alliance, and that Hamdi himself surrendered his assault rifle. Mobbs also stated that a series of "U.S. military screening team[s]" determined that Hamdi met the "criteria for enemy combatants", and that "a subsequent interview of Hamdi has confirmed that he surrendered and gave his firearm to Northern Alliance forces" (p. 2637).

The district court found that the Mobbs declaration, given its "generic and hearsay nature", fell "far short" of supporting Hamdi's detention (p. 2637). The court ordered the government to turn over, for *in camera* review, numerous materials, including copies of Hamdi's statements and notes from his interviews; the names and addresses of all of Hamdi's interrogators; statements by members of the Northern Alliance regarding Hamdi's capture; and the identity of the American officials who determined that Hamdi was an enemy combatant. The Fourth Circuit reversed, concluding that the averments in the Mobbs declaration, if accurate, sufficed to establish that the President, pursuant to his war powers, had constitutionally detained Hamdi, and that separation of powers principles barred a federal court from "delv[ing] further into Hamdi's status and capture". 316 F.3d at 473.

(3) The Array of Supreme Court Opinions. The Supreme Court vacated the Fourth Circuit's decision and remanded for further proceedings. There was no majority opinion, and the four separate opinions totaled nearly 100 pages. But all of the Justices agreed that a federal court exercising habeas corpus jurisdiction was authorized to inquire into the legality of Hamdi's detention by the Executive. And all except Justice Thomas agreed that the government could not lawfully detain Hamdi merely on the basis of the Mobbs declaration and that, accordingly, the Fourth Circuit's judgment could not stand.

In a plurality opinion that controlled the disposition of the case, Justice O'Connor (joined by the Chief Justice and Justices Kennedy and Breyer) found that the Executive could lawfully detain enemy combatants, but that individuals like Hamdi were entitled to an opportunity before a neutral decisionmaker to contest the Executive's factual assertions. She voted to vacate and remand to permit an appropriate determination of whether Hamdi was an enemy combatant. Justice Scalia (joined by Justice Stevens) dissented, concluding that Hamdi's detention was unconstitutional; accordingly, he thought the Fourth Circuit should be reversed and that Hamdi should be released from military detention. Justice Souter (joined by Justice Ginsburg) concluded that Hamdi's detention was unlawful because in violation of a federal statute; but because no position commanded a majority of the Justices, he joined with the plurality in ordering a remand to permit determination of Hamdi's status, in order "to give practical effect to the conclusions of eight members of the Court rejecting the Government's position" (p. 2660). Finally, Justice Thomas dissented; believing that Hamdi's detention was lawful, he would have affirmed the Fourth Circuit's judgment.

(4) Justice Scalia's Dissent. Of all of the opinions in the case, Justice Scalia's dissent gave the most attention to the history of the writ of habeas corpus and the broadest view of the Constitution's protections of Hamdi. (He made clear that his views applied only to citizens like Hamdi, not to aliens (on that point, see Rasul v. Bush, p. 104, *infra*), and that when citizens are detained outside the United States, the constitutional requirements may differ.)

Justice Scalia began by stressing that "[t]he very core of liberty secured by our Anglo–Saxon system of separated powers has been freedom from indefinite imprisonment at the will of the Executive" (p. 2661). He quoted Blackstone as echoing this principle and associating it with two ideas—that due process is the right that protects this liberty, and that the judicial instrument that safeguards the right to due process is habeas corpus.

"The gist of the Due Process Clause, as understood at the founding and since, was to force the Government to follow those common-law procedures traditionally deemed necessary before depriving a person of life, liberty, or property. When a citizen was deprived of liberty because of alleged criminal conduct, those procedures typically required committal by a magistrate followed by indictment and trial. * * * To be sure, certain types of permissible *non*criminal detention—that is, those not dependent upon the contention that the citizen had committed a criminal act—did not require the protections of criminal procedure. However, these fell into a limited number of well-recognized exceptions—civil commitment of the mentally ill, for example, and temporary detention in quarantine of the infectious. It is unthinkable that the Executive could render otherwise criminal grounds for detention noncriminal merely by disclaiming an intent to prosecute, or by asserting that it was incapacitating dangerous offenders rather than punishing wrongdoing" (pp. 2661–62).

He then traced the history of habeas corpus in England as a tool for challenging executive confinement, culminating in the Habeas Corpus Act of 1679. Under that Act, a prisoner charged with felony or treason had no right to *immediate* release, but the Crown was required to commence prosecution at the next term of court (and English courts sat four terms annually); failing that, the prisoner was entitled to release.

Like the English, the Americans viewed the writ as of central importance. Indeed, "[t]he writ of habeas corpus was preserved in the Constitution—the only common-law writ to be explicitly mentioned" (p. 2662). Thus, Article I, section 9, contains the Suspension Clause: "The privilege of the Writ of Habeas Corpus shall not be suspended, unless when in Cases of Rebellion or Invasion the public Safety may require it."

Justice Scalia then turned to Hamdi's case. The government's argument that enemy combatants have traditionally been detained until hostilities have ceased was, he acknowledged, "probably" accurate as to enemy aliens, but not, he insisted, as to American citizens (p. 2663). Instead, "[c]itizens aiding the enemy have been treated as traitors subject to the criminal process" (p. 2663)— traditionally for treason, although today's federal criminal code proscribes a number of other acts of warmaking or aiding the enemy. He noted that "[t]he only citizen other than Hamdi known to be imprisoned in connection with military hostilities in Afghanistan against the United States [John Walker Lindh] *was* subjected to criminal process and convicted upon a guilty plea" (p. 2664). (Later in his opinion he stressed that besides Hamdi and Walker, only one other citizen, Jose Padilla, is known to have been designated an enemy combatant.)

Justice Scalia continued by observing that English law provided a mechanism to accommodate exigencies in which resort to the traditional criminal process was impractical—the power to suspend the writ of habeas corpus. The Constitution's Suspension Clause expressly preserved that mechanism. He noted approvingly the general assumption that only Congress may suspend the writ, and observed that it has done so on rare occasions (during the Civil War and Reconstruction, and in Acts delegating suspension authority to the governors of the Philippines and Hawaii).

He admitted that even if traditionally the government had to choose between criminal prosecution and suspension of the writ when dealing with citizens like Hamdi, it did not necessarily follow that the Constitution forbade another alternative, such as the military detention here at issue. But Justice Scalia offered a set of reasons to reject that possibility, beginning with the inclusion of treason, and the absence of a wartime exception, in the Habeas Corpus Act of 1679. He gave particular attention to the Supreme Court's decision in Ex parte Milligan, 71 U.S. (4 Wall.) 2 (1866). There, a federal court exercising habeas corpus jurisdiction determined that a military tribunal lacked jurisdiction to try a U.S. citizen, living in Indiana, for having conspired, during the Civil War, to overthrow the government, seize munitions, and liberate prisoners of war. After extolling the right to jury trial and the rights protected by the Fourth, Fifth, and Sixth Amendments, the Milligan Court rejected the government's claim that military tribunals can try violations of the laws and usages of war, contending instead that such tribunals "can never be applied to citizens in states which have upheld the authority of the government, and where the courts are open and their process unobstructed" (71 U.S. at 121–22).

A more recent precedent, and one more to the government's liking, was Ex parte Quirin, 317 U.S. 1 (1942), in which eight German service members were apprehended on U.S. soil during World War II after having landed from a German submarine with the aim of sabotage. One of the saboteurs, Haupt, alleged that he was a naturalized citizen, but that did not preclude his being treated as an enemy belligerent and tried before a military commission for violation of the laws of war (for having secretly passed, without uniform, through enemy lines to wage war by destruction of life or property). Justice Scalia opined (pp. 2269–70) that "[t]he case was not this Court's finest hour. The Court upheld the commission and denied relief in a brief *per curiam* issued the day after oral argument concluded; a week later the Government carried out the commission's death sentence upon six saboteurs, including Haupt. The Court eventually explained its reasoning in a written opinion issued several months later.

"Only three paragraphs of the Court's lengthy opinion dealt with the particular circumstances of Haupt's case. * * * Quirin purported to interpret the language of Milligan quoted above (the law of war 'can never be applied to citizens in states which have upheld the authority of the government, and where the courts are open and their process unobstructed') in the following manner:

"Elsewhere in its opinion ... the Court was at pains to point out that Milligan, a citizen twenty years resident in Indiana, who had never been a resident of any of the states in rebellion, was not an enemy belligerent either entitled to the status of a prisoner of war or subject to the penalties imposed upon unlawful belligerents. We construe the Court's statement as to the inapplicability of the law of war to Milligan's case as having particular reference to the facts before it. From them the Court concluded that Milligan, not being a part of or associated with the armed forces of the enemy, was a non-belligerent, not subject to the law of war...." 317 U.S., at 45.

"In my view this seeks to revise Milligan rather than describe it. Milligan had involved * * * two separate questions: (1) whether the military trial of Milligan was justified by the laws of war, and if not (2) whether the President's suspension of the writ, pursuant to congressional authorization, prevented the issuance of habeas corpus. The Court's categorical language about the law of war's inapplicability to citizens where the courts are open * * * was contained in its discussion of the first point. The factors pertaining to whether Milligan could reasonably be considered a belligerent and prisoner of war * * * were * * * brought to bear in the Court's later discussion of whether Milligan came within the statutory provision that effectively made an exception to Congress's authorized suspension of the writ for * * * 'all parties, not prisoners of war, resident in their respective jurisdictions, ... who were citizens of states in which the administration of the laws in the Federal tribunals was unimpaired.' Milligan thus understood was in accord with the traditional law of habeas corpus I have described: Though treason often occurred in wartime, there was, absent provision for special treatment in a congressional suspension of the writ, no exception to the right to trial by jury for citizens who could be called 'belligerents' or 'prisoners of war' ".

In any event, Justice Scalia argued, Quirin was distinguishable because there it was admitted that the petitioners were enemy combatants; when, by contrast, someone like Hamdi contests his designation as such, Quirin left the civilian courts open to hear his claim. (Justice Scalia also suggested that Quirin, whatever its effect on Milligan's precedential value, "cannot undermine [Milligan's] value as an indicator of original meaning" (p. 2668 n. 1).)

All that remained for Justice Scalia was to consider whether the writ had been suspended. Congress' Authorization for Use of Military Force (AUMF), enacted one week after the September 11 attacks, "is not remotely a congressional suspension of the writ, and no one claims that it is. * * * If the Suspension Clause does not guarantee the citizen that he will either be tried or released, unless the conditions for suspending the writ exist and the grave action of suspending the writ has been taken; if it merely guarantees the citizen that he will not be detained unless Congress by ordinary legislation says he can be detained; it guarantees him very little indeed" (pp. 2671–72).

Justice Scalia concluded by criticizing the plurality opinion, which, after finding that the AUMF did authorize detention of enemy combatants, set forth the procedures that must be followed in testing Hamdi's claim that he was not an enemy combatant. Justice Scalia took the plurality to task for formulating such procedures anew in disregard of what the Constitution and common law demanded, and in particular for ruling that "in the absence of [the Executive's prior provision of procedures that satisfy due process]," a habeas court "must itself ensure that the minimum requirements of due process are achieved" (p. 2672). He objected that "[t]he role of habeas corpus is to determine the legality of executive detention * * *. It is not the habeas court's function to make illegal detention legal by supplying a process that the Government could have provided, but chose not to. If Hamdi is being imprisoned in violation of the Constitution (because without due process of law), then his habeas petition should be granted; the Executive may then hand him over to the criminal authorities, whose detention for the purpose of prosecution will be lawful, or else must release him" (pp. 2672–73). He thus would have found the detention unlawful and reversed the judgment below.

(5) Justice O'Connor's Plurality Opinion. Justice O'Connor's plurality opinion also determined that the Fourth Circuit's approach did not respect Hamdi's constitutional rights, but she presented a far less absolute understanding of the Constitution's requirements. She began by stating that the question was the authority of the Executive to detain citizens who qualify as "enemy combatants" under the laws and usages of war and who thus are subject to detention until the cessation of hostilities. She acknowledged (p. 2639) that "[t]here is some debate as to the proper scope of this term, and the Government has never provided any court with the full criteria that it uses in classifying individuals as such. It has made clear, however, that, for purposes of this case, the 'enemy combatant' that it is seeking to detain is an individual who, it alleges, was 'part of or supporting forces hostile to the United States or coalition partners' in Afghanistan and who 'engaged in an armed conflict against the United States' there".

Hamdi asserted that his detention as an enemy combatant violated 18 U.S.C. § 4001(a), which provides: "No citizen shall be imprisoned or otherwise detained by the United States except pursuant to an Act of Congress." However, Justice O'Connor found that Congress in fact authorized Hamdi's detention when, one week after the September 11 attacks, it passed the Authorization for Use of Military Force, which provides: "That the President is authorized to use all necessary and appropriate force against those nations, organizations, or persons he determines planned, authorized, committed, or aided the terrorist attacks that occurred on September 11, 2001, or harbored such organizations or persons, in order to prevent any future acts of international terrorism against the United States by such nations, organizations or persons." In her view, "detention of individuals falling into the limited category we are considering, for the duration of the particular conflict in which they were captured, is so fundamental and accepted an incident to war as to be an exercise of the 'necessary and appropriate force' Congress has authorized the President to use" (p. 2640). (She thus found it unnecessary to rule on the government's claim that it had inherent power under the Constitution to detain Hamdi quite apart from congressional authorization.)

Turning to precedents on the lawfulness of military detention, Justice O'Connor argued that the Milligan decision "does not undermine our holding about the Government's authority to seize enemy combatants" (p. 2642). She emphasized Milligan's repeated statements that the legality of the military tribunal's proceedings "turned in large part on the fact that Milligan was not a prisoner of war, but a resident of Indiana arrested while at home there. * * * Had Milligan been captured while he was assisting Confederate soldiers by carrying a rifle against Union troops on a Confederate battlefield, the holding of the Court might well have been different" (p. 2642). She added that the later, unanimous decision in Quirin makes clear that, whatever Milligan or earlier decisions might suggest, the military's power to detain and try individuals for acts committed during wartime extends to citizens as well as aliens.

Justice O'Connor set forth several reasons for rejecting Justice Scalia's approach to Hamdi's petition. First, he failed to give due weight to Quirin, a unanimous opinion that "both postdates and clarifies Milligan" (p. 2643). Second, under his approach, in which ordinary criminal prosecution or suspension of habeas corpus are the only two options, it was unclear why it should matter whether (as in Quirin) enemy status was admitted, or why adequate proof of enemy status could not substitute for an admission. Finally, Justice Scalia "largely ignores the context of this case: a United States citizen captured in a *foreign* combat zone. * * * Justice Scalia can point to no case or other authority for the proposition that those captured on a foreign battlefield (whether detained there or in U.S. territory) cannot be detained outside the criminal process * * *. [Indeed, he] presumably would come to a different result if Hamdi had been kept in Afghanistan or even Guantanamo Bay. This creates a perverse incentive. Military authorities faced with the stark choice of submitting to the full-blown criminal process or releasing a suspected enemy combatant captured on the battlefield will simply keep citizen-detainees abroad" (p. 2643).

Justice O'Connor then turned to the procedures necessary to make detention lawful. "Even in cases in which the detention of enemy combatants is legally authorized, there remains the question of what process is constitutionally due to a citizen who disputes his enemy-combatant status. Hamdi argues that he is owed a meaningful and timely hearing and that 'extra-judicial detention [that] begins and ends with the submission of an affidavit based on third-hand hearsay' does not comport with the Fifth and Fourteenth Amendments. The Government counters that any more process than was provided below would be both unworkable and 'constitutionally intolerable.' Our resolution of this dispute requires a careful examination both of the writ of habeas corpus * * * and of the Due Process Clause * * *.

" * * * [T]he parties agree that, absent suspension, the writ of habeas corpus remains available to every individual detained within the United States. Thus, it is undisputed that Hamdi was properly before an Article III court to challenge his detention under 28 U.S.C. § 2241 * * * "(pp. 2643–44).

Justice O'Connor then summarized the parties' arguments. The government contended, based on its view of the separation of powers and the limited judicial capacity in matters of military decision-making, that a habeas court should determine only whether legal authorization exists for the broader detention scheme; at most, the court should review the Executive's determination that Hamdi is an enemy combatant under a deferential 'some evidence' standard, under which it would assume the accuracy of the facts in the Mobbs declaration and assess only whether they provide a legitimate basis for detention. Hamdi urged that an individual may not be detained at the will of the Executive without some proceeding before a neutral tribunal to determine whether the asserted justifications for detention "have basis in fact and warrant in law.

"Both of these positions highlight legitimate concerns. * * * The ordinary mechanism that we use for balancing such serious competing interests, and for determining the procedures that are necessary to ensure that a citizen is not 'deprived of life, liberty, or property, without due process of law,' is the test that we articulated in Mathews v. Eldridge, 424 U.S. 319 (1976). Mathews dictates that the process due in any given instance is determined by weighing 'the private interest that will be affected by the official action' against the Government's asserted interest, 'including the function involved' and the burdens the Government would face in providing greater process. 424 U.S., at 335. The Mathews calculus then contemplates a judicious balancing of these concerns, through an analysis of 'the risk of an erroneous deprivation' of the private interest if the process were reduced and the 'probable value, if any, of additional or substitute safeguards.' *Ibid*. We take each of these steps in turn" (p. 2646).

Hamdi, Justice O'Connor said, asserts the "most elemental" liberty interest, freedom from physical detention by one's government, an interest not offset by circumstances of war or accusations of treason (p. 2646). "[T]he risk of erroneous deprivation of a citizen's liberty in the absence of sufficient process here is very real. Moreover, * * * history and common sense teach us that an unchecked system of detention carries the potential to become a means for oppression and abuse of others who do not present that sort of threat.

"On the other side of the scale are the weighty and sensitive government interests in ensuring that those who have in fact fought with the enemy during a war do not return to battle against the United States. * * * [C]ore strategic matters of warmaking belong in the hands of those who are best positioned and most politically accountable for making them" (p. 2647). She also noted the government's concern that trial-like processes would distract military officers engaged in battle half a world away and "intrude on the sensitive secrets of national defense" (p. 2648).

Stressing the importance of ensuring that the constitutional calculus "not give short shrift", during "our most challenging and uncertain moments", to the values for which we fight abroad, Justice O'Connor rejected the process followed by the government (which created an unacceptable risk of erroneous deprivation of liberty), as well as that envisioned by the district court (some of whose procedural safeguards were unwarranted in light of their limited value and the burdens they imposed) (p. 2648). Instead, she said, "a citizen-detainee seeking to challenge his classification as an enemy combatant must receive notice of the factual basis for his classification, and a fair opportunity to rebut the Government's factual assertions before a neutral decisionmaker" (p. 2648).

"At the same time, the exigencies of the circumstances may demand that, aside from these core elements, enemy combatant proceedings may be tailored to alleviate their uncommon potential to burden the Executive at a time of ongoing military conflict. Hearsay, for example, may need to be accepted as the most reliable available evidence from the Government in such a proceeding. Likewise, the Constitution would not be offended by a presumption in favor of the Government's evidence, so long as that presumption remained a rebuttable one and fair opportunity for rebuttal were provided. Thus, once the Government puts forth credible evidence that the habeas petitioner meets the enemy-combatant criteria, the onus could shift to the petitioner to rebut that evidence with more persuasive evidence that he falls outside the criteria. A burden-shifting scheme of this sort would meet the goal of ensuring that the errant tourist, embedded journalist, or local aid worker has a chance to prove military error while giving due regard to the Executive once it has put forth meaningful support for its conclusion that the detainee is in fact an enemy combatant. * * *

"We think it unlikely that this basic process will have the dire impact on the central functions of warmaking that the Government forecasts. * * * [D]ocumentation regarding battlefield detainees already is kept in the ordinary course of military affairs. Any factfinding imposition created by requiring a knowledgeable affiant to summarize these records to an independent tribunal is a minimal one. Likewise, arguments that military officers ought not have to wage war under the threat of litigation lose much of their steam when factual disputes at enemy-combatant hearings are limited to the alleged combatant's acts" (pp. 2648–49).

Thus, she rejected the government's contention that "the courts must forgo any examination of the individual case and focus exclusively on the legality of the broader detention scheme" as unwarranted "by any reasonable view of the separation of powers", and added that "unless Congress acts to suspend it, the Great Writ of habeas corpus allows the Judicial Branch to play a necessary role in maintaining this delicate balance of governance, serving as an important judicial check on the Executive's discretion in the realm of detentions. See [INS v. St. Cyr, 533 U.S. 289, 301 (2001), Fifth Edition p. 353] ('At its historical core, the writ of habeas corpus has served as a means of reviewing the legality of Executive detention, and it is in that context that its protections have been strongest'). Thus, while we do not question that our due process assessment must pay keen attention to the particular burdens faced by the Executive in the context of military action, it would turn our system of checks and balances on its head to suggest that a citizen could not make his way to court with a challenge to the factual basis for his detention by his government, simply because the Executive opposes making available such a challenge. * * *

"Because we conclude that due process demands some system for a citizen detainee to refute his classification, the proposed 'some evidence' standard is inadequate. Any process in which the Executive's factual assertions go wholly unchallenged or are simply presumed correct without any opportunity for the alleged combatant to demonstrate otherwise falls constitutionally short" (pp. 2650–51). The "some evidence" standard has been used, she stressed, as a standard of review of a prior determination made after an adversary proceeding; it is ill-suited as a standard of proof in a situation "in which a habeas petitioner has * * * had no prior opportunity to rebut the Executive's factual assertions before a neutral decisionmaker" (p. 2651).

Justice O'Connor concluded by noting "the possibility that the standards we have articulated could be met by an appropriately authorized and properly constituted military tribunal. Indeed, it is notable that military regulations already provide for such process in related instances, dictating that tribunals be made available to determine the status of enemy detainees who assert prisoner-of-war status under the Geneva Convention. In the absence of such process, however, a court that receives a petition for a writ of habeas corpus from an alleged enemy combatant must itself ensure that the minimum requirements of due process are achieved. * * * We anticipate that a District Court would proceed with the caution that we have indicated is necessary in this setting, engaging in a factfinding process that is both prudent and incremental" (p. 2651).

(6) Justice Souter's Opinion. Joined by Justice Ginsburg, Justice Souter concurred in part and concurred in the judgment. Unlike the plurality, he did not think that the Authorization for Use of Military Force constitutes an authorization of detention that satisfies the requirements of the Non–Detention Act, 18 U.S.C. § 4001(a). "The threshold issue is how broadly or narrowly to read the Non–Detention Act, the tone of which is severe: 'No citizen shall be imprisoned or otherwise detained by the United States except pursuant to an Act of Congress.' * * * For a number of reasons, the prohibition within § 4001(a) has to be read broadly to accord the statute a long reach and to impose a burden of justification on the Government" (pp. 2253–54).

First, he stressed that the Act superseded a cold-war statute, the Emergency Detention Act of 1950, that "was repealed in 1971 out of fear that it could authorize a repetition of the World War II internment of citizens of Japanese ancestry", background that "provides a powerful reason to think that § 4001(a) was meant to require clear congressional authorization before any citizen can be placed in a cell" (p. 2654). More broadly, he argued (p. 2655) that "[i]n a government of separated powers, deciding finally on what is a reasonable degree of guaranteed liberty whether in peace or war (or some condition in between) is not well entrusted to the Executive Branch of Government * * *. For reasons of inescapable human nature, the branch of the Government asked to counter a serious threat is not the branch on which to rest the Nation's entire reliance in striking the balance between the will to win and the cost in liberty on the way to victory * * *. A reasonable balance is more likely to be reached on the judgment of a different branch * * *. Hence the need for an assessment by Congress before citizens are subject to lockup, and likewise the need for a clearly expressed congressional resolution of the competing claims".

Justice Souter then turned to the question whether the Force Resolution specifically authorized detention in the present circumstances. While "[i]t is fairly read to authorize the use of armies and weapons, whether against other armies or individual terrorists * * * it never so much as uses the word detention, and there is no reason to think Congress might have perceived any need to augment Executive power to deal with dangerous citizens within the United States, given the well-stocked statutory arsenal of defined criminal offenses covering the gamut of actions that a citizen sympathetic to terrorists might commit" (p. 2657). (Justice Souter cited numerous federal criminal offenses that would apply to the conduct in which Hamdi was alleged to have engaged.)

Finally, Justice Souter rejected the government's position that the Force Resolution's authorization of war encompasses authority to deal with enemy belligerents according to the laws of war, which permit detention of captives. Whatever the merits of that position in other circumstances, he stated, the government, in holding Hamdi incommunicado, has not been treating him as a prisoner of war under the Geneva Convention, and thus "has not made out its claim that * * * it is acting in accord with the laws of war authorized to be applied against citizens by the Force Resolution" (p. 2659).

Thus concluding that Hamdi's detention violated the Non–Detention Act, Justice Souter found no need to "reach any questions of what process he may be due in litigating disputed issues in a proceeding under the habeas statute or prior to the habeas enquiry itself"; he would simply vacate and remand on the basis that detention was unauthorized. However, "[s]ince this disposition does not command a majority of the Court, * * * the need to give practical effect to the conclusions of eight members of the Court rejecting the Government's position calls for me to join with the plurality in ordering remand on terms closest to those I would impose" (p. 2660).

(7) Justice Thomas' Dissent. Only Justice Thomas voted to affirm the judgment below and uphold the government's authority to detain without further process. He agreed with the plurality that the AUMF authorized the President to detain enemy combatants, and for him, it sufficed that the Executive Branch had determined, within the scope of its war powers, that Hamdi was an enemy combatant. Stressing the breadth of the President's power to protect national security and conduct foreign affairs, he reasoned that while Congress too has a substantial role to play, "*judicial* interference in these domains destroys the purpose of vesting primary responsibility in a unitary Executive" (p. 2676). Because much intelligence is appropriately secret, courts lack the information needed to make judgments in these domains, and even if they could require some form of disclosure, " 'the very nature of executive decisions as to foreign policy is political, not judicial' "(p. 2676, quoting Chicago & Southern Air Lines, Inc. v. Waterman S.S. Corp., 333 U.S. 103, 111 (1948)).

Thus, while he agreed that "the question whether Hamdi's executive detention is lawful is a question properly resolved by the Judicial Branch, * * * we lack the information and expertise to question whether Hamdi is actually an enemy combatant, a question the resolution of which is committed to other branches" (p. 2678).

Although he therefore thought the plurality's balancing approach was not appropriate, he added that even under that framework, the plurality had not adequately credited the government's interest in gathering intelligence from detainees and in avoiding its disclosure. (He later added that provision of counsel might not be warranted because it would often impair intelligence gathering.) He also objected that the plurality's assurance that hearings limited to the alleged combatant's acts would not be intrusive ignored the fact that "the meaning of the combatant's acts may become clear only after quite invasive and extensive inquiry" (p. 2684).

(8) Questions about Hamdi and Habeas Corpus. The Hamdi opinions canvass a broad set of issues in a context of considerable complexity and difficulty. But note that all nine of the Justices agreed that it was appropriate for the courts, in exercising habeas corpus jurisdiction, to inquire into the legality of executive detention. Plainly, though, the Justices had very different views about the appropriate inquiry to be made in ascertaining the legality of detention.

In considering the availability of habeas corpus in a particular case, note the many difficult questions that may arise.

(a) Has Congress conferred habeas corpus jurisdiction on the court in these circumstances? Although not at issue in Hamdi, that question was very much in dispute in the two cases decided the same day, Rasul v. Bush, 124 S.Ct. 2686 (2004) and Rumsfeld v. Padilla, 124 S.Ct. 2711 (2004). See pp. 104–13, *infra.*

(b) In cases in which no habeas jurisdiction has been statutorily conferred, does the Suspension Clause of the Constitution itself confer a right to habeas corpus review? *Cf.* INS v. St. Cyr., Fifth Edition p. 353? And if so, may that constitutional right to habeas review be exercised in the federal courts, which ordinarily exercise only that jurisdiction that Congress has conferred? In a state court (notwithstanding uncertainties about its constitutional power to issue the writ to a federal official, see Tarble's Case, Fifth Edition p. 433)?

(c) Was the Executive's detention of the petitioner lawful? Note how complex that question may be on the merits. The Executive's authority might be grounded in the Constitution, a statute, or some combination of the two. For Justices Scalia and Justice Thomas, quite different understandings of the Constitution were central to their opposing views of the legality of detention, while for the plurality, the constitutional inquiry turned on accommodating the needs of the Executive and the interests of the individual. Justices O'Connor and Souter appeared to agree that Congress' action bore importantly on the legality of detention, although they disagreed about whether the Force Resolution authorized the detention at issue.

The lawfulness of detention may depend on other factors as well. Hamdi's case involved the rights of a citizen. The scope of constitutional or statutory rights of aliens may be quite different. And still other factors—whether the petitioner was captured overseas or in the United States, and whether the present detention is inside the United States or abroad—may affect the determination of legality.

(d) What is the appropriate scope of inquiry for a habeas court asked to determine the lawfulness of detention? In many cases, as in Hamdi, the general grant of habeas jurisdiction in 28 U.S.C. § 2241 is interpreted as providing such review as the Constitution demands. In general, habeas courts engage in de novo review of constitutional or statutory questions where a detainee has not previously obtained a judicial resolution of those questions. But it is harder to offer a simple generalization about the scope of review of questions of fact or of the application of law to fact, such as whether Hamdi is an enemy combatant.

Note, too, that a statute may confer on individuals a right to litigate in habeas corpus that extends beyond constitutional requirements. For example, in federal habeas corpus actions brought by prisoners convicted of criminal offenses in state courts, federal habeas courts have for many decades engaged in relitigation of federal constitutional issues that the state court resolved adversely to the prisoner. Few observers think that such relitigation is constitutionally required, but Congress is free to authorize federal courts to engage in broader review.

(e) Where the lawfulness of detention depends on a prior individualized determination, what kind of determination suffices? Justice Thomas alone suggested that the Executive's unilateral determination of enemy combatant status sufficed. Justice O'Connor's opinion suggests that some form of adversary hearing before a military tribunal, in which "normal" rules of proof were adjusted in view of the needs of the military, could provide all the process that Hamdi is due. (In that case, the habeas court would judge the detention to be lawful on the basis that the military had lawfully determined that Hamdi was an enemy combatant, and the court would not reexamine that question, even if Hamdi asserted that the military tribunal's determination was erroneous.)

(f) Justice Scalia mentions the historic intersection of the writ of habeas corpus and the protections of due process: detention, to be lawful, must comport with due process (or with the Constitution generally), and habeas corpus provides a judicial remedy through which inquiry into constitutionality can be made. In this respect, habeas corpus is a procedural vessel for the vindication of legal rights rooted elsewhere. But can one sharply distinguish right and remedy here? Does the tradition of habeas corpus, and its recognition in the Suspension Clause, have some substantive bearing on the legality of detention?

The lower courts have not had occasion to address these or other questions concerning the application of the Hamdi decision. Following the Supreme Court's decision, Hamdi himself was released, on condition that he return to Saudi Arabia, renounce his U.S. citizenship, and not travel to the United States, Afghanistan, Iran, or several other countries. (For consideration of the scope of the right of *alien* detainees, captured on the battlefield and determined by the government to be enemy combatants, to habeas review, see p. 104, *infra.*)

(9) Detention of Citizens Arrested and Detained in the United States: The Padilla Case. Jose Padilla, one of the few American citizens detained in connection with the war on terror, was arrested not on a foreign battlefield but rather in Chicago, as a material witness in connection with an investigation in New York of the 9/11 attacks. He was transported initially to New York and then, after designation as an enemy combatant, to South Carolina. He filed a habeas petition in New York, but when his case reached the Supreme Court, the majority ruled that only the federal district court in South Carolina had jurisdiction. See p. 110, *infra.* Four days later, Padilla re-filed his habeas petition in the District of South Carolina.

In Padilla v. Hanft, No. Civ.A. 2:04–2221–26A, 2005 WL 465691 (D.S.C. Feb. 28, 2005), the district court ordered Padilla released within forty-five days. The court rejected the government's efforts to treat Padilla as an enemy combatant, stressing that the criminal justice system was fully available to detain and try Padilla. The court distinguished Hamdi on the grounds that Padilla had been "captured in the United States," "[h]is alleged terrorist plans were thwarted at the time of his arrest," and "[t]here were no impediments whatsoever to the Government bringing charges against him for any one or all of the array of heinous crimes that he has been effectively accused of committing" (p. *7). It distinguished the military jurisdiction upheld in Ex parte Quirin as resting on "express congressional authorization" that was, in its view, absent in Padilla's case, as the court did not view the AUMF as constituting such authorization (pp. *7–*8). Concluding that Padilla's detention violated the Non–Detention Act, 18 U.S.C. § 4001(a) and was unsupported by the Executive's "inherent powers," the court found Ex parte Milligan to be a much closer analog than Quirin. Finally, it sharply rejected the government's calls for deference to the Executive's position on these questions as inconsistent with the judicial duty to protect individual liberties.

————

Pages 1293–96. Substitute, for the "Note on Courts, Justices, and Judges Authorized to Grant The Writ", the following material:

NOTE ON COURTS, JUSTICES, AND JUDGES
AUTHORIZED TO GRANT THE WRIT

(1) Territorial Jurisdiction: Location of the Petitioner. Section 2241(a) vests authority to grant the writ in the Supreme Court and the district courts, any Justice of the Supreme Court and any circuit judge, but only "within their respective jurisdictions".[1] In Ahrens v. Clark, 335 U.S. 188 (1948), the Court held that the District Court for the District of Columbia could not issue the writ because the petitioners, who were being held at Ellis Island, New York, by order of the U.S. Attorney General, were not detained within the district court's territorial jurisdiction. Over time, however, amendments to the habeas statute and judicial decisions have eroded Ahrens' restriction of each district court's jurisdiction to applications filed by petitioners physically located within the district.

(a) Legislative Revisions. The provisions construed in Ahrens have been legislatively modified in two important respects. First, as to prisoners "in custody under sentence of a court established by Act of Congress"—ordinarily those convicted of federal crimes—Congress added, in 1948, 28 U.S.C. § 2255, which requires that such prisoners file in the sentencing court, not in the district of incarceration. Second, a 1966 amendment, codified in § 2241(d), provides that state prisoners attacking convictions in states containing more than one federal district may seek habeas in the district where incarcerated *or* where the convicting court sat.

(b) The Braden Decision. Neither of the amendments just described applied to the facts in Braden v. 30th Judicial Cir. Ct., 410 U.S. 484 (1973)(6–3). But there, the Court overruled, or at least sharply limited, Ahrens' interpretation of § 2241(a) and recognized the territorial jurisdiction of a district court to entertain a petition from a prisoner physically confined in another state.

In Braden, a detainer had been filed against an Alabama prisoner to assure that he would be turned over to Kentucky for trial when his Alabama sentence expired. He filed a petition in federal district court in Kentucky, alleging denial of his constitutional right to a speedy trial in Kentucky and seeking an order compelling his immediate trial there. The Supreme Court upheld the district court's jurisdiction, concluding that § 2241(a) requires only that the court "have jurisdiction over the custodian" (p. 495). The Court stated that "developments since Ahrens have had a profound impact on the continuing vitality of that decision" (p. 497). It pointed to §§ 2255 and 2241(d) as exemplifying Congress' recognition of the desirability of resolving habeas cases in a court having close contact with the underlying controversy. And "the emergence of new classes of prisoners who are able to petition for habeas corpus because of

---

1. This represents a change from prior law in the unexplained exclusion of the district judges, see 28 U.S.C. § 452 (1940). The courts of appeals (as distinguished from their judges) have never been authorized to grant the writ, see Whitney v. Dick, 202 U.S. 132 (1906), except under the "all writs" provision, 28 U.S.C. § 1651, in aid of appellate jurisdiction in a pending case, see Adams v. United States, 317 U.S. 269 (1942); Price v. Johnston, 334 U.S. 266 (1948). (From 1911 until corrected by the Judiciary Act of 1925, 43 Stat. 940, circuit judges lacked authority to grant the writ unless specially assigned to hold a district court. See Craig v. Hecht, 263 U.S. 255, 271 (1923).)

the adoption of a more expansive definition of the 'custody' requirement", see Fifth Edition pp. 1395–98, permitted a "petitioner held in one State to attack a detainer lodged against him by another" (p. 498). The Court concluded that Ahrens should be confined to its facts—on which it was correctly decided, since not only the prisoners but those holding them were located in New York, and no showing had been made that the District of Columbia was a more convenient forum. In Braden, by contrast, "[w]e cannot assume that Congress intended" to require "Kentucky to defend its action in a distant State" (p. 499).[2]

(2) The Location of the Petitioner (II): Persons Held Outside of the United States.

The foregoing statutory provisions and decisions concern detainees located within American territory. What is the reach of habeas jurisdiction over detainees held by the federal government outside of the United States?

(a) Johnson v. Eisentrager. In Johnson v. Eisentrager, 339 U.S. 763 (1950), the Court held that the United States District Court for the District of Columbia (and, by implication, all district courts) lacked jurisdiction to issue a writ of habeas corpus on the application of German citizens being held abroad. The petitioners had been captured in China and tried and convicted by a U.S. military tribunal there for violating the laws of war by continuing military activity against the United States after the surrender of Germany in 1945. After conviction, they were sent to an American military prison in Germany, where they were being held at the time the petitions were filed. The precise basis for the Supreme Court's decision—how far it rested on a lack of statutory jurisdiction, and how far it was based on a determination that the petitioners' had suffered no violation of their constitutional rights—was not clear.

(b) Rasul v. Bush. Insofar as Eisentrager was interpreted as closing the habeas jurisdiction to all aliens held overseas, it was limited by Rasul v. Bush, 124 S.Ct. 2686 (2004), in which the majority and the dissent debated just what Eisentrager had held. The Rasul decision involved two Australians and twelve Kuwaitis captured during hostilities between the United States and the Taliban regime in Afghanistan, and held (along with about 640 other aliens) at the United States Naval Base at Guantanamo Bay in Cuba. (The United States' agreements with Cuba, from 1903 and 1934, recognize the ultimate sovereignty of Cuba over the leased areas but grant the United States, as long as it retains a naval base there, "complete jurisdiction and control".) The petitioners, alleging that they had never been combatants against the United States or engaged in any acts of terrorism, filed (through their next friends) various actions in the United States District Court for the District of Columbia, challenging the legality of their detention. Treating all of the filings as habeas corpus petitions, the lower courts ruled that under Eisentrager, they lacked jurisdiction.

(i) The Supreme Court reversed. Justice Stevens' opinion for the Court began by closely examining the Eisentrager decision, in which the court of appeals had upheld habeas jurisdiction. "In reversing that determination, this Court summarized the six critical facts in the case:

2. A footnote suggested that the district of confinement had concurrent habeas jurisdiction—subject to possible transfer under § 1404(a) to a more convenient venue (p. 499 n. 15).

'We are here confronted with a decision whose basic premise is that these prisoners are entitled, as a constitutional right, to sue in some court of the United States for a writ of *habeas corpus*. To support that assumption we must hold that a prisoner of our military authorities is constitutionally entitled to the writ, even though he (a) is an enemy alien; (b) has never been or resided in the United States; (c) was captured outside of our territory and there held in military custody as a prisoner of war; (d) was tried and convicted by a Military Commission sitting outside the United States; (e) for offenses against laws of war committed outside the United States; (f) and is at all times imprisoned outside the United States'" (p. 2693, quoting 339 U. S. at 777).

The Guantanamo detainees, Justice Stevens reasoned, differed from the Eisentrager petitioners in important respects: "They are not nationals of countries at war with the United States, and they deny that they have engaged in or plotted acts of aggression against the United States; they have never been afforded access to any tribunal, much less charged with and convicted of wrongdoing; and for more than two years they have been imprisoned in territory over which the United States exercises exclusive jurisdiction and control" (p. 2693).

The Court then stated a critical premise of its opinion: that the six factors mentioned in Eisentrager "were relevant only to the question of the prisoners' *constitutional* entitlement to habeas corpus" (p. 2693). The court of appeals in Eisentrager "implicitly conceded" that under Ahrens, the district court lacked statutory jurisdiction over petitioners detained outside of its territory, ruling that the Constitution's Suspension Clause gave the petitioners a constitutional right to habeas review, which could not be denied by a statutory gap (p. 2694). It was that constitutional ruling, Justice Stevens contended, that the Supreme Court had reversed in Eisentrager, but "[t]he Court had far less to say on the question of the petitioners' *statutory* entitlement to habeas review", stating only that the statute conferred no such right (p. 2694).

Any "statutory gap" that the Eisentrager petitioners had faced by virtue of the Ahrens decision had since been filled, Justice Stevens argued, by the Braden decision, Paragraph (1), *supra*. Braden overruled Ahrens and held that "the petitioner's physical presence within the territorial jurisdiction of the district court is not an 'invariable prerequisite' "to a district court's authority to exercise habeas jurisdiction under § 2241, which exists so long as the custodian can be reached by service of process. "Because Braden overruled the statutory predicate to Eisentrager's holding, Eisentrager plainly does not preclude the exercise of § 2241 jurisdiction over petitioner's claims" (p. 2695, quoting Braden).

Turning to the respondents' claim that § 2241 should be construed in light of the principle that federal statutes are presumed to lack extraterritorial application, Justice Stevens found the principle inapposite because the Guantanamo detainees were, in light of the terms of the lease agreements, within the territorial jurisdiction of the United States. Noting that the respondents had conceded that habeas jurisdiction would lie over a petition by an American citizen held at Guantanamo, and that § 2241 does not distinguish citizens from aliens, he said that "there is little reason to think that Congress intended the geographical coverage of the statute to vary depending on the detainee's citizenship" (p. 2696).

Thus, the Court concluded that "petitioners contend that they are being held in federal custody in violation of the laws of the United States. No party questions the District Court's jurisdiction over petitioners' custodians. Section 2241, by its terms, requires nothing more" (p. 2698). The Court expressed no view on "[w]hether and what further proceedings may become necessary after respondents make their response to the merits of petitioners' claims" (p. 2699).

(ii) Justice Scalia, joined by the Chief Justice and Justice Thomas, filed a detailed dissent. He pointed to two statutory provisions that, he said, presuppose that a petitioner must be within the district court's territorial jurisdiction: § 2241(a), which provides that "the order of a circuit judge shall be entered in the records of *the* district court of *the district wherein the restraint complained of is had*"; and § 2242, which provides that a petition addressed to an appellate court or judge thereof "shall state the reasons for not making application to *the* district court of *the district in which the applicant is held*" (p. 2701; emphasis in Justice Scalia's opinion).

Turning to the Court's discussion of Eisentrager, Justice Scalia contended that the court of appeals had ruled that there was statutory jurisdiction, although that conclusion was premised on the need to avoid difficult constitutional questions that otherwise would have arisen. (In response, Justice Stevens, without agreeing with that contention, said that "what is most pertinent for present purposes is that this Court clearly understood the Court of Appeals' decision to rest on constitutional and not statutory grounds" (p. 2694 n. 8).) By the same token, Justice Scalia insisted that the Supreme Court's disposition in Eisentrager, reversing the court of appeals' determination that there was jurisdiction, necessarily had to rest on a determination, however briefly discussed, that § 2241 conferred no jurisdiction over the petitioners.

The dissent also disputed the Court's contention that Braden had "overruled the statutory predicate to Eisentrager's holding" that a petitioner must be within the territorial jurisdiction of the district court. In Justice Scalia's view, Braden, facing a new form of custody not foreseen when Ahrens was decided, merely held that a petitioner in custody in multiple jurisdictions within the United States may challenge his legal confinement in the jurisdiction within which that confinement originates, even if he is physically confined elsewhere. "Outside that class of cases, Braden did not question the general rule of Ahrens (much less that of Eisentrager). Where, as here, present physical custody is at issue, Braden is inapposite, and Eisentrager unquestionably controls" (pp. 2704–05).

Justice Scalia acknowledged that Eisentrager had distinguished the rights of aliens and those of citizens. The constitutional doubt about whether a citizen held abroad could be denied access to habeas review might "justify[] a strained construction of the habeas statute, or (more honestly) a determination of the constitutional right to habeas. * * * [B]ut the possibility of one atextual exception thought to be required by the Constitution is no justification for abandoning the clear application of the text to a situation in which it raises no constitutional doubt" (p. 2706).[3]

The dissent then turned to the consequences of the majority's decision: "an alien captured in a foreign theater of active combat [may] bring a § 2241

---

3. [Ed.] Given that the federal courts are courts of limited jurisdiction, even were Justice Scalia to conclude that citizens held abroad do have a constitutional right to habeas review, does it follow that they have a right to be heard in *federal* court? See Fifth Edition pp. 330–37. But if not, would a state court have power to entertain a habeas petition? See Tarble's Case, Fifth Edition p. 433.

petition against the Secretary of Defense. * * * From this point forward, federal courts will entertain petitions from these prisoners, and others like them around the world, challenging actions and events far away, and forcing the courts to oversee one aspect of the Executive's conduct of a foreign war" (pp. 2706–07). He included a long quotation from Eisentrager highlighting the practical difficulties that could ensue, and concluded: "[T]oday's clumsy, countertextual reinterpretation * * * confers upon wartime prisoners greater habeas rights than domestic detainees. The latter must challenge their present physical confinement in the district of their confinement, see Rumsfeld v. Padilla, [Paragraph (3)(a), *infra*], whereas under today's strange holding Guantanamo Bay detainees can petition in any of the 94 federal judicial districts.[4] * * * For this Court to create such a monstrous scheme in time of war, and in frustration of our military commanders' reliance upon clearly stated prior law, is judicial adventurism of the worst sort" (p. 2711).

(iii) In an opinion concurring in the judgment, Justice Kennedy took an intermediate view. He agreed with Justice Scalia that Braden had not overruled the statutory predicate to Eisentrager, and thus he rejected the Court's recognition of "automatic statutory authority" to adjudicate claims of persons held outside the United States. But he read Eisentrager as indicating, on the one hand, "that there is a realm of political authority over military affairs where the judicial power may not enter", and, on the other hand, that there are circumstances in which it falls to the courts to protect individuals from unlawful detention, even where military affairs are involved. In this case, he recognized jurisdiction, distinguishing Eisentrager on two bases: "First, Guantanamo Bay is in every practical respect a United States territory, and it is one far removed from any hostilities" (p. 2700). Second, the detainees were being held indefinitely without trial or other proceedings, which suggests a weaker case of military necessity and "much greater alignment with the traditional function of habeas corpus" (p. 2700).

(iv) It is not easy to determine whether the majority's result depends on the fact that the detainees were held at Guantanamo Bay, rather than, for example, in Afghanistan, where the United States would not exercise complete jurisdiction and control. Early in his opinion, Justice Stevens says: "The question now before us is whether the habeas statute confers a right to judicial review of the legality of Executive detention of aliens in a territory over which the United States exercises plenary and exclusive jurisdiction, but not 'ultimate sovereignty' "(p. 2693). He then turns, in what might be viewed as the heart of his analysis, to consideration of Eisentrager, Ahrens, and Braden. As noted above, that discussion, in distinguishing Eisentrager, refers to the special status of Guantanamo Bay, but it proceeds more broadly thereafter in suggesting that Braden removed the statutory predicate for the view that Eisentrager excludes petitioners held outside a district court's territorial jurisdiction from seeking habeas review. The next section of his opinion begins by saying: "Putting Eisentrager and Ahrens to one side, respondents contend" that § 2241 should

---

4. [Ed.] In Gherebi v. Bush, 374 F.3d 727, 739 (9th Cir. 2004), decided after Rasul, the Ninth Circuit upheld the power of the District Court in the Central District of California to exercise jurisdiction over the habeas petition of a Guantanamo detainee "and transfer[] the proceedings to the appropriate forum"—in this case, the U.S. District Court for the District of Columbia. That court, in turn, agreed that it was a proper forum (citing Rasul, which was also filed in D.C.), despite the fact that the Secretary of Defense, who the government claimed was the only properly-named respondent, works at the Pentagon in Arlington, Virginia. See 338 F.Supp.2d 91, 96 (D.D.C. 2004).

not be interpreted to have extraterritorial reach (p. 2696); in rejecting that contention, he relies in part on the control that the United States exercises at Guantanamo Bay, and in part on the intersection of the government's concession that a U.S. citizen held at Guantanamo could seek habeas with his observation that § 2241 does not distinguish aliens from citizens.

In considering whether aliens detained, for example, in Afghanistan would have the same rights as the Guantanamo detainees, note that several distinct questions are involved: (i) Do the federal courts have jurisdiction under the habeas corpus statute? (ii) To what extent do aliens held overseas possess rights under the Constitution, or under federal law more generally, that could support a claim of illegal detention? (Did Rasul read Eisentrager as having held that in the circumstances there presented, the petitioners had suffered no violation of their rights so as to call the legality of detention into question?) (iii) What is the appropriate scope of habeas review of a claim of illegal detention (an issue the Court expressly reserves in Rasul)?

(c) Post–Rasul Adjudication of Petitions of Guantanamo Detainees. Nine days after the Rasul, decision, the government established Combatant Status Review Tribunals (CSRTs)—panels of three "neutral" military officers. A detainee may contest before the CSRT the government's prior determination of enemy combatant status. (The order establishing CSRTs defines an enemy combatant as an "individual who was part of or supporting Taliban or al Qaeda forces, or associated forces that are engaged in hostilities against the United States or its coalition partners. This includes any person who has committed a belligerent act or has directly supported hostilities in aid of enemy armed forces.") While the government's prior determination is presumed to be correct, a detainee may hear the factual basis for detention (to the extent that that basis does not involve classified information), may testify and present evidence, and may have assistance from a military officer, serving as a "Personal Representative", in understanding the process.

But creation of the CSRTs did not put an end to habeas litigation by Guantanamo detainees. A number of such cases in the District Court for the District of Columbia were consolidated for certain administrative purposes before Judge Joyce Hens Green. The government moved to dismiss the cases, arguing that "the Rasul decision resolved only whether individuals detained at Guantanamo Bay had the right merely to *allege* in a United States District Court under the *habeas* statute that they are being detained in violation of the Constitution and other laws," but "was silent on the issue of whether the detainees actually *possess* any underlying substantive rights." Judge Green rejected the government's contention that the detainees possessed no such rights, holding instead that in view of the Rasul decision, "it is clear that Guantanamo Bay must be considered the equivalent of a U.S. territory in which fundamental constitutional rights [including the Due Process Clause] apply". In re Guantanamo Detainee Cases, 355 F.Supp.2d 443, 453–54, 464 (D.D.C. 2005).

Judge Green proceeded to find that review by a CSRT failed to provide due process, because detainees were not permitted to review classified evidence supporting their classification as enemy combatants and because they were not permitted to have counsel review that evidence (even on the condition that counsel not disclose it to the client). While the Personal Representative may review classified evidence, that representative is "neither a lawyer nor an advocate" and thus not "an effective surrogate to compensate for a detainee's inability to personally review and contest classified evidence against him" (p. 472).

Judge Green further held that some detainees had stated plausible claims that (a) some of the evidence used against them was the product of torture or other coercion and thus could not, consistently with due process, be considered, and (b) the definition of "enemy combatant" was vague and overly broad and could not be applied consistently with due process. On the second point, she noted that "[i]n response to [a series of hypothetical questions at the oral hearing on the Government's motion to dismiss], counsel for [the government] argued that the Executive has the authority to detain the following individuals until the conclusion of the war on terrorism: '[a] little old lady in Switzerland who writes checks to what she thinks is a charity that helps orphans in Afghanistan but [what] really is a front to finance al-Qaeda activities,' a person who teaches English to the son of an al Qaeda member, and a journalist who knows the location of Osama Bin Laden but refuses to disclose it to protect her source" (p. 475).

Judge Green concluded that given the Executive's failure to provide a military tribunal that comports with due process, a habeas court is obliged to provide petitioners with a fair opportunity to challenge the government's factual basis for detention. She sought input from counsel about how to proceed in view of the conclusions reached in her opinion.

Finally, while agreeing with the government that the Geneva Conventions do not apply to members of al Qaeda, she held that detainees determined to be Taliban members had stated a claim that their exclusion from POW status violated Geneva Convention requirements, which she found to be self-executing.

However, Judge Green's colleague, Judge Richard J. Leon, took a quite different view of these issues in a very similar case. In Khalid v. Bush, 355 F.Supp.2d 311 (D.D.C. 2005), he granted the government's motion to dismiss habeas petitions filed by Guantanamo detainees. Unlike Judge Green, Judge Leon viewed Guantanamo not as equivalent to U.S. territory but as a U.S. base located in a foreign sovereignty. And also unlike Judge Green, he agreed with the government that Rasul was silent as to whether non-resident aliens captured and detained outside the U.S. have any cognizable constitutional rights. Rejecting the petitioners' view that Rasul had overruled Eisentrager v. Johnson, he ruled that Rasul merely recognized the existence of statutory habeas jurisdiction, without limiting Eisentrager's holding that petitioners lack any constitutional rights that can be vindicated in a habeas proceeding. He proceeded to find that the petitioners failed to identify any U.S. law or treaty that would support their claim, or that would even provide a private right of action to bring such a claim, and that it was up to the political branches to address any complaints petitioners might have about the conditions of their detention.

Appeals are pending both in In re Guantanamo Detainee Cases and in Khalid.

(d) Transfer of Alien Detainees to Foreign Nations. A number of Guantanamo detainees with pending habeas petitions have resisted their possible transfer to foreign nations, in some cases for release and in others for continued detention and possible trial by foreign authorities. The government has stated that its policy is not to transfer individuals when it believes it is more likely than not that they will be tortured, but the petitioners have supplied newspaper articles and other material that they claim substantiates their position that detainees already transferred have been tortured and that future transferees might be as well. On this basis, the petitioners have sought injunctive orders requiring the government to provide 30 days notice before any transfer from Guantanamo to any location outside the United States. A majority of district court decisions have granted these motions, citing petitioners' interests in having a meaningful opportunity to contest transfer to countries that might engage in torture, in obtaining release (not merely release from American custody), and in not having their habeas claims eliminated, see, *e.g.*, Al–Marri v. Bush, No. Civ.A. 04–2035(GK), 2005 WL 774843 (D.D.C. April 4, 2005), and the court's interest in protecting its jurisdiction over pending petitions against elimination by executive action, see, e.g., Abdah v. Bush, No. Civ.A. 04–1254(HHK), 2005 WL 711814 (D.D.C. March 29, 2005). See also Al–Joudi v. Bush, No. Civ.A. 05–301(GK), 2005 WL 774847 (D.D.C. April 4, 2005); Kurnaz v. Bush, Nos. Civ. 04–1135(ESH) & 05–0392 (ESH), 2005 WL 839542 (D.D.C. April 12, 2005) (notice required unless transfer is for release only). Nearly all of these rulings left open the questions whether subsequent attempts to block transfer would succeed or whether a transfer would in fact extinguish the court's jurisdiction.

However, two district judges have refused to grant the requested order. In Almurbati v. Bush, 366 F.Supp.2d 72 (2005), the court noted that the petitioner had submitted no evidence beyond news reports to support claims about possible torture abroad, while the government had submitted declarations setting forth its policy, noted above, and explaining how that policy is pursued. The court ruled that it lacked authority "to interfere with the respondents' prerogative to release any of the petitioners", particularly since this was precisely "the result requested" by petitioners, and thus petitioners had very little likelihood of success on the merits of any attempt to block transfer to a foreign country (pp. 80–81). Accord, Al–Anazi v. Bush, 370 F.Supp.2d 188, 2005 WL 1119602 (D.D.C. April 21, 2005).

(3) Territorial Jurisdiction: The Proper Respondent. When a prisoner challenges the lawfulness of custody, who is the proper respondent? The official who operates the facility of detention? That official's supervisor? How far up the chain of authority may a detainee go in naming a respondent?

(a) The Padilla Decision. In Rumsfeld v. Padilla, 124 S.Ct. 2711 (2004), decided the same day as Rasul, Padilla, an American citizen, was arrested as a material witness in connection with a federal grand jury investigation in New York of the September 11 terrorist attacks and was transported to New York. While his motion to vacate the material witness warrant was pending in the Southern District of New York, President Bush ordered Secretary of Defense Rumsfeld to designate Padilla an "enemy combatant" and detain him in military custody; Padilla was then taken into military custody and transported to the Naval Brig in Charleston, South Carolina. Two days later, his lawyer filed on his behalf a habeas corpus petition in the Southern District of New York, naming as respondents President Bush, Secretary Rumsfeld, and Melanie Marr, Commander of the Naval Brig. The government moved to dismiss, arguing (a) that only Commander Marr, the immediate custodian, was a proper respondent, and (b) that the district court in New York lacked jurisdiction over her. When the case reached the Supreme Court, it upheld the government's position on both points.

(i) On the former point, Chief Justice Rehnquist, writing for the majority, emphasized that the habeas statute consistently refers to "the" custodian, and cited longstanding authority and practice confirming "that in habeas challenges to present physical confinement—'core challenges'—the default rule is that the proper respondent is the warden of the facility where the prisoner is being held, not the Attorney General or some other remote supervisory official" (p. 2718). Cases departing from that rule involved challenges to something other than present physical confinement—as, for example, in Braden, whether the petitioner challenged future confinement.

The Court was required to distinguish Strait v. Laird, 406 U.S. 341 (1972), which held that an inactive Army reservist could petition for habeas (to review a failure to grant discharge as a conscientious objector) in California, where he was domiciled. Although all of his superior officers, and thus his nominal custodian, were in Indiana (where they had charge of the petitioner's records), the Court in Strait held that they were "present" in California because they processed his discharge application through Army personnel in that state.[5] In Padilla, the Court characterized Strait as holding that "the immediate custodian rule had no application because petitioner was not challenging any present physical confinement" and thus, as in Braden, *"there was no immediate physical custodian* with respect to the 'custody' being challenged" (p. 2720).

The majority also distinguished Ex parte Endo, 323 U.S. 283 (1944), in which the petitioner sought the writ in the Northern District of California, where she was being held during the relocation of persons of Japanese ancestry during World War II. On appeal from denial of the writ, the Supreme Court in Endo held that the district court retained jurisdiction, despite her subsequent removal to Utah, because a custodian—the assistant director of the War Relocation Authority—remained within the district.[6] In Padilla, the Court said that "Endo stands for the important but limited proposition that when the Government moves a habeas petitioner after she properly files a petition naming her immediate custodian, the District Court retains jurisdiction and may direct the writ to any respondent within its jurisdiction who has legal authority to effectuate the prisoner's release" (p. 2721).

(ii) Having determined that only Commander Marr was a proper respondent, the Court proceeded to rule that the Southern District lacked jurisdiction to entertain a petition naming her, resting on the "traditional rule" that the writ may be issued only in the district in which the immediate custodian is located (p. 2722). The Court relied in part on precedent, and in part on a variety of statutory provisions that presupposed that a petition must be filed only in the district of confinement—in this case, the federal district of South Carolina.[7] "In habeas challenges to *present* physical confinement, [unlike the

---

5. Strait seemed to have drawn the teeth from the earlier decision in Schlanger v. Seamans, 401 U.S. 487 (1971), where the Court had held that a federal district court in Arizona could not entertain a petition from an Air Force enlisted man on temporary duty in Arizona, since nobody who could be deemed his "custodian" (*i.e.*, his commanding officer or the Secretary of the Air Force) was in the state.

6. The decision was explained in Ahrens v. Clark, Paragraph (1), *supra*, 335 U.S. at 193, as "in conformity with the policy underlying [then] Rule 45(1) of the Court", which provided that pending "review of a decision refusing a writ of habeas corpus, the custody of the prisoner shall not be disturbed." (For the current, somewhat different, provision, see Sup.Ct.R. 36.)

7. Those provisions included §§ 2241(d) and 2255, see Paragraph (1)(a), *supra,* which

situation in Braden], the district of confinement is synonymous with the district court that has territorial jurisdiction over the proper respondent" (p. 2733).

Padilla argued that just as the Court in Strait had found that Strait's "nominal custodian" in Indiana was "present" in California "through the officers who processed [Strait's] application for discharge", so Secretary Rumsfeld was present in the Southern District through his subordinates who took Padilla into custody. Rejecting that claim, the Chief Justice said that the Strait Court contrasted the presence of the nominal custodian with that of "a commanding officer who is responsible for the day to day control of his subordinates" and who would be subject to jurisdiction only in the district where he resides (p. 2724). Only in the "limited circumstances" in Strait— "when Strait had always resided in California and had his only meaningful contacts with the Army there * * * did we invoke concepts of personal jurisdiction to hold that the custody was present in California through the actions of his agents" (p. 2724). There was no need to do so here, as both the petitioner and Commander Marr were in South Carolina.

(iii) In a concurring opinion joined by Justice O'Connor, Justice Kennedy said that the rules set forth by the Court were more like personal jurisdiction or venue than subject matter jurisdiction, and thus were subject to exceptions and to waiver by the government. He indicated that he would recognize an exception if the government were not forthcoming about the location where someone was detained or if it moved a detainee to try to make it difficult for the detainee's lawyer to file in the proper district.

(iv) Justice Stevens, joined by Justices Souter, Ginsburg, and Breyer, dissented. While agreeing that "the immediate custodian rule should control in the ordinary case," (p. 2731), he noted that the government moved *ex parte* to vacate the material witness warrant and transfer custody to the military on June 9, 2002, two days before a scheduled hearing on Padilla's motion challenging the legality of his detention under that warrant. On June 10, the Attorney General announced Padilla's detention and transfer to the Defense Department, and when on June 11 Padilla's lawyer filed a habeas petition, she apparently had not received official notice of Padilla's whereabouts. Justice Stevens objected that if the government had given her notice of its intention to transfer Padilla to military custody, she would presumably have filed immediately, at a time when Padilla's immediate custodian would have been within the Southern District; the government should not, he contended, be able to obtain an advantage by having proceeded *ex parte*.

Justice Stevens stressed that the Court's "bright line rule" admits many exceptions—when physical custody is not at issue (as in Braden), when citizens are confined overseas (see Paragraph (3)(b), *infra*), when the petitioner is transferred after filing (as in Endo), or when the custodian is present in the district through his agent's conduct (as in Strait). He added that while the Court treats this detention as run-of-the-mill, in fact it "is singular not only because it calls into question decisions made by [Secretary Rumsfeld] himself, but also because those decisions have created a unique and unprecedented

in some circumstances permit state or federal convicts to file in districts other than the district of confinement; both provisions would have been unnecessary, the Court said, if § 2241 generally permits a prisoner to file outside the district of confinement. The Court also relied on §§ 2241(a) and 2242, both discussed in Justice Scalia's dissent in Rasul, Paragraph (2)(b), *supra*.

threat to the freedom of every American citizen" (pp. 2732–33). The dissenters thus would have departed from the immediate custodian rule, and concluded that Secretary Rumsfeld had sufficient contacts to bring him within the jurisdiction of the Southern District on the basis of his order to military personnel to seize Padilla and remove him to South Carolina.[8]

(b) Custodians of Persons Held Overseas by the United States. What happens when the petitioner and the immediate custodian are both overseas? In Padilla, the Court acknowledged that "[w]e have long implicitly recognized an exception to the immediate custodian rule in the military context where an American citizen is detained outside the territorial jurisdiction of any district court" (p. 2718 n. 9), citing two Supreme Court decisions in which the District Court for the District of Columbia had exercised jurisdiction over superior officials in the United States. In Burns v. Wilson, 346 U.S. 137 (1953), two servicemen convicted for crimes committed in Guam and detained overseas named the Secretary of Defense as respondent. Although in the end refusing to grant the writ, the Supreme Court did not question its jurisdiction, and the jurisdictional issue, though not mentioned in the opinion, was discussed by Justice Frankfurter in his opinion dissenting from the denial of rehearing, 346 U.S. 844 (1953). Similarly, in United States ex rel. Toth v. Quarles, 350 U.S. 11 (1955), habeas relief against the Secretary of the Air Force was granted to an ex-serviceman arrested in the U.S. and taken to Korea for military trial. See also the discussion in Braden, Paragraph (1), *supra,* 410 U.S. at 498.

Would a similar exception to the immediate custodian rule apply if the petitioner were an alien? Reconsider the facts of Rasul, Paragraph (2)(b), where the Guantanamo detainees named as respondents the President, the Secretary of Defense, the Chairman of the Joint Chiefs of Staff, the Commandant of Camp X–Ray/Camp Delta at Guantanamo, and other military officials. The question of which if any of these officials was a proper respondent was not joined in the Supreme Court, which said only that no challenge had been made to the district court's jurisdiction over the petitioner's custodians. (Does that suggest that the Rasul Court agrees with the view Justice Kennedy expressed, in his concurrence in Padilla, that these kinds of "jurisdictional" defects are waivable?)

(c) Citizens Detained Abroad by Foreign Nations, but Allegedly with American Involvement. Abu Ali v. Ashcroft, 350 F.Supp.2d 28 (D.D.C. 2004), involved a habeas petition on behalf of an American citizen arrested and detained by Saudi Arabian authorities, allegedly at the request of American officials. The government sought dismissal, arguing that federal courts have "no jurisdiction to consider the habeas petition of a United States citizen if he is in the hands of a foreign state" and that judicial intervention would interfere with the Executive's foreign affairs power (p. 31). The court rejected these

---

8. For concern about the implications of Padilla for immigration cases, see Morawetz, *Detention Decisions and Access to Habeas Corpus for Immigrants Facing Deportation,* 25 B.C. Third World L.J. 13 (2005). Morawetz notes that many detainees in immigration cases are held at a federal facility in the Western District of Louisiana, that that district's judges take the view that they lack power to stay removal orders, regardless of the merits, and that once a person has been deported, the Fifth Circuit refuses, even if it finds the deportation was illegal, to order the immigrant's return. If this is a problem, is the answer to permit detainees to file in the federal district of their choice, or at least in any district to which they have some connection (*e.g.,* where they had resided or were taken into custody)? Or is the solution for the court of appeals to exercise more supervision over the district court's refusal to stay deportations?

arguments, noting that both Padilla and Rasul "recognize an exception" to the normal territorial limitations of habeas jurisdiction "when the petitioner and his immediate custodian are 'outside the territory of any district court'" (p. 44, quoting Braden). "Constructive custody," if it did exist here, could satisfy the habeas statute's custody requirement, and "[t]here is simply no authority or precedent . . . for [the government's] suggestion that the executive's prerogative over foreign affairs can overwhelm to the point of extinction the basic constitutional rights of citizens of the United States to freedom from unlawful detention by the executive" (pp. 48, 61–62).

(4) Original Application in the Supreme Court. Since 1789, the Supreme Court and its Justices have had authority to issue the writ directly. See Fifth Edition p. 1286. In Ex parte Yarbrough, 110 U.S. 651, 653 (1884), the Court stated that "it is not only within the authority of the Supreme Court, but it is its duty to inquire into the cause of commitment * * *, and if found to be as charged, a matter of which such a court had no jurisdiction, to discharge a prisoner from confinement." (The Supreme Court issues an "original" writ of habeas corpus as an exercise of its "appellate" jurisdiction, reviewing a decision of a lower federal court. See Fifth Edition p. 1286.)

By the time of its decision in Ex parte Abernathy, 320 U.S. 219, 219 (1943), the Court's concept of judicial duty had changed drastically: "the jurisdiction conferred on this Court * * * to issue writs of habeas corpus in aid of its appellate jurisdiction * * * is discretionary * * * and this Court does not, save in exceptional circumstances, exercise it in cases where an adequate remedy may be had in a lower federal court, or, if the relief sought is from the judgment of a state court, where the petitioner has not exhausted his remedies in the state courts."[9]

The present Sup.Ct.R. 20.4(a) states: "To justify the granting of a writ of habeas corpus, the petitioner must show that exceptional circumstances warrant the exercise of the Court's discretionary powers, and that adequate relief cannot be obtained in any other form or from any other court.[10] This writ is rarely granted."[11] Since 1900, the Court appears to have granted relief in cases involving direct recourse to its habeas jurisdiction in only three instances, most recently in 1925.[12]

---

9. Three major factors seem to have produced the change: (1) the Act of March 3, 1885, 23 Stat. 437, restoring an appeal to the Supreme Court from circuit court judgments in habeas cases, as provided by the Act of 1867 but withdrawn in 1868, see Fifth Edition p. 328; (2) the decision in Ex parte Royall, 117 U.S. 241, 254 (1886), affirming broad discretion to deny the writ to a state prisoner contesting, in advance of trial, the validity of the state statute under which the indictment was brought; and (3) the establishment in 1889 and 1891 of an appeal from convictions in federal criminal cases, see Fifth Edition p. 1552.

10. [Ed.] Since 1948, the Supreme Court, its Justices, and circuit judges have been authorized to "decline to entertain an application for the writ" and to transfer it to the district court "having jurisdiction to entertain it." 28 U.S.C. § 2241(b).

11. The power of a Justice to grant a writ returnable before the full Court was affirmed in Ex parte Clarke, 100 U.S. 399, 403 (1879). For a statement that the principles guiding the Court on original applications for the writ are followed by its members in the exercise of their authority as Justices, see United States ex rel. Norris v. Swope, 72 S.Ct. 1020 (1952)(Douglas, J.); cf. Rosoto v. Warden, 83 S.Ct. 1788 (1963) (Harlan, J.).

12. See Ex parte Grossman, 267 U.S. 87 (1925)(commitment for criminal contempt despite presidential pardon; prisoner dis-

SECTION 2. COLLATERAL ATTACK ON STATE JUDGMENTS OF CONVICTION

Page 1297. Add to footnote 2:

A recurrent question is whether a federal habeas court may entertain a prisoner's claim of violation of the treaty obligation, set forth in the Vienna Convention on Consular Relations, that states notify criminal defendants of their right to access of the consulate of their home country. See generally pp. 125–27, *infra.*

Page 1298. Add to the end of Paragraph (2) a new footnote 4a:

4a. As modified by rule amendments that took effect on December 1, 2004, Rule 11 now reads: "The Federal Rules of Civil Procedure, to the extent that they are not inconsistent with any statutory provisions or these rules, may be applied to a proceeding under these rules."

Page 1298. Add to footnote 5:

For application of the limitations period to cases involving recognition of a new constitutional right, see Dodd v. United States, 125 S.Ct. 2478 (2005), p. 128, *infra* (discussing the same question in a *federal* prisoner's postconviction proceeding).

Page 1298. Add to footnote 6:

In Pace v. DiGuglielmo, 125 S.Ct. 1807 (2005), the Court (5–4) ruled that a state postconviction petition dismissed as untimely by the state court is not "properly filed" within the meaning of § 2244(d) and hence its filing does not toll the federal statute's limitations period. The Court further ruled that equitable tolling was not appropriate in the circumstances presented.

For discussion of complexities lying at the intersection of the statute of limitations and the exhaustion requirement, see Fifth Edition p. 1392, and the corresponding material in this Supplement.

Page 1298. Add to the end of Paragraph (3) a new footnote 6a:

6a. The intersection of the statute of limitations with the § 2254 Rules and with the Federal Rules of Civil Procedure was at issue in Mayle v. Felix, 125 S.Ct. ___ (2005). Felix's initial habeas petition alleged that the introduction of a witness' videotaped testimony violated the Confrontation Clause. Five months after expiration of the limitations period, he filed an amended petition adding a claim that the introduction of his confession violated the Fifth Amendment. Felix argued that the amended petition was timely under Fed. R. Civ. Proc. 15(c)(2), which provides that an amended pleading "relates back" in time to the original pleading when both arise out of the same conduct, transaction, or occurrence. The Supreme Court, per Ginsburg, J., held that the amended petition did not relate back and hence was

charged); Ex parte Hudgings, 249 U.S. 378, 384–85 (1919)(district court had summarily adjudged petitioner in contempt for committing perjury; ruling that perjury as such is not contempt and noting the danger to liberty posed by the district court's approach, the Court reached the merits); Matter of Heff, 197 U.S. 488 (1905)(petitioner's attack on constitutionality of statute under which he was convicted had already been rejected by court of appeals in another case; statute held unconstitutional and prisoner discharged). See also Felker v. Turpin, 518 U.S. 651 (1996), Fifth Edition p. 1387 (discussing the availability of the original writ but ultimately denying the petition); Oaks, *The "Original" Writ of Habeas Corpus in the Supreme Court,* 1962 Sup.Ct.Rev. 153.

time-barred. The Court noted that most decisions under Rule 15 permit relation back only when there is a common core of operative facts. While Felix contended that both claims related to the admission of evidence at trial, the Court responded that the dispositive facts for his confession claim related to out-of-court police interrogation. A broad approach to the relation back of habeas claims, Justice Ginsburg argued, was in tension with Rule 2(c) of the § 2254 Rules, which provides that a petition must "specify all the grounds for relief available" and "state the facts supporting each ground", and also with the statute of limitations.

Justice Souter, joined by Justice Stevens, dissented, contending that "the imposition of the conviction that justifies the challenged custody" was the relevant transaction within the meaning of Rule 15 and that neither Habeas Rule 2(c) nor the statute of limitations demanded a narrower standard. Rule 2(c) is merely designed, he said, to help habeas courts identify meritless petitions by specifying discrete claims. Nor did the statute of limitations argue for a narrower standard, as the very purpose of Rule 15(c) is to qualify limitations periods. He noted that most petitioners lack counsel, and that even when a lawyer is appointed, it is usually only after the judge's preliminary review of the petition; Congress, in authorizing the appointment of counsel, would not have wanted the lawyer to have "one hand tied behind his back, as compared with an attorney hired by a prisoner with money" (p. ___ n. 9).

Page 1300. Add to footnote 14:

In Miller–El v. Cockrell, 537 U.S. 322 (2003), the Court reversed a court of appeals' decision refusing to issue a certificate of appealability (COA), stressing that a court asked to issue such a certificate should conduct only " 'a threshold inquiry into the underlying merit of [the prisoner's] claims' "to determine if the petitioner has made, in the words of § 2253(c)(2), "a substantial showing of the denial of a constitutional right"—*i.e.,* a showing that reasonable jurists could debate whether the petition should be resolved differently (p. 327, citing Slack v. McDaniel, 529 U.S. 473, 481 (2000)). The COA stage, the Court indicated, was not the place for "full consideration of the factual or legal bases adduced in support of the claims" (p. 336).

Justice Scalia joined the Court's opinion but wrote a concurrence discussing the effect on the availability of a COA of § 2254(d), which generally precludes habeas courts from issuing relief unless the state-court determination challenged in the habeas proceeding was not merely wrong but unreasonable. In his view, whether a COA should issue depends upon whether the habeas court's denial of relief (rather than the state court's decision) was debatable to jurists of reason, who might all agree that a state court's rejection of a constitutional claim was debatable but also that the state court's determination was not unreasonable and, therefore, that habeas relief was unavailable. That approach, he suggested, was consistent with § 2253(c)(2)'s purpose of preventing meritless appeals. Acknowledging that § 2253(c)(2) refers to "a substantial showing of the denial of a constitutional right" rather than a substantial showing that the habeas court erred, he noted that the provision says only that a COA *may* issue upon that showing, not that it must.

It is unclear what position the majority opinion takes on the issue raised by Justice Scalia, as different passages seem to point in opposite directions. However, in Medellín v. Dretke, 125 S.Ct. 2088 (2005), Justices O'Connor, Stevens, Souter, and Breyer said that whether a prisoner has cleared the hurdles imposed by § 2254(d) "is an appropriate consideration for an appellate court contemplating whether to grant a COA, and for this Court reviewing the denial of a COA. See Miller–El, 537 U.S. at 349–350 (Scalia, J., concurring) ('A circuit justice or judge must deny a COA . . . if all reasonable jurists would conclude that a substantive provision of the federal habeas statute bars relief)'" (p. 2099). The other Justices had no occasion to consider this question.

The Miller–El case returned to the Supreme Court in 2005. See p. 120, *infra.*

Pages 1321–22. Add to footnote 6:

The Seventh Circuit has overruled its decision in Holman v. Page, cited in the Fifth Edition. See Owens v. United States, 387 F.3d 607 (7th Cir.2004).

Pages 1324–25. Add to Paragraph (7):

See also Thomas *et al., Is It Ever Too Late for Innocence? Finality, Efficiency, and Claims of Innocence,* 64 U.Pitt.L.Rev. 263 (2003) (arguing that due process "require[s] courts to be open to powerful claims of innocence without regard to whether procedural deadlines for challenging a conviction have expired" (p. 264) and noting a trend in recent decisions toward "finding a basis to allow powerful claims of innocence to be heard even if filed too late under the rules of procedure" (p. 280)).

Pages 1332–33. Add to Paragraph (3):

In Schriro v. Summerlin, 124 S.Ct. 2519 (2004)—a case filed before the AEDPA was enacted and thus not covered by the present version of § 2254(d)—although the first Teague exception was not at issue, the Court broadly recharacterized it this way: "New *substantive* rules generally apply retroactively. This includes decisions that narrow the scope of a criminal statute by interpreting its terms, see Bousley v. United States, [Fifth Edition p. 1401], as well as constitutional determinations that place particular conduct covered by the statute beyond the State's power to punish". A footnote added: "We have sometimes referred to rules of this latter type as falling under an exception to Teague's bar on retroactive application of procedural rules; they are more accurately characterized as substantive rules not subject to the bar" (p. 2523 & n. 4).

The Court in Schriro held that the constitutional rule on which the prisoner relied—that a jury, not a judge, must find the presence of an aggravating factor necessary to qualify a defendant for a death sentence, see Ring v. Arizona, 536 U.S. 584 (2002)—did not satisfy Teague's second exception. Justice Breyer, for four dissenters, disagreed, arguing that the requirement of a jury in a capital sentencing procedure was a watershed rule, *inter alia*, because (i) of the jury's "special role * * * [in] making the death-related, community based value judgments", (ii) in capital cases, equal justice is of special importance, while "the risk of error that the law can tolerate is * * * diminished", and (iii) any harm to the administration of justice from retroactive application is relatively small (pp. 2528–29). The majority's responded (per Justice Scalia) that although many observers view juries as more accurate factfinders, others take the opposite view, and that the evidence is "too equivocal" to support a conclusion that "judicial factfinding so 'seriously diminishe[s]' accuracy that there is an 'impermissibly large risk' of punishing conduct the law does not reach" (p. 2525, quoting Teague).

In view of the Court's reformulation of Teague's first exception, and so long as Teague's second exception remains a null set, would it be accurate to restate the operative doctrine on retroactivity this way: new substantive rules apply retroactively; new procedural rules do not.

Page 1335. Add to Paragraph (5)(e):

For citations to circuit decisions disagreeing on whether a habeas court must always, before discussing the constitutional merits, first determine whether Teague precludes relief, see Campiti v. Matesanz, 333 F.3d 317, 321 & n. 4 (1st Cir.2003). There, Judge Boudin noted that decisions like Caspari v. Bohlen, Fifth Edition p. 1335 n. 8, reproving lower courts for failing to address the *Teague* issue, involved a decision to *grant* relief without first determining whether the rule relied upon was "new". He rejected the state's invitation to read those cases as requiring a habeas court always to address the *Teague* issue first, even when relief could be denied on a narrower or easier ground, and he proceeded to deny the prisoner's petition on the merits. He added: "Only as a

last resort should the circuit courts read Supreme Court decisions to create
* * * mandatory priorities. * * * Anything that precludes judges from taking
the shortest distance to a result impairs their ability to give truly difficult cases
the time they require'' (pp. 321–22). Compare Lockyer v. Andrade, 538 U.S. 63
(2003), p. 120, *infra* (discussing a similar question with respect to the limitation
on the scope of habeas review contained in 28 U.S.C. § 2254(d)).

Page 1349. Add to footnote 1:

For detailed review of the Court's decisions under § 2254(d), see Ides, *Habeas Standards
of Review Under 28 U.S.C. § 2254(d)(1): A Commentary on Statutory Text and Supreme Court
Precedent,* 60 Wash. & Lee L.Rev. 677 (2003).

Page 1350. Add to Paragraph (2):

The Court has interpreted the "unreasonable application" clause in three
subsequent decisions.

(a) In Lockyer v. Andrade, 538 U.S. 63 (2003), the prisoner claimed that
the imposition of two consecutive terms of 25 years to life, under California's
"three strikes" law, for each of two thefts of a handful of videotapes violated
the Cruel and Unusual Punishment Clause. Justice O'Connor's opinion
stressed that the Supreme Court's decisions "in this area have not been a
model of clarity" and "have not established a clear or consistent path for courts
to follow" (p. 72). The only "clearly established" doctrine is a "gross disproportionality principle, the precise contours of which are unclear, applicable only in
the 'exceedingly rare' and 'extreme' case" (p. 73; internal citations omitted).
Finding that the facts here at issue fell between two Supreme Court precedents, one invalidating a life sentence without parole and the other upholding a
life sentence with the possibility of parole, the Court held that the state court's
application of the gross disproportionality principle was not unreasonable. In so
ruling, the Court rejected the Ninth Circuit's view that "objectively unreasonable" means "clear error", saying that a clear error standard "fails to give
proper deference to state courts by conflating error (even clear error) with
unreasonableness" (p. 75).

Justice Souter's dissent (joined by Justices Stevens, Ginsburg, and Breyer)
argued that the two thefts, separated by only two weeks and involving the same
victim and a continuing effort to finance a drug habit, could be understood only
as punishment for the total amount stolen (some $150). He then argued that a
sentence of 50 years without possibility of parole for a 37–year–old prisoner was
tantamount to life without parole and plainly invalid under the Court's precedents. The majority rejected that characterization of the sentence, responding
that here parole was ultimately available and that under the dissent's view, a
ten-year sentence of a 77–year–old defendant would be equivalent to life
without parole. The majority also rejected the dissent's treatment of the two
25–year sentences as a single package.

Note that for the majority, it does not suffice that the principle forbidding
gross disproportionality is clearly established; instead, the "precise contours" of
the principle's application must also, apparently, be clear. On that view, isn't
§ 2254(d)(1) especially likely to preclude habeas relief when the state court
decision in question involves a constitutional doctrine that is framed as a
standard rather than as a rule?

(b) The Court suggested as much the next Term in Yarborough v. Alvarado, 124 S.Ct. 2140 (2004). There, the Ninth Circuit had ruled that the state

courts, in finding a prisoner not to have been in custody for purposes of the Miranda rules, had unreasonably applied clearly established law. The Supreme Court, in reversing, observed that "[a]pplying a general standard to a specific case can demand a substantial element of judgment. As a result, evaluating whether a rule application was unreasonable requires considering the rule's specificity. The more general the rule, the more leeway courts have in reaching outcomes in case by case determinations" (p. 2149).

In Alvarado, Justice Kennedy, writing for the majority, and Justice Breyer, writing for the four dissenters, offered sharply conflicting appraisals of the circumstances that bear on the custody determination. Their differences appear to turn more on the substance of the custody inquiry than on the proper application of § 2254(d), with the majority declaring that the Ninth Circuit was "nowhere close to the mark" when it found the state courts' application of existing law to be unreasonable (p. 2150), and the dissenters suggesting that it was "obvious" that the prisoner had been in custody during the police questioning (p. 2152).

One important issue in the case was whether, in determining whether Alvarado was in custody, a court should consider his youth (he was 17). The Ninth Circuit had noted that the Supreme Court had held juvenile status relevant when evaluating the voluntariness of confessions and the validity of a purported waiver of the privilege against compulsory self-incrimination, and had reasoned that these precedents demanded "extension of the principle that juvenile status is relevant" to Miranda custody determinations (p. 2147). In rejecting that view, Justice Kennedy said that there was "force" to the warden's argument that "if a habeas court must extend a rationale before it can apply to the facts at hand then the rationale cannot be clearly established at the time of the state-court decision" (pp. 2150–51). The majority proceeded to stress, however, not only that its Miranda precedents had not previously mentioned the suspect's age or mandated its consideration but also that the Miranda inquiry, unlike the precedents on which the Ninth Circuit relied, is an objective inquiry and that consideration of a suspect's age could be viewed as requiring the kind of subjective inquiry that prior decisions had rejected.

(c) However, in Rompilla v. Beard, 125 S.Ct. 2456 (2005), the Court awarded habeas relief to a prisoner based upon his claim of ineffective assistance of counsel at the capital sentencing hearing, even though, as the Court acknowledged, the governing Sixth Amendment standard—reasonable performance under prevailing professional norms considering all of the circumstances—"spawns few hard-edged rules" (p. 2462). In Rompilla, defense counsel had made significant efforts to develop mitigating evidence for the sentencing hearing, even though the defendant and his family had suggested that no mitigating evidence was available. Nonetheless, the majority (per Souter, J.) found that counsel's performance fell short because of the failure to examine the court file on the defendant's prior rape and assault conviction. Counsel knew that the prosecution planned to introduce the transcript of the rape victim's testimony as evidence in aggravation, and the case file was readily available. In these circumstances, the Court ruled that a reasonable lawyer would surely review the file to learn what the prosecution knew, to ensure the prosecution was not quoting selectively, and to seek to downplay the earlier conviction—particularly when the defense strategy at sentencing was to focus on residual doubt about the defendant's guilt, a strategy that could be undermined by evidence of a prior similar crime. The Court included only the briefest discussion of § 2254(d): after its very detailed argument that counsel's performance was inadequate under the Sixth Amendment, the Court simply added that "the state courts were objectively unreasonable in concluding that counsel could reasonably decline to make any effort to review the file" (p. 246).

In dissent, Justice Kennedy, joined by the Chief Justice and Justices Scalia and Thomas, objected (p. 2475): "Today's decision is wrong under any standard, but the Court's error is compounded by the fact that this case arises on federal habeas. * * * Rompilla must show that the Pennsylvania Supreme Court decision was not just 'incorrect or erroneous,' but 'objectively unreasonable.' Lockyer v. Andrade, 538 U.S. 63, 75 (2003) (citing Williams v. Taylor, 529 U.S. 362, 410, 412 (2000)). He cannot do so. The Court pays lip service to the Williams standard, but it proceeds to adopt a rigid, per se obligation that binds counsel in every case and finds little support in our precedents".

Note that three cases in which the Court has found state court determinations to be unreasonable under § 2254(d)—Terry Williams, Rompilla, and Wiggins v. Smith, p. 121, *infra* (finding state court *factual* determinations to be unreasonable)—involved the ineffectiveness of defense counsel at capital sentencing hearings. In these cases, particularly Rompilla, is there anything to Justice Kennedy's charge that the Court pays only lip service to the limits that § 2254(d) places on habeas review?

Pages 1352–53. Add to Paragraph (6):

In Lockyer v. Andrade, 538 U.S. 63 (2003), discussed at p. 118, *supra,* the Court disapproved the Ninth Circuit's approach, described in the Fifth Edition, under which habeas courts must first review the state court decision de novo before applying § 2254(d)'s standard of review. The Court declared (p. 71): "AEDPA does not require a federal habeas court to adopt any one methodology in deciding the only question that matters under § 2254(d)(1)—whether a state court decision is contrary to, or involved an unreasonable application of, clearly established federal law. See Weeks v. Angelone, 528 U.S. 225 (2000)". (In Weeks, the majority had analyzed the prisoner's constitutional claim in some detail and suggested that it lacked merit, and then had concluded its opinion by stating that "[f]or the reasons stated above, it follows *a fortiori*" that the state court's determination was neither "contrary to" nor an "unreasonable application of" Supreme Court precedent (528 U.S. at 237).) In Lockyer, the Court did not reach the question whether the state court erred, ruling only that § 2254(d) foreclosed relief in any event.

Page 1353. Add to the end of Paragraph (7) a new footnote 6:

6. For criticism of the circuit decisions noted in text, see Sloane, *AEDPA's "Adjudication on the Merits" Requirement: Collateral Review, Federalism, and Comity*, 78 St.John's L. Rev. 615 (2004) (arguing that a summary dismissal is not an "adjudicat[ion] on the merits" for purposes of § 2254(d)). For broader arguments that review under § 2254(d) should focus on the reasonableness of the state court's analysis, and not simply on the reasonableness of the result reached, see Lee, *Section 2254(d) of the Federal Habeas Statute: Is It Beyond Reason?*, 56 Hastings L.J. 283 (2004); Semeraro, *A Reasoning–Process Review Model for Federal Habeas Corpus*, 94 J.Crim.L. & Criminology 897 (2004).

Page 1355. Add to Paragraph (2):

In Miller–El v. Dretke, 125 S.Ct. 2317 (2005), which involved allegations that the prosecution had exercised peremptory challenges to potential jurors based upon race, the majority and dissent sparred about the application of

§ 2254(d)(2). The state trial court held two hearings on the discrimination issue: one at the time of jury selection, and a second after the Supreme Court, in Batson v. Kentucky, 476 U.S. 79 (1986), substantially extended the Equal Protection Clause's application to the use of race in exercising peremptory challenges. In the second hearing, the court reviewed the voir dire record and, deeming the government's race-neutral explanations for its challenges "completely credible" (p. 2323), found no discrimination. The Texas Court of Criminal Appeals affirmed.

On habeas, the district court denied relief. The court of appeals' initial denial of a certificate of appealability was reversed by the Supreme Court, see p. 116, *supra*, after which the Fifth Circuit affirmed the denial of relief on the merits. In its second look at the case, the Court reversed. The majority (per Souter, J.) carefully analyzed the record and, after comparing the prosecution's treatment of black and white jury panelists, found the race-neutral explanations not credible. Central to that analysis were juror questionnaires and juror information cards, most of which had not been introduced into evidence in state court. Those documents were lodged in the record in the federal habeas proceeding, although no determination had been made under § 2254(e)(2) that a federal evidentiary hearing was warranted.

Justice Thomas' dissent (joined by the Chief Justice and Justice Scalia) accused the Court of flouting § 2254(d)(2), which precludes relief unless the state court's factual determination was unreasonable "in light of the evidence presented in the State court proceeding". The Court's analysis, he complained, rested heavily on three types of evidence not presented in state court: the alleged similarity of blacks struck by the prosecution to whites who were not; disparate questioning of whites and blacks about their views of the death penalty; and the prosecution's use of the "jury shuffle" (which permits either side to rearrange the order in which potential jurors are seated) when a predominant number of black jurors were seated in the front of the panel.

The majority responded that "the dissent conflates the difference between evidence that must be presented to the state courts * * * and theories about that evidence. There can be no question that the transcript of the *voir dire*, recording the evidence on which Miller–El based his arguments and on which we base our result, was before the state courts * * *. Only as to the juror questionnaires and information cards is there question about what was before the state courts" (p. 2326 n. 2). The majority offered a blend of justifications for considering these items of evidence: the state had not objected and indeed had referred to the material in its arguments in federal court; "it is not clear to what extent the lodged material expands upon what the state judge knew; the same judge presided over the *voir dire* [and both of the hearings], and the jury questionnaires were subjects of reference at the *voir dire*" (p. 2335 n. 15). While Justice Thomas contended that § 2254(d)(2) is addressed to the courts and that its strictures are not waivable, the Court, after alluding to the issue of waivability, did not, in the end, resolve it.

Page 1355. Add to Paragraph (3):

In Wiggins v. Smith, 539 U.S. 510 (2003), the Court, as in the Terry Williams decision, reversed the Fourth Circuit and upheld a claim of ineffective assistance of counsel in connection with a capital sentencing hearing. The decision sparked a dissent by Justice Scalia (joined by Justice Thomas) accusing the majority of misconstruing a state court's factual findings and of disregarding the limitations on habeas review set forth in §§ 2254(d) and 2254(e)(1).

At the capital sentencing hearing, defense lawyers did not introduce evidence relating to the prisoner's life history. His habeas petition was based on the factual premise that counsel's investigation of that history (which included sexual abuse as a child) had been limited to review of a pre-sentence investigation (PSI) and of Department of Social Services (DSS) records, neither of which revealed the sexual abuse, and on the legal position that any tactical decision not to present evidence of the prisoner's life history had been based on an inadequate investigation.

Upholding that claim, Justice O'Connor's majority opinion found that the Maryland Court of Appeals' conclusion that counsel had made a reasonable tactical decision was based, "in part, on a clear factual error—that the 'social service records ... recorded incidences of ... sexual abuse' "(p. 528). In view of the state's concession in the habeas proceedings that the DSS records lacked that information, she found that the state court's factual assumption "has been shown to be incorrect by 'clear and convincing evidence,' 28 U.S.C. § 2254(e)(1), and reflects 'an unreasonable determination of the facts in light of the evidence presented in the State court proceeding,' § 2254(d)(2)" (p. 528).

On the habeas issue, an important factual question was the extent of the investigation that counsel had performed before deciding not to present evidence concerning life history. The Maryland Court of Appeals had stated that trial counsel "did investigate and were aware of [the prisoner's] background" and that "[c]ounsel were aware that [he] had a most unfortunate childhood" (pp. 528, 530). Parsing the state court opinion, the majority declared that the state court "clearly assumed * * * that counsel's investigation began and ended with the PSI and the DSS records" (p. 544), and thus concluded that "[w]e therefore must determine, *de novo*, whether counsel reached beyond" those documents (p. 531). The Court proceeded to find that they had not done so and that the limited scope of their investigation violated the Sixth Amendment.

Justice Scalia's dissent read the same passages of the state court opinion very differently: "absolutely nothing in the state-court opinion * * * says (or assumes) that [the PSI and DSS records] were the only sources on which counsel relied" (p. 544). He highlighted aspects of the record that, he contended, supported his view that the state courts had found that counsel's investigation reached more broadly, and he objected that the state court's "failure to recite what is obvious from the record surely provides no basis for believing that it stupidly 'assumed' the opposite of what is obvious from the record" (p. 545).

Page 1358. Add to Paragraph (4):

In Bryan v. Mullin, 335 F.3d 1207 (10th Cir.2003), the court expressly rejected the approach of Valdez v. Cockrell, noted in the Fifth Edition, that state court findings are entitled to deference even if not the product of a full and fair hearing. Instead, the court held that "because the state court did not hold any evidentiary hearing, * * * we need not afford those findings any deference" (p. 1216). The court added that when a prisoner did not "fail" to present evidence in state court within the meaning of § 2254(e)(2), the availability of a federal evidentiary hearing is governed by pre-AEDPA standards (see Keeney v. Tamayo–Reyes, Fifth Edition p. 1356).

Pages 1378. Add to Paragraph (4)(e):

(e) In connection with the material in this Paragraph, consider the decision in Massaro v. United States, 538 U.S. 500 (2003). There, a *federal* prisoner filed a collateral attack under 28 U.S.C. § 2255, asserting the ineffectiveness of his trial counsel. Noting that his lawyer on direct review had not asserted that claim on appeal, the Second Circuit had affirmed the district court's dismissal of the claim, following its precedents under which the failure of new counsel on appeal to raise an ineffective assistance claim based solely on the trial record constitutes a procedural default that (absent cause and prejudice) bars relief under § 2255.

The Supreme Court unanimously reversed, declaring that the general rule that claims not raised on direct appeal ordinarily may not be raised on collateral review "is neither a statutory nor a constitutional requirement" but is doctrine to which courts adhere "to conserve judicial resources and to respect the law's important interest in the finality of judgments" (p. 504). However, the Second Circuit's application of this general rule to claims of ineffective assistance of counsel, rather than promoting those objectives, would "creat[e] the risk that defendants would feel compelled to raise the issue before there has been an opportunity fully to develop the factual predicate for the claim. Furthermore, the issue would be raised for the first time in a forum not best suited to assess those facts. This is so even if the record contains some indication of deficiencies in counsel's performance", for a trial record focusing on guilt or innocence may not reveal the facts necessary to determine whether counsel's performance was "not supported by a reasonable strategy" or whether any constitutional deficiency in performance was prejudicial (pp. 504–05). By contrast, in a § 2255 proceeding, the evidence relevant to the claim of ineffective assistance can be fully developed and will often be evaluated by the district judge who presided at trial.

The Court also noted practical objections to the Second Circuit's approach. Under that approach, trial counsel, if they fear that their effectiveness may be impugned on appeal, may be unwilling to provide assistance needed by appellate counsel (who often operate under short deadlines). Moreover, that approach would require the § 2255 court to determine whether the record on direct review was sufficient to support the ineffectiveness claim; the gain from eliminating from collateral review the few claims that could properly have been resolved on direct review would be far outweighed by the increased burden of scrutinizing the trial record in the larger number of cases in which the ineffectiveness claim could not properly have been resolved on appeal. Without holding that defendants may never raise ineffectiveness claims on direct review, the Court concluded that the failure to do so does not bar collateral review under § 2255.

The policy considerations that the Court adduced are equally applicable to state prisoners, and the Court's opinion noted that "[a] growing majority of state courts now follow the rule we adopt today" (p. 508). But what of those that don't and instead require new counsel on direct review to raise at least some kinds of ineffective assistance claims before a state appellate court? Would failure to comply with such a requirement bar direct review by the Supreme Court? Habeas review?

Consider, also, Massaro's suggestion that adequate opportunity to challenge the effectiveness of trial counsel exists only on collateral and not on direct review. Doesn't that suggestion reinforce the doubts raised in the Fifth Edition pp. 1377–78, about holdings that prisoners on collateral review have no right to counsel—even when they are litigating claims of ineffective assistance that, Massaro suggests, could not practically have been litigated earlier? See Dripps, *Ineffective Litigation of Ineffective Assistance Claims: Some Uncomfortable Reflections on Massaro v. United States*, 42 Brandeis L.J. 793 (2004).

Page 1379. Add a new footnote 9a at the end of Paragraph (5)(b):

9a. In Banks v. Dretke, 540 U.S. 668 (2004), which, like Strickler, involved a claim that the prosecution had withheld exculpatory evidence, the Court found that all three factors on which Strickler had based its finding of cause were present. Indeed, Justice Ginsburg said for the Court, the case was stronger than Strickler because the prosecution allowed untruthful testimony to stand uncorrected. The state contended that the prisoner was barred from obtaining relief because he had failed, during his state postconviction proceedings, to exercise due diligence in investigating possible concealment by the prosecution. Rejecting that contention, the Court stressed that the prosecution had represented that it would disclose all exculpatory material: "A rule * * * declaring 'prosecutor may hide, defendant must seek,' is not tenable in a system constitutionally bound to accord defendants due process" (p. 696).

Page 1379. Add to Paragraph (6):

For a decision finding that prejudice was established, see Banks v. Dretke, 540 U.S. 668 (2004). There, the prisoner alleged that the prosecution had unconstitutionally suppressed exculpatory evidence in violation of Brady v. Maryland, 373 U.S. 83 (1963). After finding cause for his failure to have raised the claim earlier, see immediately above, the Court stated that "prejudice within the compass of the 'cause and prejudice' requirement exists when the suppressed evidence is 'material' for Brady purposes"—which in turn requires a " 'reasonable probability of a different result' "(pp. 691, 699, quoting Kyles v. Whitley, 514 U.S. 419, 434 (1995)).

Page 1380. Add a new sub-Paragraph (7)(c):

(c) In Dretke v. Haley, 541 U.S. 386 (2004), the Court had before it the question, on which the circuits had divided, of "the availability and scope of the actual innocence exception in the noncapital sentencing context" (p. 392). The prisoner should have received a sentence of no more than two years, but had been sentenced to 16 1/2 years under an habitual offender statute that, the state later acknowledged, did not apply to his case. Nonetheless, the state resisted post-conviction attacks on the sentence on the basis that defense lawyers had failed, at sentencing and on direct review, to contest the applicability of the habitual offender statute.

On federal habeas, the lower courts excused the default and granted relief, with the Fifth Circuit holding narrowly that the actual innocence exception "applies to noncapital sentencing procedures involving a career offender or habitual felony offender" (306 F.3d at 264). But the Supreme Court vacated and remanded, holding that "a federal court faced with allegations of actual innocence, whether of the sentence or of the crime charged, must first address all nondefaulted claims for comparable relief and other grounds for cause to excuse the procedural default" (pp. 393–94). Here the state acknowledged that the petitioner had a "viable and 'significant' ineffective assistance of counsel claim" that, if sustained, would provide the same relief (re-sentencing) that the lower courts had provided (p. 394, quoting the oral argument). Justice O'Connor's majority opinion expressed concern about "licens[ing] district courts to riddle the cause and prejudice standard with ad hoc exceptions whenever they perceive an error to be 'clear' "(p. 394). She stressed that the applicability of the actual innocence exception in this case raised difficult constitutional questions better avoided if possible, and noted that the state had promised not to re-incarcerate the prisoner during the pendency of his ineffective assistance of counsel claim.

Justice Stevens (joined by Justices Kennedy and Souter) dissented. He noted, *inter alia*, that the prisoner had already served more than six years although it was now undisputed that he could not lawfully be sentenced to more than two years and that the miscarriage of justice was manifest. He charged (p. 398) that the Court's "attempt to refine the boundaries of the judge-made doctrine of procedural default" caused it to lose sight of the basic office of habeas corpus, to ensure fundamental fairness. Justice Kennedy also dissented separately.

Page 1384. Add, after Paragraph (D)(2), the following new sub-section:

E. Treaty Obligations under International Law and Procedural Default

The Vienna Convention on Consular Relations, to which the United States is a signatory, requires that aliens who are detained be informed without delay of their rights under the Convention, which include their right to ask that authorities inform the consulate of the detainee's home country. Many states have failed to comply with that obligation, and in a number of cases convicted defendants have later raised that failure for the first time in seeking habeas relief. These cases raise complex problems about the relationship of international law to domestic procedural default doctrine and of international courts to domestic tribunals.

In Breard v. Greene, 523 U.S. 371 (1998) (per curiam), a Paraguayan citizen sentenced to death filed a federal habeas corpus petition alleging for the first time that his conviction and sentence should be overturned because the state had failed to comply with the Vienna Convention. After the lower courts had denied relief, the International Court of Justice (ICJ), acting on a complaint by Paraguay, issued an order requesting the United States to take all measures at its disposal to prevent execution pending final decision in the ICJ proceeding. Breard then sought leave to file a petition in the U.S. Supreme Court for an original writ of habeas corpus, relying on the ICJ order; he had previously filed a petition for certiorari.

On the eve of execution, the Supreme Court issued a per curiam opinion denying both petitions on the ground that Breard had forfeited his claim under the Treaty by having failed to raise it in state court. The Court rejected Breard's submission that the procedural default doctrine is inapplicable to treaty obligations. In response to Breard's contention that the claim was "novel" and hence there was cause for the default, the Court relied on Teague as holding that the habeas court should not entertain a claim based on new law.

However, at the time of Breard, the Supreme Court did not confront a final ICJ judgment. That changed by the time the Court heard Medellín v. Dretke, 125 S.Ct. 2088 (2005), where the prisoner also raised a Vienna Convention claim for the first time in a federal habeas proceeding. While Medellín's appeal from the district court's denial of relief was pending, the ICJ issued a final decision in an action brought by Mexico against the United States, asserting violations of the Convention in Medellín's and in other cases. The ICJ ruled that the "the Vienna Convention guaranteed individually enforceable rights, that the United States had violated those rights, and that the United States must 'provide, by means of its own choosing, review and reconsideration of the convictions and sentences of the [affected] Mexican nationals' to determine whether the violations 'caused actual prejudice,' without allowing procedural default rules to bar such review" (p. 2090, quoting the ICJ decision). Thereafter, the court of appeals, relying on Breard and the fact of Medellín's procedural default, refused to issue a certificate of appealability.

The Supreme Court granted certiorari from the court of appeals' judgment, to consider whether (1) a federal court is bound by the ICJ's ruling that U.S. courts must reconsider Medellín's claim for relief free from the bar of procedural default doctrine, and (2) whether as a matter of comity a federal court should give effect to the ICJ's judgment to promote uniform treaty interpretation. Thereafter, Medellín sought postconviction review in the Texas state courts, relying in part on a memorandum issued by President Bush, after the ICJ decision, "that stated the United States would discharge its international obligations ... by 'having State courts give effect to the [ICJ] decision in accordance with general principles of comity in cases filed by the 51 Mexican nationals addressed in that decision' " (p. 2090). (What is the source of Presidential authority to issue such a memorandum? Is a state court obliged under the Supremacy Clause to comply with it? *Cf.* Garamendi, p. 40, *supra.*)

Following this action, the Supreme Court dismissed the writ of certiorari in Medellín's case as improvidently granted. It noted five hard questions presented by the case: (1) whether a violation of the Vienna Convention is a "fundamental defect" cognizable on habeas corpus, (2) whether the state court's determinations that the Vienna Convention creates no individually enforceable rights, that procedural default rules bar Medellín's claim, and that Medellín was not harmed by any lack of notification of the Mexican consulate, were "contrary to, or an unreasonable application of, clearly established Federal law, as determined by the Supreme Court", 28 U.S.C. § 2254(d); (3) how the ICJ judgment relates to the "new law" jurisprudence of Teague v. Lane; (4) whether a claim of treaty violation can support a certificate of appealability, which requires a "substantial showing of the denial of a *constitutional* right", and (5) whether Medellín had exhausted state court remedies. In view of the possibility that the state courts would provide relief and of the availability of review in the Supreme Court after the state court proceedings, the Court viewed it as "unwise to reach and resolve the multiple hindrances to dispositive answers to the questions here presented" (p. 2092).

Justice O'Connor, joined by Justices Stevens, Souter, and Breyer, dissenting, would have vacated the court of appeals' denial of the certificate of appealability and remanded for resolution of "questions of national importance [that] are bound to recur"—namely, whether the ICJ judgment is binding on American courts, whether the Vienna Convention creates a judicially enforceable individual right, and whether the Convention sometimes requires state procedural default rules to be set aside (p. 2096).[17] She saw no barrier to issuance of a certificate of appealability, since the state had belatedly raised the

---

17. Opinions by Justice Ginsburg (joined by Justice Scalia), Justice Souter, and Justice Breyer suggested the proper course was simply to stay the case before the Supreme Court, pending the state court proceedings. But as a majority did not favor that course, Justices Ginsburg and Scalia joined the per curiam and Justices Souter and Breyer joined the dissent.

question whether violation of a treaty, rather than the constitution, can support issuance of a certificate and since she did not think that the presence of other, difficult issues on remand provided a reason not to reverse the court of appeals' erroneous denial of a certificate.

Pages 1390–91. Add to Paragraph (3)(a):

In Baldwin v. Reese, 541 U.S. 27 (2004), the Court stated that "ordinarily a state prisoner does not 'fairly present' a claim to a state if that court must read beyond a petition or a brief (or a similar document) that does not alert it to the presence of a federal claim" (p. 32). Thus, the Court ruled that the prisoner failed to exhaust his Sixth Amendment claim of ineffective assistance of counsel when his papers before the state supreme court, on discretionary review of a denial of postconviction relief, asserted that his counsel had been ineffective in violation of state law. Rejecting the Ninth Circuit's view that the federal claim had been presented to the state supreme court because, had it read the lower state court opinions, it would have seen the federal basis for the ineffective assistance claim, the Court contended that such an approach would burden state appellate judges by effectively requiring them to read such opinions.

Page 1389. Add to the end of Paragraph (5) a new footnote 7:

7. For discussion of when a motion for relief from judgment under Fed. R. Civ. Proc. 60(b) will be treated as a second or successive petition, and thus may be filed only in accordance with the limitations of § 2244(b), see Gonzalez v. Crosby, 125 S.Ct. ___ (2005).

Page 1392. Add to Paragraph (4):

In Rhines v. Weber, 125 S.Ct. 1528 (2005), the Supreme Court gave qualified approval to the stay-and-abeyance procedure noted in the Fifth Edition. Rhines, who was under a death sentence, filed a federal habeas corpus petition 11 months before the one-year limitation period would expire, and filed an amended petition 9 months later. Eighteen months thereafter, the district court found that 8 of his 35 claims were unexhausted. Had the district court dismissed the mixed petition so as to permit exhaustion of the 8 claims, the statute of limitations would have barred refiling in federal court. Therefore, the district court held Rhines' petition in abeyance conditioned upon his commencing state court exhaustion proceedings within 60 days and returning to federal court within 60 days of completing such exhaustion. The court of appeals reversed, but was in turn reversed by the Supreme Court.

Justice O'Connor's opinion for the Court, after noting the risks (described in the Fifth Edition) posed by the interplay of the Court's 1982 decision in Rose v. Lundy and the 1996 enactment of a one-year limitations period, found that AEDPA did not deprive the district courts of their customary authority to stay proceedings. However, she contended that a stay like the one ordered by the district court could undermine AEDPA's purposes of reducing delays in executing sentences, especially capital sentences, and of encouraging litigants to be sure that all claims are exhausted before filing in federal court. Accordingly, the Court held that the stay-and-abeyance procedure is appropriate only "when the district court determines there was good cause for the petitioner's failure to exhaust his claims first in state court", and, further, that a district court would abuse its discretion if it issued a stay with respect to "plainly meritless" unexhausted claims (p. 1535). (Where no stay issues, the district court should allow the prisoner to delete the unexhausted claims and proceed with the exhausted ones.[a]) The Court added that to avoid delay, in which capital petitioners might have a special incentive to engage, district courts should impose "reasonable time limits on a petitioner's trip to state court and back", and should not grant a stay "if a petitioner engages in abusive litigation tactics or intentional delay" (*id.*). But the Court added that a district court would abuse its discretion by denying a stay to a prisoner who had good cause for failure to exhaust potentially meritorious claims and who had not engaged in intentional dilatory tactics.

Concurring in part and concurring in the judgment, Justice Souter (who did not join the Court's opinion), joined by Justices Ginsburg and Breyer (who did join the Court), would not have conditioned a stay on demonstration of good cause: given the difficulties posed for pro se prisoners in addressing tricky exhaustion issues, he thought a threshold inquiry into good cause "will give the district courts too much trouble to be worth the time"; he would instead have denied a stay only when "intentionally dilatory litigation tactics" have been established (p. 1536). Justices Ginsburg and Breyer also joined a concurring opinion of Justice Stevens stating that he joined the Court on the understanding that the good cause requirement would not prove to be trap for unwary pro se petitioners.

SECTION 3.   COLLATERAL ATTACK ON FEDERAL JUDGMENTS OF CONVICTION

Page 1402. Add to Paragraph (5)(c):

See also Massaro v. United States, p. 123, *supra.*

Page 1404. Add to footnote 8:

In Clay v. United States, 537 U.S. 522 (2003), the Court resolved the circuit conflict noted in the Fifth Edition, ruling unanimously that when a federal defendant whose conviction has been affirmed by the court of appeals does not petition for a writ of certiorari, the conviction becomes final (and thus the one-year limitations period begins to run) on the date on which the time for filing a petition for a writ of certiorari expired, rather than on the date on which the court of appeals issued its mandate.

Under § 2255, the one-year period runs from the latest of four dates, one of which is "the date on which the right asserted was initially recognized by the Supreme Court, if that right has been newly recognized by the Supreme Court and made retroactively applicable to cases on collateral review". In Dodd v. United States, 125 S.Ct. 2478 (2005)(5–4), the Court held that the one-year period runs from the date on which the Supreme Court recognizes the new right, rather than the date on which the right is made retroactive in a subsequent proceeding. Justice O'Connor's majority opinion viewed the statute as clear, recognizing "one date and one date only" (p. 2482). The second clause—"if that right has been newly recognized by the Supreme Court and made retroactively applicable to cases on collateral review"—imposes a further condition on bringing actions but "has no impact whatsoever on the date from which

----

a. A decision the prior Term in Pliler v. Ford, 542 U.S. 225 (2004), had held narrowly that habeas courts are not required, when they determine after the limitations period has run that some claims in a mixed petition are unexhausted, to provide petitioners with specific advice about their options.

the 1–year limitation period * * * begins to run" (*id.*). Here, the motion was time-barred because the prisoner, whose conviction became final in 1997, sought in his 2001 motion to invoke a right recognized by the Supreme Court in 1999 (although the right was not made applicable on collateral review by the Eleventh Circuit, within which the case arose, until 2002). The Court recognized that often more than a year passes between the Supreme Court's recognition of a new right and that right's being made retroactively applicable, and that where that is so, the decision will preclude a prisoner from ever being able to bring a habeas claim. However, Justice O'Connor declared that the Court was "not free to rewrite the statute that Congress has enacted" (p. 2483).

In dissent, Justice Stevens (joined by Justices Souter, Ginsburg, and Breyer) refused to believe accept the conclusion that Congress should be understood, "in the same provision, both to recognize a potential basis for habeas relief and also to make it highly probable that the statute of limitation would bar relief before the claim can be brought" (p. 2488).

How likely is it that Congress contemplated that the two conditions necessary to bring this provision into play would occur on different dates? If it did, would it have provided that the one-year period could run before both events had occurred? If it didn't, couldn't the statutory language referring to "initial" recognition of the right be read to include the occurrence of both of the events necessary to the petitioner's cause of action?

Page 1404. Add to footnote 10:

A distinctive problem for federal prisoners arises when, as is not uncommon, a district court treats as a § 2255 motion a filing that a pro se prisoner has labeled differently. In Castro v. United States, 540 U.S. 375 (2003), the Court ruled that unless the district court (i) informs a pro se prisoner of its intent to recharacterize the filing as a § 2255 motion, (ii) warns the prisoner that doing so means that any subsequent § 2255 motion will have to meet the strict limitations on successive petitions, and (iii) offers the prisoner a chance to withdraw or amend the filing, "a recharacterized motion will not count as a § 2255 motion for purposes of applying § 2255's 'second or successive' provision" (p. 377).

————

CHAPTER XII

ADVANCED PROBLEMS IN JUDICIAL FEDERALISM

SECTION 1.   PROBLEMS OF RES JUDICATA

Page 1408. Add to Paragraph (2):

Arguing in favor of a restrictive reading of the Semtek decision, Professor Woolley contends that the decision should require reliance on the preclusion rules of the initial forum state in only two contexts: judgments involving dismissal of claims on the basis of the statute of limitations and judgments turning on rules of privity between parties stemming from state substantive law. Woolley, *The Sources of Federal Preclusion Law After Semtek*, 72 U.Cin.L.Rev. 527 (2003). Thus, he sees a significant role for federal preclusion law not only to implement the procedural obligations imposed by the Federal Rules (*e.g.*, with respect to compulsory counterclaims), but also to give due recognition to a range of other federal interests (including the proper allocation of federal judicial resources).

Page 1429. Add a new footnote 2a at the end of Paragraph (2):

2a.   For further evidence of the impact of § 1738, as interpreted in McCurry and Kremer, see San Remo Hotel, L.P. v. City and County of San Francisco, 125 S.Ct. 2491 (2005), also discussed at pp. 16, 87, *supra*. In this case, plaintiffs had brought a federal court action challenging the constitutionality of a city ordinance both on its face and as applied. (The challenge was based on the Takings Clause of the Fifth Amendment, as incorporated in the Fourteenth.) The Ninth Circuit decided that Pullman abstention was appropriate on the facial challenge, and that the as-applied challenge was unripe because the plaintiffs had not yet sought compensation under state law (see Fifth Edition p. 229). The plaintiffs then went to state court and argued that the ordinance violated the Takings Clause of the California constitution. Noting that it had interpreted that clause to be co-extensive with the federal Takings Clause, the state supreme court upheld the ordinance both on its face and as applied. Plaintiffs then returned to federal court on their federal claims. But the Supreme Court, affirming the decisions of the courts below, held that the issues determined in the state proceedings were entitled to preclusive effect and, as a result, the federal suit was effectively barred.

On the facial challenge, the Court held that while the England case (Fifth Edition p. 1200) allowed plaintiffs to renew their facial challenge following federal court abstention, it did not protect against issue preclusion on issues actually determined in the state courts. On the as-applied challenge, the rule of the England case was not relevant at all, since the original claim was dismissed for lack of ripeness, and the Court held that issue preclusion was required by § 1738 even though existing doctrine compelled the plaintiffs to seek compensation in state court before asserting their federal claim. In answer to plaintiffs' argument that they should not lose their ability to litigate their federal claim in federal court as a result of being forced to go to state court first, the Court said: "We have repeatedly held, to the contrary, that issues actually decided in valid state-court judgments may well deprive plaintiffs of the 'right' to have their federal claims relitigated in federal court. This is so even when the plaintiff would have preferred not to litigate in state court, but was required to do so * * *. The relevant question * * * is whether the state court actually decided an issue of fact or law that was necessary to its judgment (p. ___)." "Even when the plaintiff's resort to state court is involuntary and the federal interest in denying finality is robust, we have held that Congress 'must "clearly manifest" ' its intent to depart from § 1738' " (p. ___)(quoting Kremer).

Page 1436. Add to footnote 11:

In Dow Chem. Co. v. Stephenson, referred to in the last paragraph of this footnote, the lower court's decision (allowing an absent class member to collaterally attack a class action judgment on grounds of the adequacy of representation) was affirmed without opinion by an equally divided Supreme Court. 539 U.S. 111 (2003)(Stevens, J., not participating). (The affirmance related to the Stephenson respondents. With respect to certain other respondents, the judgment was remanded for reconsideration on procedural grounds, *i.e.*, the Supreme Court's holding in Syngenta Crop Prot., Inc. v. Henson, Fifth Edition p. 1538, that a case may not be removed from a state court under the All Writs Act, 28 U.S.C. § 1651.)

SECTION 2. OTHER ASPECTS OF CONCURRENT OR SUCCESSIVE JURISDICTION

Page 1440. Add to Paragraph (4):

In Exxon Mobil Corp. v. Saudi Basic Industries Corp., 125 S.Ct. 1517 (2005), the Court—noting that "lower federal courts have variously interpreted the Rooker–Feldman doctrine to extend far beyond the contours of [those] cases" (p. 1519)—held the doctrine inapplicable to a case involving parallel state and federal proceedings relating to the same controversy.

In this case, Saudi Basic Industries (SABIC) had sued subsidiaries of Exxon Mobil in state court, seeking a declaratory judgment upholding the validity of SABIC's claim for royalties. Shortly after, Exxon Mobil and the subsidiaries sued SABIC in federal court, alleging that the royalties in question constituted improper overcharges, and the subsidiaries filed counterclaims on the same claims in the state proceeding. SABIC's motion to dismiss the federal action— alleging, *inter alia*, immunity under the Foreign Sovereign Immunities Act— was denied, and SABIC took an interlocutory appeal to the Third Circuit. Before argument on that appeal, a substantial state trial court judgment was rendered in favor of the subsidiaries, and the Third Circuit ruled that because that judgment preceded any federal court judgment on the same claims, Rooker–Feldman deprived the federal court of jurisdiction.

On certiorari, the Supreme Court unanimously reversed. The Court, per Justice Ginsburg, noted first that Rooker and Feldman were the only Supreme Court decisions relying on the doctrine bearing their names. After discussing the two cases in some detail, the Court stated that the doctrine is "confined to cases of the kind from which [it] derived its name: cases brought by state-court losers complaining of injuries caused by state-court judgments rendered before the district court proceedings commenced and inviting district court review and rejection of those judgments" (pp. 1521–22). Neither case, the Court continued, "supports the notion that properly invoked concurrent jurisdiction vanishes if a state court reaches judgment on the same or related question while [as in the case at bar] the case remains *sub judice* in a federal court" (p. 1527). And in dicta, the Court noted that while Rooker–Feldman was inapplicable in such a case, (a) principles of comity or abstention [see Fifth Edition pp. 1179–1271] might require stay or dismissal, and (b) once the state court adjudication is complete, disposition of the federal action would be governed by the law of preclusion.

The Exxon–Mobil decision, in both its holding and its general tone, is likely to temper the enthusiasm of many lower courts for applying the Rooker–Feldman doctrine in some doubtful cases, but there are still a number of unresolved questions. For example, does the doctrine apply to bar federal actions commenced after the grant of interlocutory relief in a state court proceeding, or after final judgment in a lower state court? And what is the precise relationship between the state court judgment and the subsequently commenced federal action that will bring the doctrine into play?

Page 1451. Add to Paragraph (2)(c):

Despite the views expressed by a majority of the Court in Spencer v. Kemna (as discussed in this Paragraph in the Fifth Edition), the Court in Muhammad v. Close, 540 U.S. 749, 752 n. 2 (2004)(discussed below), indicated that the question of the availability of § 1983 for a prisoner who had fully served his sentence, or a defendant who had been fined but not imprisoned, was still open. Citing Spencer, and the expression there by "[m]embers of the Court" of the view that "unavailability of habeas for other reasons [i.e., reasons other than those in the Muhammad case] may also dispense with the habeas requirement", the Court went on to state that "[t]his case is no occasion to settle the issue."

Page 1452. Add a new footnote 2a at the end of Paragraph (3):

2a.   Edwards v. Balisok was distinguished in Muhammad v. Close, 540 U.S. 749 (2004). In this case, a prisoner brought a § 1983 damages action against a prison guard for certain injuries allegedly sustained during a period of prehearing detention that culminated in the imposition of disciplinary sanctions for misconduct prior to the detention. In a per curiam decision reversing the decision below that the § 1983 action was barred by the Heck rule, the Court said that the lower court's decision was flawed "as a matter of fact and as a matter of law" (p. 754). The factual error lay in the assumption that the prisoner had sought expungement of the misconduct charge from his prison record, and the legal error lay in the view that Heck "applies categorically" to all suits challenging prison disciplinary proceedings (*id.*). In this instance, the Heck rule did not apply because the relief sought did not raise any question about the validity of the underlying conviction, since the federal magistrate judge had found or assumed that as a matter of state law, "no good-time credits were eliminated by the prehearing action" brought into question by the prisoner's suit (*id.*).

Page 1452. Add a new Paragraph (4):

(4) The Application of Preiser–Heck to Method of Execution Claims. In Nelson v. Campbell, 541 U.S. 637 (2004), petitioner Nelson, a state prison inmate in Alabama, had been sentenced to execution, and denial of his application for federal habeas was affirmed by the court of appeals. One month after that decision, the state changed its method of execution from electrocution to lethal injection (but allowed inmates to opt for electrocution, an option not exercised by petitioner). Because Nelson's veins had been badly damaged by drug use, the question of how access to his veins would be obtained was discussed with the prison warden, but six days before his scheduled execution, the warden announced that a different procedure was being substituted for that previously indicated. Three days later, Nelson filed a federal court § 1983 action against the state commissioner of corrections and others, complaining that (especially in light of the availability of safer and less invasive means) the newly announced procedure for obtaining venous access violated his rights under the Eighth Amendment. Nelson sought a permanent injunction against use of this method, a temporary stay of execution to allow consideration of his claim, and other injunctive relief. The district court dismissed the complaint and the court of appeals affirmed, ruling that since such a claim necessarily sounded in habeas, Nelson should have sought permission to file a second or successive habeas application and that had he done so, permission would have been denied under the test laid down in 28 U.S.C. § 2244(b)(2)(B)(ii).

A unanimous Supreme Court, in an opinion by Justice O'Connor, reversed. She noted that under the Preiser doctrine (as elaborated in Heck), claims that effectively challenge the fact of conviction or the duration of a sentence "fall within the 'core' of habeas corpus and are thus not cognizable when brought pursuant to § 1983" (p. 643). But "claims that merely challenge the conditions of a prisoner's confinement, whether the inmate seeks monetary or injunctive relief, fall outside of that core and may brought pursuant to § 1983 in the first instance" (*id.*, citing Muhammad v. Close, note 2a, *supra*).

Justice O'Connor then stated that the question whether a civil suit seeking to enjoin a particular method of execution fell within the core of habeas corpus was not squarely governed by these prior decisions but did not have to be resolved in this case with respect to method-of-execution claims generally. "Even were we to accept as given respondents' premise that a challenge to lethal injection sounds in habeas, * * * [the fact that] venous access is a necessary prerequisite [to lethal injection] does not imply that a particular means of gaining such access is likewise necessary. Indeed, the gravamen of petitioner's entire claim is that use of the [challenged method of venous access] would be gratuitous. * * * If on remand and after an evidentiary hearing the District Court concludes that use of the [challenged] procedure * * * is necessary for administering the lethal injection, the District Court will need to address the broader question, left open here, of how to treat method-of-execution claims generally" (pp. 645–46).[a] (Query: what of the fact that a convicted prisoner in Alabama also has the option of electrocution?)

Clearly, the opinion in this case does not explicitly take a position on the question of the availability of a § 1983 action to challenge the constitutionality of the only means of execution available under state law. But could the allowance of such an action be squared with the Court's existing rule that the action is not a substitute for (or alternative to) habeas when the outcome of the action, if successful, would affect the "duration" of a sentence?

Page 1452. Add a new Paragraph (5):

(5) The Application of Preiser–Heck to Challenges to the Validity of Parole Procedures. In Wilkinson v. Dotson, 125 S.Ct. 1242 (2005), the

---

a. The Court went on to uphold as appropriate the prayer for injunctive relief to enjoin an allegedly unnecessary procedure, but to hold that the requested stay of execution was unnecessarily broad because it sought to enjoin the execution entirely. The matter was effectively moot, however, since the execution warrant had expired, and no new date had been set. The Court also rejected respondents' "floodgates" argument in view of the "extremely limited" nature of its holding (p. 649).

Preiser–Heck doctrine was further confined in the context of challenges to the constitutionality of state parole procedures. In this consolidated case involving two § 1983 actions, one Ohio prisoner, Dotson, challenged the validity of a parole officer's determination that he was not presently eligible for consideration for parole, and another Ohio prisoner, Johnson, challenged the validity of a parole board determination that he was not suitable for parole. Both prisoners argued that the constitutional error consisted of the retroactive application of new, harsher guidelines, and each sought a parole hearing free from the alleged constitutional defect. In each case, the federal district court decided, and the court of appeals agreed, that the prisoner could seek relief only in a habeas proceeding. In an 8–1 decision, the Supreme Court reversed.

Writing for the Court, Justice Breyer summarized the prior holdings as focusing "on the need to ensure that state prisoners use only habeas corpus (or similar state) remedies when they seek to invalidate the duration of their confinement—either *directly* through an injunction compelling speedier release or *indirectly* through a judicial determination that necessarily implies the unlawfulness of the State's custody" (p. 1247). Such cases, he observed, seek "core" habeas corpus relief (*id.*). But in the present case, he continued, neither prisoner seeks an injunction ordering immediate or speedier release, nor will a favorable judgment "necessarily imply" the invalidity of their convictions or sentences (p. 1248). Success for Dotson will mean at most a speedier consideration of his parole application, and success for Johnson will mean at most a new parole hearing. Thus neither action lies at "the core of habeas corpus" (*id.*).

Concurring, Justice Scalia (joined by Justice Thomas) went further than Justice Breyer and argued that in the circumstances, a habeas remedy should not lie at all because the relief sought "neither terminates custody, accelerates the future date of release from custody, nor reduces the level of custody" (p. 1250). Thus, "a contrary holding would require us to broaden the scope of habeas relief beyond recognition" (*id.*). Dissenting, Justice Kennedy argued that Preiser–Heck should govern because "[c]hallenges to parole proceedings are cognizable in habeas" (p. 1252).

Isn't Justice Scalia correct, at least as a matter of precedent and the traditional conception of habeas? Is there a case in which the Supreme Court has recognized habeas as an available remedy even though the relief sought would neither require immediate or accelerated release nor reduce the level of custody? Is Justice Scalia's point undermined by the fact that a habeas court upholding a petitioner's claim may issue a *conditional* writ ordering the petitioner released *unless* a new proceeding (*e.g.*, a trial on the merits or a sentencing proceeding) is conducted? Would a federal court sustaining Dotson's or Johnson's claim have authority to require *release* of the petitioner unless the constitutional defect is remedied?

CHAPTER XIII

THE DIVERSITY JURISDICTION OF THE FEDERAL DISTRICT COURTS

SECTION 1. INTRODUCTION

Page 1454. Add at the end of the Note on Statutory Development:

In 2005, Congress enacted the Class Action Fairness Act, Pub.L. 109–2, 119 Stat. 4 (2005)(discussed in detail at pp. 136, 145, *infra*). As part of this Act, § 1332 was amended, moving former subsection (d)(defining "States") to subsection (e), and adding a new subsection (d) significantly expanding federal court jurisdiction over certain class actions, as well as certain "mass action[s]" in which "monetary relief claims of 100 or more persons are proposed to be tried jointly".

SECTION 2. ELEMENTS OF DIVERSITY JURISDICTION

Page 1457. Add a new footnote a at the end of Section B(5):

a. One commentator has argued that present § 1332(e) (until 2005, § 1332(d))—which purports to bring all these cases within the diversity jurisdiction by defining the District of Columbia, the territories, and Puerto Rico as "States" for purposes of that jurisdiction—should be conceived "less as a grant of diversity jurisdiction than as permissible legislation, adopted pursuant to Section 5 of the Fourteenth Amendment, to enforce the Privileges or Immunities Clause." Pfander, *The Tidewater Problem: Article III and Constitutional Change*, 79 Notre Dame L.Rev. 1925, 1930 (2004). (Note that this theory, standing alone, would not support the result in the Tidewater case itself, since the litigants there were corporations not entitled to the benefits conferred by the Privileges or Immunities Clause. But Professor Pfander suggests "work[ing] around the corporate gap * * * by relying upon the equal protection-based limit on discrimination against out-of-state corporations" (p. 1973)).

If the ability of an out-of-state U.S. citizen to obtain access to federal diversity jurisdiction is viewed, as Professor Pfander suggests, as a privilege of national citizenship, what are the implications of that thesis with respect to a claim that the Constitution itself requires such access? Can any such implication be squared with the generally accepted view that lower federal courts are not themselves constitutionally mandated? With the statutory limitations on the diversity jurisdiction that have existed since the first Judiciary Act? Does acceptance of Professor Pfander's thesis at least furnish a basis for congressional creation of federal jurisdiction in the case described in subsection (7), Fifth Edition p. 1458—an action between a citizen of a state and a citizen of the U.S. who is domiciled abroad?

Page 1463. Add a new footnote 5 at the end of Paragraph (3)(b):

5. For the view that in many of their applications, various enactments and proposals basing federal jurisdiction on "minimal diversity" (including § 1369 and the subsequently enacted Class Action Fairness Act of 2005, discussed immediately below) "present significant issues in terms both of congressional power to enact them, and the appropriateness of its doing so", see Floyd, *The Limits of Minimal Diversity*, 55 Hastings L.J. 613, 616 (2004). The problem, Professor Floyd argues, is that in part, substantial aspects of these enactments and proposals "baldly are predicated on the need to achieve judicial and litigant economy and consistent outcome between federal and state litigation arising from the same events or transactions" and are not sufficiently focused on whether the expansion of jurisdiction is necessary and proper to achieve the purposes of the Diversity Clause (pp. 692–94). He extends the argument to the use of the concept of supplemental jurisdiction to authorize the exercise of jurisdiction over non-diverse state law claims, questioning whether the existence of a formal relationship among jurisdictional and non-jurisdictional claims is sufficient to satisfy the requirements of a "necessary and proper" test (pp. 678–92). In appraising this thesis, consider how stringent the test should be of the authority of Congress to utilize the diversity jurisdiction (and related notions of supplemental jurisdiction) to achieve a wide range of goals consistent with a reasonable view of the needs of judicial federalism.

Page 1463. Add a new subparagraph (c) at the end of Paragraph (3):

(c) The Class Action Fairness Act of 2005.

● **Background and Summary.** For a number of years, there had been intense debate, and lobbying, on the question whether federal court jurisdiction should be expanded with respect to class actions (particularly plaintiff class actions) involving significant sums of money and class members and/or defendants from several states. Arguments favoring such expansion focused on claims that many state courts were too willing to certify inappropriate, even frivolous, class actions, and then to approve settlements that were either forced on defendants in order to avoid litigation, or benefitted the lawyers for the plaintiff class far more than the class members themselves, or both. Early in the Session following the 2004 election, Congress responded to these arguments by enacting the Class Action Fairness act of 2005 (CAFA), Pub.L. 109–2, 119 Stat. 4. The Act considerably expands the original and removal jurisdiction of the federal courts over certain class actions (and related actions) and adopts a number of special provisions regarding the settlement of such actions and the award of attorney's fees. Following is a brief summary of the Act's principal provisions.

—Section 2 of the Act contains findings of the importance of class actions, and of abuses of the device that have adversely affected interstate commerce, plaintiff class members, and defendants, and includes among the purposes of the Act the assurance of prompt and fair recovery for class members and of "Federal court consideration of interstate cases of national importance under the diversity jurisdiction".

—Section 3, which adds new §§ 1711–15 to Title 28, deals with the settlement of class actions in the federal courts. Section 1712 imposes substantive and procedural limitations on settlements that involve the recovery of "coupons" (to be used, for example, in purchasing the defendant's product(s)) and on the calculation of attorney's fees in such cases. Sections 1713 and 1714 provide protection against a net loss by class members as a result of a settlement (see, *e.g.*, Kamilewicz v. Bank of Boston Corp., Fifth Edition p. 1440), and against discrimination in settlements based on the geographic locations of class members. Section 1715 provides that particular state and federal officials, and certain institutions, must be given notice and opportunity for comment on certain proposed settlements.

—Section 4 inserts into the original jurisdiction provision of 28 U.S.C. § 1332 a new subsection(d) [moving present subsection (d) to new subsection (e)]. This new subsection (d)—the heart of the expansion of federal diversity jurisdiction—confers original federal court jurisdiction over class actions (as defined) in which the matter in controversy (after *aggregating* the claims of all class members) exceeds $5,000,000, and in which any member of a class of plaintiffs is (a) a citizen of a state different from any defendant, *or* (b) a foreign state or citizen of a foreign state if any defendant is a citizen of a state, *or* (c) is a citizen of a state if any defendant is a foreign state or citizen of a foreign state. The provision then goes on (a) to *authorize* the district court, after consideration of six enumerated factors, to decline to exercise jurisdiction in any case in which more than 1/3 but less than 2/3 of the plaintiff class members, as well as the "primary defendants", are citizens of the forum state; and (b) to *mandate* the decline of jurisdiction if more than 2/3 of the plaintiff class members are citizens of the forum state, if at least one defendant from whom significant relief is sought is also a citizen of the forum state, and if certain other conditions are met. Remaining provisions of new § 1332(d) serve, among other things, (a) to exempt certain class actions from the section's coverage (including classes consisting of fewer than 100 members), (b) to define an unincorporated association as a citizen of the state where it is organized and of the state where it has its principal place of business, and (c) to include in the definition of "class action" certain "mass action[s]" involving the joinder of 100 or more plaintiffs.

—Section 5, dealing with removal of class actions from state to federal court, is designed to complement the original jurisdiction provisions of § 4 by facilitating removal of actions falling within its scope. It adds a new § 1453 to Title 28, and is discussed at p. 145, *infra*.

—Finally, § 6 requires the Judicial Conference to submit a report to the House and Senate Judiciary Committees, within one year of enactment of the Act, containing recommendations for ensuring fair settlements and fair awards of attorney's fees, and specifying the actions taken and proposed to implement those recommendations. (The remaining three sections of the Act confirm the 2003 amendments to Federal Rule 23 (on class actions), reaffirm the role of the Judicial Conference and the authority of the Supreme Court in promulgating rules of practice and procedure, and provide that the Act shall apply to any civil action commenced on or after the date of enactment.)

● **Comments and Questions.** Note the departures in the CAFA from such decisions interpreting § 1332 as Snyder v. Harris (Fifth Edition p. 1481), Zahn v. International Paper Co. (Fifth Edition p. 1483 and p. 139, *infra*), and United Steelworkers v. R.H. Bouligny, Inc. (Fifth Edition p. 792). (There are also significant departures from existing statutory limitations on removal, see p. 145, *infra*).

Among the broad policy questions raised by this Act are: whether, and to what extent, the Act is warranted by state court abuses and overreaching in class action cases; whether the Act may overburden federal courts with the adjudication of matters not involving federal law; and whether Congress should have considered addressing not only procedural and remedial issues in class action cases significantly affecting commerce but also issues of substantive tort liability (particularly in the area of responsibility for defective products).

In addition, a number of more specific problems are bound to confront the courts as they attempt to deal with these new provisions. For example: Who is a "primary" defendant? Does it matter, in making this determination, whether the case is one involving joint and several liability under state law? How does the Court determine—particularly in cases involving large classes, at least some of whose members are not known or may not even have been born—what percentage of class members are citizens of the forum state?

Moreover, since the Act applies "to any class action before or after the entry of a class certification order by the court", what happens if, say, in a removed action, the federal court refuses to certify under Rule 23? Must the entire action be remanded to state court, or are there situations in which any remaining individual action(s) by the named plaintiff(s) may remain in federal court? In the event of remand, is it still open to the state court to certify the action as a class action under state rules? If so, would the result undermine one of the goals of the CAFA ? If not, would the result unconstitutionally interfere with state administration of a case not governed by federal law?

SECTION 3.   JURISDICTIONAL AMOUNT

Page 1483. Add to Paragraph (4):

After many years of uncertainty and disagreement among courts and commentators, the Supreme Court, in Exxon Mobil Corp. v. Allapattah Services, Inc., 125 S.Ct. ___ (2005), held, 5–4, that Congress, in enacting § 1367, overruled the holdings of both the Zahn case and its predecessor, Clark v. Paul Gray, Inc. (Fifth Edition p.1482). Exxon Mobil is discussed in detail in Section 4, below.

SECTION 4. SUPPLEMENTAL JURISDICTION

Page 1490. Substitute the following for Paragraph (2):

(2) Supplemental Jurisdiction in Diversity Cases Under § 1367:

(a) Background. The genesis of the supplemental jurisdiction provision enacted by Congress in 1990 is described at Fifth Edition pp. 924–30, and the reader should refer to that discussion for consideration of a number of problems that arise in both the federal question and diversity contexts. The legislative history indicates, however, that the provision was designed primarily to deal with the "pendent party" question in the context of federal question litigation and, by and large, not to change the law dramatically in the diversity context. As it turned out, a number of questions have arisen involving the provision's application in diversity cases, and the questions have generated both vigorous debate in the law reviews and disagreement in the lower federal courts about the meaning (and wisdom) of the provision in that context.[a] Some of the more difficult questions raised both by the general coverage of subsection (a) and the exceptions in subsection (b), including that presented in Stromberg, are discussed in the remainder of this Paragraph.

(b) Preservation of the Kroger Rule. Both the wording of subsection (b) and the legislative history indicate that the drafters did not intend to change the result in Kroger. But was that decision a sound one, in view of the powerful arguments Justice White makes in dissent? Can it be justified by a general predisposition against any expansion of the diversity jurisdiction?

Does the intent to preserve the Kroger result mean that a plaintiff cannot assert a direct claim against a third-party nondiverse defendant even if the action was originally brought in a state court and then removed? Does the statute affect the answer to the question asked at the end of Paragraph (1)(f), *supra*, about the ability of a plaintiff to assert a claim against a nondiverse third party defendant if the claim is asserted as a *counterclaim* to a claim by the third party? As a *compulsory* counterclaim to such a claim?

(c) Resolution of the Issue in Stromberg. By the time the the Supreme Court decided the question presented in Stromberg, in 2005, the federal courts of appeals were almost evenly divided. In a 5–4 decision, the Court agreed with the Stromberg result. Exxon Mobil Corp. v. Allapattah Services, Inc., 125 S.Ct. ___ (2005).

• **The Exxon Mobil Opinions.** Exxon Mobil consisted of two companion cases in which federal jurisdiction was based on diversity. In the first, Exxon Mobil was the defendant in a plaintiff class action in which at least one of the representative plaintiffs claimed damages in excess of the jurisdictional amount but the claims of some class members fell below that amount (and thus under Zahn, the Court would have lacked jurisdiction). In the second case, Ortega v. Star–Kist Foods, Inc., the plaintiffs were a child claiming damages in excess of the jurisdictional amount (as a result of an injury from an allegedly defective product), and her family, whose related claims for emotional distress and

---

a. For a selected bibliography of law review articles dealing with § 1367 in general and diversity cases in particular, see Fifth Edition p. 930 n. 11.

expenses fell below that amount (and thus under the rule of Clark v. Paul Gray (prohibiting aggregation), jurisdiction over the suit was lacking).[b]

The Court, per Justice Kennedy, held that under § 1367, the requirements for federal jurisdiction were satisfied in both cases. The Court first concluded that the case fell within the general provisions of § 1367(a): "When the well-pleaded complaint contains at least one claim that satisfies the amount-in-controversy requirement, and there are no other relevant jurisdictional defects, the district court, beyond all question, has original jurisdiction over that claim" (p. ___). It responded to what it described as the "indivisibility theory"—the view that "all claims in the complaint must stand or fall as a single, indivisible 'civil action' " in order for § 1367(a) to come into play at all—by dismissing the theory as "inconsistent with the whole notion of supplemental jurisdiction" (p. ___). The Court found it especially unconvincing to say (as the theory required if the subsection were to have its clearly intended effect in the federal question context) that it applied to diversity claims but not to federal question claims. Obviously concerned that its rationale might lead to the partial overruling (in the case of multiple plaintiffs) of the complete diversity requirement, the Court then discussed what it referred to as "the contamination theory"—that a lack of jurisdiction over one claim "contaminated" the entire action; that theory, it stated, "can make some sense in the special context of the complete diversity requirement because the presence of nondiverse parties on both sides of a lawsuit eliminates the justification [bias in favor of the home state party] for providing a federal forum" (p. ___). Thus an absence of complete diversity precludes the application of § 1367(a) because "unlike the failure of some claims to meet the requisite amount in controversy, [this absence] contaminates every claim in the action" (p. ___). In both cases before the Court, however, complete diversity existed (in the class action, as a result of the rule established in Ben Hur, Fifth Edition p. 1471, that the citizenship of the named representative of the class is controlling).

Having decided that § 1367(a) applied, the Court found the rest to be relatively clear sailing. The exceptions listed in § 1367(b) did not include the joinder of plaintiffs under Rule 20, nor did that subsection refer to class actions under Rule 23. And the legislative history, so heavily relied on by those resisting jurisdiction, was irrelevant "because § 1367 is not ambiguous" and because the history was in any event "far murkier" than the selective quotation relied on by its advocates would suggest (pp. ___–___). Finally, the Class Action Fairness Act of 2005, discussed at p. 136, *supra*, had no bearing on the question because the Act was not retroactive and because, in any event, there remained cases not covered by the Act that would fall within the scope of § 1367 as interpreted by the Court.

Justice Ginsburg, joined by Justices Stevens, O'Connor, and Breyer, dissented. While recognizing that the majority's reading of the statute was a plausible one, she urged that "another plausible reading" would be "less disruptive of our jurisprudence" (p. ___). Relying in significant part on a theory advanced by Professor Pfander, in *Supplemental Jurisdiction and Section 1367: The Case for a Sympathetic Textualism*, 148 U.Pa.L.Rev. 109 (1999)(referred to in the majority opinion as the "indivisibility" theory), she urged that the operative phrase "civil actions of which the district courts have original jurisdiction" in subsection (a) is "a formulation that in diversity cases, is sensibly read to incorporate [not only the requirement of complete diversity but

b. The child and her family were citizens of Puerto Rico, and all courts and parties in the case assumed without discussion that Puerto Rico was a state for diversity purposes. *Cf.* The Tidewater case, Fifth Edition p. 416.

also] the rules on joinder and aggregation tightly tied to § 1332 at the time of § 1367's enactment" (p. ___). So read, the general provision of § 1367(a) does not apply, and the exceptions to supplemental jurisdiction in subsection (b)—whose provisions are designed to "stop plaintiffs from * * * using another's claim as a hook to add a claim that the plaintiff could not have brought in the first instance [as in Kroger]"—need not be considered (p. ___). This reading did not affect the applicability of § 1367(a) to cases in which a *federal question* claim was joined with a non-federal claim involving either existing or additional parties because (quoting the court below in the Ortega case) "[u]nder § 1331, the sole issue is whether a federal question appears on the face of the plaintiff's well-pleaded complaint * * *. Section 1332, by contrast, predicates original jurisdiction on the identity of the parties * * * and their [satisfaction of the amount-in-controversy specification]" (p. ___).

Justice Stevens, joined by Justice Breyer, wrote a separate dissent in which he stressed the significance of the legislative history that the majority had described as both irrelevant and murky. He particularly relied on the statement in the House and Senate Reports that "[t]he section is not intended to affect the jurisdictional requirements of 28 U.S.C. § 1332 in diversity-only class actions, as those requirements were interpreted prior to Finley [citing Ben Hur and Zahn]" (p. ___).

● **Comments and Questions on Exxon Mobil.** The close division in this case reflects the difficulty of interpreting a statute that tried perhaps too hard to deal in elaborate detail with an area that did not easily yield to codification. Indeed, both sides had to confront several difficulties in reaching their conclusions.[c]

For the majority, perhaps the major problem lay in explaining why its "contamination theory" precluded subsection (a) from affecting the complete diversity requirement but did not preclude the overruling of Zahn and of Clark v. Paul Gray. The majority's argument was that (unlike the absence of the requisite jurisdictional amount with respect to one plaintiff's claim) the presence of co-citizens as adversaries dispels the concern that underlies diversity jurisdiction because it obviates the danger that home state citizen(s) will be unfairly preferred. The statutory availability of diversity jurisdiction in the plaintiff's home state is difficult to square with this view, as is the strained definition of complete diversity in class actions under the Ben Hur rule. (And see also Fifth Edition pp. 1498–1503.) But even assuming the majority's premise, will the presence of citizens of the same state—even the forum state—on both sides of a case guarantee that a party from another state will not be disfavored in the consideration of questions of liability and/or the measure of relief? Wouldn't it often be possible to prefer a forum-state defendant at the expense of an out-of-state defendant? Moreover, if the majority is right that the absence of complete diversity means that the entire action has been jurisdictionally contaminated from the start, how does one justify the decisions in cases like Newman–Green (Fifth Edition p. 1463), allowing dismissal of the non-diverse party on appeal and the upholding of the relief awarded against the remaining defendants? And finally, how does the Court's decision apply in a case in which there is not one defendant (as in both Exxon Mobil and Ortega), but multiple defendants who have been joined under Rule 20? Doesn't the exception of § 1367(b) apply in that situation? Does that distinction make sense?

c. Although the Class Action Fairness Act of 2005 was held not relevant to the outcome, and did not moot the case, that Act, in authorizing aggregation in many diversity class actions, clearly reduced the significance of the Exxon Mobil decision.

For the dissent, the principal problem was to distinguish between the meaning of subsection (a) in diversity cases and in federal question cases, for if the term "civil action over which the district courts have original jurisdiction" always requires reference to all claims in the case, then the provision does not even overrule Finley, given the holding in Finley itself that the district court lacked original jurisdiction. Justice Ginsburg grapples with this problem, but does her explanation account for the fact that, prior to the enactment of § 1367, a case like Finley, if brought in a state court, could not have been removed under § 1441(a) as a case over which the district courts had "original jurisdiction"? Moreover, her theory of subsection (b) is, as she recognizes, difficult to square with some of its provisions, *e.g.*, the exception for claims by plaintiffs *against* persons made parties under Rule 20—even in the original complaint.

What conclusions, if any, do you draw from this experience concerning the difficulty and desirability of detailed codification of complex jurisdictional doctrine?

(d) The Applicability of § 1367 to Removed Cases. Despite some uncertainty in the language of the provision, the Supreme Court held, in City of Chicago v. International College of Surgeons, 522 U.S. 156 (1997), that § 1367(a) applies to removed cases. But the question remains whether the limitations in § 1367(b) apply to claims asserted in state court before removal. For a forceful argument that they do not, see Steinman, *Supplemental Jurisdiction in § 1441 Removed Cases: An Unsurveyed Frontier of Congress' Handiwork*, 35 Ariz.L.Rev. 305 (1993). Professor Steinman's argument is supported by the phrasing of § 1367(b) in terms of the relationship of the *Federal* Rules of Civil Procedure to the assertion of claims and the joinder of parties. Indeed, given this terminology, rejection of her argument might raise difficult questions of the application of subsection (b) to removed cases in which claims have been asserted and/or parties joined under state rules that differ significantly from the relevant federal rules.

(e) Additional Problems of Interpreting § 1367(b). Difficult questions are also raised under subsection (b) with respect to the addition of parties under Rule 19 and intervention under Rule 24. For example, are *all* claims excluded if they are asserted by plaintiffs against persons made parties under these rules, or only those that "would be inconsistent" with the requirements of § 1332? (And what are those?) An aspect of this question is grammatical: does the final clause of subsection (b) relate to the entire subsection, or only to claims by persons joined as, or seeking to intervene as, plaintiffs? As another example, since subsection (b) does not purport to affect claims made by persons seeking to intervene as *defendants*, the problem of alignment, and possible realignment, becomes critical.

———

CHAPTER XIV

ADDITIONAL PROBLEMS OF DISTRICT COURT JURISDICTION

SECTION 1. CHALLENGES TO JURISDICTION

Page 1507. Add at the end of footnote 1:

See also Lee, *The Dubious Concept of Jurisdiction*, 54 Hastings L.J. 1613, 1638 (2003) (arguing that, although there may be "good policy reasons for having a bright line 'jurisdiction-first' rule", there is nothing inherent in the concept of jurisdiction that requires a federal court to establish jurisdiction before passing on the merits); Mullenix, *Standing and Other Dispositive Motions After Amchem and Ortiz: The Problem of "Logically Antecedent" Inquiries*, 2004 Mich.St.L.Rev. 703 (2004) (criticizing the Amchem and Ortiz decisions for their lack of clarity on whether or not the class certification issue must be considered first, and arguing that the cases need not, and should not, be read as foreclosing prior consideration of standing and other jurisdictional issues); Schwartz, *Limiting Steel Co.: Recapturing a Broader "Arising Under" Jurisdictional Question*, 104 Colum.L.Rev. 2255 (2004)(arguing that the question whether a complaint states a cause of action is itself sufficiently jurisdictional in character to permit its resolution, when appropriate, before ruling on other jurisdictional issues).

Page 1509. Add to Paragraph (2)(e):

The tension between the doctrine that a jurisdictional defect may be cured by dropping the party whose presence precluded jurisdiction and the doctrine that jurisdiction is determined at the time the action is brought was reflected in the sharply divided decision denying jurisdiction in Grupo Dataflux v. Atlas Global Group, L.P., 541 U.S. 567 (2004). In that case, a federal court action was brought against a Mexican corporation by a partnership containing partners who were U.S. citizens and partners who were Mexican citizens. Jurisdiction was alleged on the basis of diversity, but the parties and the Supreme Court agreed that at the outset of the case, diversity was lacking because of the presence of aliens on both sides.[a] Before trial, however, the Mexican partners

---

a. The citizenship of a partnership, even a limited partnership like the plaintiff in this case, is determined by looking to the citizenship of each partner. See Carden v. Arkoma Associates, Fifth Edition p. 1471. And in Grupo Dataflux, the Supreme Court, citing Mossman v. Higginson, 4 U.S. (4 Dall.) 12, 14 (1800), stated that diversity jurisdiction cannot exist if there are aliens on both sides of the case. But the one-paragraph decision in Mossman does not squarely support that proposition. Is the proposition sound? Should the statutory requirement of complete diversity between adversaries (see Fifth Edition p. 1459) preclude jurisdiction in an action by a citizen against an alien because the citizen plaintiff is joined by an alien co-plaintiff? *Cf.* 28 U.S.C. § 1332(a)(3) (authorizing jurisdiction "in an action between citizens of different States in which citizens or subjects of a foreign state are additional parties").

left the partnership, and in rejecting a post-verdict motion to dismiss for lack of jurisdiction, the courts below reasoned that on the basis of the decisions in Newman–Green (Fifth Edition pp. 1463, 1509) and Caterpillar Inc. v. Lewis (Fifth Edition p. 1550), it was sufficient, given the delay in filing the motion, that diversity existed when the verdict was rendered.

The Court, per Justice Scalia, reversed, holding those cases inapplicable because they involved the dismissal of a separate, dispensable party while in the present case, "[t]he purported cure arose not from a change in the parties to the action, but from a change in the citizenship of a continuing party [the plaintiff partnership]" (p. 574). The case, in the majority's view, was therefore analogous to one in which an individual plaintiff changes his citizenship after the filing of the action in an attempt to remedy a jurisdictional defect—a change that all members of the Court agreed would not cure the original defect. Turning to the practical aspects of its decision, the Court stated: "The policy goal of minimizing litigation over jurisdiction is thwarted whenever a new exception to the time-of-filing rule is announced, arousing hopes of further new exceptions in the future" (p. 580).

Justice Ginsburg, joined by Justices Stevens, Souter, and Breyer, dissented. The partnership situation presented by the case, she argued, was a novel one, and need not be analogized to the case of an individual plaintiff. Rather, in resolving this "subconstitutional" issue of jurisdiction (p. 589), it was equally plausible to regard a partnership not as an " 'entity' comprising its members" but as an " 'aggregation' composed of its members" (p. 591 n.6), and if the latter approach were adopted, the Newman–Green and Caterpillar cases would be squarely in point. Such a ruling would avoid the necessity of a new action and, perhaps, an additional trial, and "in procedural rulings generally, even on questions of a court's adjudicatory authority in particular, salvage operations are ordinarily preferable to the wrecking ball" (p. 592).

The rule that subject matter jurisdiction is ordinarily determined at the time of filing is one devised by the courts and not mandated by Congress. If the rule is therefore one that may be shaped in order best to achieve the goals of efficiency and fairness in adjudication, who has the better of the argument on this aspect of the case?

SECTION 2.   PROCESS AND VENUE IN ORIGINAL ACTIONS

Page 1524. Add a new footnote 2 at the end of Paragraph (2):

2.   One commentator has argued that it conflicts with tradition and sound policy to read federal provisions permitting nationwide service of process against corporations in certain federal actions in combination with § 1391(c) to authorize nationwide venue in such actions as well. Janutis, *Pulling Venue Up by Its Own Bootstraps: The Relationship Among Nationwide Service of Process, Personal Jurisdiction, and § 1391(c)*, 78 St. John's L.Rev. 37 (2004). Professor Janutis would limit venue in such cases to those districts with which the defendant has minimum contacts. (Even if such a result is desirable, can it be squared with the language of the venue statute? Is the availability of transfer under § 1404(a) an adequate remedy for

the problem? Professor Janutis, dealing with both issues, answers yes to the first question, and no to the second.)

SECTION 3.   REMOVAL JURISDICTION AND PROCEDURE

Page 1537. Add a new footnote 2 at the end of Paragraph (3):

2. In Breuer v. Jim's Concrete of Brevard, Inc., 538 U.S. 691 (2003), the Court unanimously upheld the removability of a private state court action for recovery of unpaid wages and other relief under the Fair Labor Standards Act (FLSA). Resolving a conflict among the circuits, the Court held that the provision of the FLSA that such an action "may be maintained * * * in any state court of competent jurisdiction" did not constitute a sufficiently unambiguous prohibition of removal to satisfy the requirement of § 1441(a) that removal of certain actions was allowed "[e]xcept as otherwise expressly provided by Act of Congress". The Court contrasted the language of the FLSA with the very explicit prohibition on removal of FELA actions in § 1445.

Page 1539: Add a new Paragraph (9) at the end of the Introductory Note:

(9) In the Class Action Fairness Act of 2005 (discussed in detail at p. 136. *supra*), Congress added to Title 28 a new § 1453, containing removal provisions designed to complement the new provisions for original jurisdiction in § 1332(d). Section 1453 authorizes removal of certain class actions (as defined in § 1332) "by any defendant without the consent of all defendants" and "without regard to whether any defendant is a citizen of the State in which the action is brought". Also, specific exception is made to the prohibition (in § 1447(d)) of appellate review of a remand order: "a court of appeals may accept an appeal from an order of a district court granting or denying a motion to remand * * * if application is made to the court of appeals not less than [more than?] 7 days after entry of the order." The section also requires prompt disposition of such an appeal if the district court's order is accepted for review.

Page 1545. Add a new subparagraph (c) at the end of Paragraph (2):

(c) New § 1453, discussed immediately above, provides with respect to the removal of class actions that "the 1–year limitation under section 1446(b) [see Fifth Edition p. 1544, footnote 4] shall not apply."

Page 1551. Add to Paragraph (1)(f):

In the 2003 Term, however, a sharply divided Court refused to extend the rationale of the Caterpillar and Newman–Green cases to a case in which diversity was originally lacking in a federal court action by a partnership against a foreign corporation, but the defect was allegedly "cured" when, prior to trial, the partners who were responsible for the lack of diversity jurisdiction left the partnership. Grupo Dataflux v. Atlas Global Group, L.P., 541 U.S. 567 (2004) (holding, 5–4, that the change after filing of the action did not cure the lack of jurisdiction)(discussed in more detail in this Supplement under Section 1 of this Chapter, addition to page 1509).

CHAPTER XV

APPELLATE REVIEW OF FEDERAL DECISIONS AND THE CERTIORARI POLICY

SECTION 2. JURISDICTION OF THE COURTS OF APPEALS

Page 1562. Add to footnote 5:

Compare also Sell v. United States, 539 U.S. 166 (2003), a case involving a district court pretrial order requiring the administration of antipsychotic drugs involuntarily to a mentally ill criminal defendant in order to render that defendant competent to stand trial. Before considering the merits of the defendant's constitutional claim under the Due Process Clause, the majority held that the district court order satisfied the three prongs of the Cohen "collateral order" rule and thus could be appealed to the court of appeals as a "final" decision. The order, said the majority, conclusively determined the disputed issue [whether the defendant had a right to refuse the medication]; the issue was an important one that was completely separate from the merits; and the issue was "effectively unreviewable" after final judgment because the harm (involuntary medication) would already have occurred and constituted a serious intrusion, the issue would be mooted by an acquittal, and the question after conviction (whether the medication *did* make the trial unfair) was different from the question before trial (whether the medication *might* make the trial unfair).

Justice Scalia, joined in dissent by Justices O'Connor and Thomas, did not reach the merits but took strong issue with aspects of the majority's holding on appealability—especially with its conclusion that the third prong (effective unreviewability after final judgment) was satisfied. Justice Scalia contended (surely correctly) that the possibility that an acquittal would moot the issue was not controlling, and further contended that under the Court's own precedent, the issue on appeal after conviction would be the same as at an interlocutory stage. Finally, he argued, the Court's implication that the Cohen rule applied because the trial court order, if implemented, would cause an immediate violation of the defendant's constitutional rights was a "breathtaking expansion of appellate jurisdiction over interlocutory orders" (p. 191), even if limited to the fuzzy category of severe intrusions.

Granted that the standard articulated by the Court in Sell is not a clearly predictable one, wasn't the approach followed in Sell inaugurated in Abney (Fifth Edition pp. 1562–63), where the Court stated that a denial of a double jeopardy claim was immediately appealable because the right asserted was one that would be effectively destroyed if not vindicated before trial?

Page 1576. Add at the end of Paragraph (2):

The notion that issues implicating separation of powers considerations may tilt the scales in favor of early appellate review[a] was invoked in Cheney v.

a. A notion expressed in both United States v. Nixon, Fifth Edition p. 1568 (authorizing immediate appeal by President Nixon from denial of his motion to quash a subpoena), and Ex parte Peru, Fifth Edition p. 307 (authorizing the filing of an original writ of mandamus in the Supreme Court in a case in which the Executive Branch objected to alleged interference with its conduct of foreign affairs by the district court).

United States District Court for the District of Columbia, 124 S.Ct. 2576 (2004), a case involving discovery orders directed to the Vice President and other senior officials. In that case, two private organizations filed suit against the Vice President and others, seeking to enforce the open meeting and disclosure requirements of the Federal Advisory Committee Act (FACA) with respect to the proceedings of a national energy policy group headed by the Vice President and consisting of other government officials, but allegedly also including—as "de facto" members—a number of private persons. The individual official defendants, including the Vice President, moved to dismiss on the grounds that FACA (which exempts groups consisting wholly of federal officers or employees) did not apply to this group and that to apply it would violate the separation of powers. The court deferred decision on that motion, ruling instead that discovery should be allowed in order to determine whether the "de facto membership doctrine"—a doctrine adopted by the D.C. Circuit—applied in the circumstances. The district court noted that the defendants could, if they wished, assert executive privilege to protect sensitive materials from disclosure.

Rather than raising any specific claims of privilege or seeking to narrow the discovery orders, the defendants sought certification for an interlocutory appeal under § 1292(b), and when that was denied, filed both a notice of appeal under the Cohen doctrine (see Fifth Edition pp. 1558, 1562) and a petition for a writ of mandamus in the court of appeals to vacate the discovery orders and for other relief. A divided panel of the court of appeals dismissed both the appeal and the mandamus petition, ruling with respect to the latter that such a petition would not be entertained until and unless specific claims of executive privilege had been made and rejected by the district court.

In a 7–2 decision, the Supreme Court (without reaching the question of appealability under the Cohen doctrine) reversed the judgment below with respect to the denial of the mandamus petition. Justice Kennedy, for the Court, stressed that although the writ of mandamus should be used only in exceptional circumstances, and that the case might be different were the Vice President not a party, the petition's allegation that the discovery orders "threaten 'substantial intrusions on the process by which those in closest operational proximity to the President advise the President' * * * [removes the case] from the category of ordinary discovery orders where interlocutory appellate review is unavailable through mandamus or otherwise" (p. 2587). Neither precedent nor policy, he continued, required a specific invocation of executive privilege in order to challenge the discovery as "an unwarranted impairment of another branch in the performance of its constitutional duties" (p. 2592). In a brief concluding portion speaking only for five Justices, Justice Kennedy ordered the case remanded with directions to consider the challenge to the "de facto membership doctrine" and to the discovery orders as well as to other matters bearing on whether the writ should issue.

Justice Stevens concurred, but noted that in his view the court of appeals would have been justified in vacating the district court's approval of the discovery sought because the broad scope of that discovery effectively prejudged the merits of plaintiffs' claim. Justice Thomas, joined by Justice Scalia (who earlier had written an opinion rejecting plaintiffs' request that he recuse himself), concurred in part and dissented in part. He agreed with the majority that mandamus was improperly denied but went on to contend that the court of appeals should be instructed to issue the writ because the only relief that plaintiffs could seek on the merits in the District Court was unavailable to them. Justice Ginsburg, joined by Justice Souter, dissented, contending that any form of appellate review was premature given the failure of the defendants to seek to narrow discovery at the District Court level and, as a result of that failure, the hypothetical nature of their separation-of-powers concerns.

Did the Court in Cheney let down the barriers to interlocutory review too far in light of the defendants' failure to narrow the issues by seeking more specific relief from the scope of discovery in the district court? Or did the Court display a laudable flexibility in allowing early review of a case raising difficult questions of inter-branch relations?

Section 3. Review of Federal Decisions by the Supreme Court

Page 1590. Add a new footnote a at the end of the second paragraph of Paragraph (1):

a. The Supreme Court has also held that the 90–day time limit for filing a certiorari petition is tolled, even if no petition for rehearing is filed in the court below, if the lower court itself recalls its mandate and asks for briefing on whether the case should be reheard en banc; in such a case, if the lower court ultimately denies rehearing, the period begins to run anew on the date of that denial. Hibbs v. Winn, 542 U.S. 88 (2004) (also discussed at p. 86, *supra*). (The holding in Hibbs, as it relates to the effect of a lower court decision considering rehearing on its own motion, was codified by the Court in a revision of Rule 13.3 in 2005.)

Page 1595. Add a new footnote 6 at the end of Paragraph (3):

6. In Ballard v. Commissioner of Internal Revenue, 125 S.Ct. 1270 (2005), the Court relied on the provision of Rule 14.1(a)—that "[t]he statement of any question presented is deemed to comprise every subsidiary question fairly included therein"—to warrant reversal on the basis of the Tax Court's noncompliance with a regulation in a case in which the questions presented on certiorari were limited to the Tax Court's compliance with the governing statutes and with the Constitution. The meaning of the regulation, the Court said, was "a question anterior to all other questions the parties raised" (p. 1275 n.2). The Chief Justice, joined by Justice Thomas in dissent, suggested on this point (at p. 1287 n.1) that the Court was in fact disregarding the very same rule (14.1(a)) that it invoked in support of its conclusion, since that rule also states that "[o]nly the questions set out in the petition, or fairly included therein, will be considered by the Court."

Section 4. The Certiorari Policy

Page 1596. Add to Paragraph (2):

See also Merrill, *The Making of the Second Rehnquist Court: A Preliminary Analysis*, 47 St. Louis U.L.J. 569, 640–44 (2003)(concluding that the primary factor responsible for the precipitous decline in the Court's plenary docket is, as Professor Hellman suggests, the application of a new and more rigorous standard for granting certiorari, and that Justice Scalia has been the principal architect of this standard, perhaps because of his heavy personal involvement in the preparation and revision of opinions issuing under his name).

Page 1610. Add to Paragraph (2):

Professor Hartnett, opposing a "blanket rule obliging the Court to preserve its jurisdiction" whenever a case is accepted for review, urges that "[i]n the death penalty context, however, Congress could, and should, determine that if the Supreme Court grants certiorari, a stay of execution is always appropriate." Hartnett, *Ties in the Supreme Court*, 44 Wm. & Mary L.Rev. 644, 675–76 (2002). (In the same article, Hartnett forcefully defends against recent criticism the Supreme Court's long-standing practice (even in capital cases) of affirming the decision below whenever—as result of the recusal of a Justice or for other reasons—the Court is equally divided.)

Page 1611. Add to footnote 8:

In an article critical of the result in the Tarver case, Professor Robbins proposes that the Rule of Four be applied to all writ petitions, including petitions for extraordinary writs, and further proposes that the Court publish all of its rules concerning the number of votes needed to grant plenary review or other relief with regard to particular filings. Robbins, *Justice by the Numbers: The Supreme Court and the Rule of Four—Or Is It Five?*, 36 Suffolk U.L.Rev. 1 (2002).

Page 1618. Add to footnote 15:

See also Price v. United States, 537 U.S. 1152, 1153 (2003), in which Justice Scalia, dissenting from a decision granting the writ of certiorari, vacating the judgment below, and remanding for further proceedings, said that he was writing in part to "record [his] continuing conviction that, in general, we have no power to vacate a judgment that has not been shown to be (or been conceded to be) in error" simply because the Court disagrees with the reasoning below. Though joined by only two other Justices on this point, Justice Scalia asserted that a total of five sitting Justices had (in prior dissents) expressed agreement with this view.

Two recent articles critique the Court's increasing use of the "GVR" (grant of certiorari, vacation of the decision below, and remand for further consideration). See Martin, *Gaming the GVR*, 36 Ariz.St.L.J. 551 (2004)(documenting the increased use of the GVR practice and criticizing the practice on the ground that it encourages litigants to petition for certiorari in the hope that some intervening event will occur before the Court acts on the petition); Chemerinsky & Miltenberg, *The Need To Clarify the Meaning of U.S. Supreme Court Remands: The Lessons of Punitive Damages Cases*, 36 Ariz.St.L.J. 513 (2004)(contending, on the basis of a study of varying lower court treatment of a series of related GVRs—all resulting from an intervening Supreme Court decision—that the Court needs to make clear that a GVR is intended not to convey any disapproval of the lower court's decision but only to ask for reconsideration in the light of the intervening event).

†